Jazz

A Beginner's Guide

ONEWORLD BEGINNER'S GUIDES combine an original, inventive, and engaging approach with expert analysis on subjects ranging from art and history to religion and politics, and everything in-between. Innovative and affordable, books in the series are perfect for anyone curious about the way the world works and the big ideas of our time.

Beginners
GUIDES

Jazz

A Beginner's Guide

Stuart Nicholson

ONEWORLD

A Oneworld Paperback Original

First published by Oneworld Publications, 2017

ISBN 978–1–78074-998-3
eISBN 978–1–78074-999-0

Typeset by Silicon Chips
Printed and bound in Great Britain by Clays Ltd, St Ives plc

Oneworld Publications
10 Bloomsbury Street
London, WC1B 3SR
England

Stay up to date with the latest books,
special offers, and exclusive content from
Oneworld with our monthly newsletter

Sign up on our website
www.oneworld-publications.com

To Dear Kath (and Gwladys)

Contents

Introduction

Somehow it's impossible to feel neutral about jazz. Love it or hate it, it always seems to provoke strong emotions. Depending on your point of view it can be downmarket or upmarket, monotonous or momentous, baffling or blatant and it's been that way since its emergence in the early years of the twentieth century. Its arrival couldn't have been better timed. Commercial radio was spreading across the United States and would bring jazz into the homes of millions, while the sales of recorded music were taking off in a big way, not just in America but around the world. As soon as a recording came out in the United States, the rest of the world got to hear it within weeks. As cultural historian Donald Sassoon has pointed out, 'The spread of jazz ... in the 1920s was the first great trend in music history to occur mainly through recording.'[1] Today, practically every country in the world boasts an active jazz scene and international jazz stars are now just as likely to come from outside America as they are from inside it. Walt Whitman once wrote of each voice 'singing what belongs to him or her and none else',[2] and today the jazz world is singing in just such a way, creating a rich and diverse music that speaks of its continuing vibrancy into the twenty-first century.

Jazz: A Beginner's Guide is a step-by-step guide to help you get the most out of listening to this remarkable music. It has its roots in a course I was invited to give some years ago at a college of further education. It was an experience I greatly valued and the students' responses, observations and suggestions – plus the notes and modifications I made as the course progressed – have coloured my thinking on what follows. The first thing that

I quickly learned was that when we hear a new piece of music for the first time we subconsciously compare it with what we know so as to form an opinion about it, but if we've not heard anything like it before then we're not certain what to think. So when I played the students tracks jazz aficionados fondly imagine will make believers out of non-believers I was greeted with looks of polite bewilderment, since their previous listening experiences had not encompassed the kind of music they were now hearing. Clearly a more cautious musical approach was needed, and I soon came up with a selection of tracks that they found interesting and engaging, and by the end of the first semester I was more than pleasantly surprised by how quickly they had embraced jazz, formed their own musical preferences and were talking about their favourite recordings like experts!

Although there is no magic switch to 'instantly' improve our understanding of music with which we are unfamiliar, we do know our ability to understand music has been subconsciously developing below our threshold of conscious perception throughout our lifetime, beginning in our mother's womb. By the sixth month of pregnancy an *in utero* baby becomes aware of auditory stimulation and it appears that after twenty-eight weeks the majority of foetuses can detect frequency changes in the range of 250Hz.[3] One experiment involved playing a piano melody to twenty-five women twice daily during their final weeks of pregnancy. A separate control group of twenty-five pregnant women were not exposed to the piano melodies. Six weeks after birth, the same melodies were played to all fifty babies. While the melody had a relaxing effect on all of them, the effect was twice as relaxing to the twenty-five who had had the melody played to them *in utero*.[4]

Music researchers tell us that our early listening habits are influenced by osmosis, or the gradual and unconscious assimilation of the music we're surrounded with as we grow up. By our early teenage years, we are surprisingly sure about music that conforms to our taste expectations and are equally sure about music that does not. You might think that these musical preferences are set in stone, but they're not. Of course, whether we decide to broaden our musical taste as we get older is an entirely personal decision, but modern research tells us that our auditory, cognitive and motor functions are well able to undertake this through active listening, when 'parts of the brain that evolved for other purposes such as language, skill learning and auditory analysis are gradually co-opted into doing something new'.[5] Emmanuel Bigand is just one of many psychologists to discover that humans are more skilled in understanding music than was previously thought, even those without any musical training. After conducting many experiments in the area of music cognition he discovered the reactions of musicians and non-musicians were closer than anybody had ever anticipated.[6] One of his early experiments[7] was how listeners interpreted complex pieces, and he discovered that while the response of trained musicians was along expected lines, untrained listeners intuitively, albeit less precisely, reached more or less the same conclusions and were nearly as good as trained listeners. While they were not able to explain any musical processes involved, they were nevertheless able to make pretty good sense of what was going on. Bigand conducted dozens more experiments looking at various aspects of music and a similar pattern emerged: experts were better than non-experts, but the non-experts were a lot better than might reasonably have been expected. Although there are clearly differences between trained and untrained listeners, Bigand concluded the gap was narrowed between the two groups because 'the human brain is already intensively trained to music through everyday life experience'.[8] So, whatever misgivings you might be harbouring about getting into jazz – 'you need a music degree to understand what's going on,' or 'it's a difficult listen' – then you can comfortably forget about them, as you're actually better equipped to get into jazz than you thought.

Throughout this book I've been very conscious of how the digitization of recorded sound has created a cultural landscape quite unlike anything in the past, or even the near past. Today, the immediacy of the Internet and the portability and sophistication of laptops, tablets, iPods and 4G smartphones means we're all able to engage with computer games, social networking sites, movies or music at any time of the day or night. And when it comes to music, chances are many of us listen to it on the go. It's a trend that shows no sign of slowing with sales of mobile MP3 players growing exponentially year by year,[9] yet most people would probably be surprised – offended even – to learn that when consuming music in this way 'the act of listening' ceases to be 'exclusive' and the prime focus of their attention, but instead becomes 'inclusive' as we interact with reality around us.

For many, music today is overheard rather than listened to – a way of avoiding the silence of the daily commute, the daily jog or doing the housework, functioning as 'a form of "sonic wallpaper" that [provides] an undemanding backdrop to some other task'.[10] This is known as 'secondary listening' and it's changing the nature of musical experience and the value we now attach to it. In their study 'Uses of Music in Everyday Life', Adrian North and his colleagues wrote that this reflected 'a rather passive attitude to music, which perhaps indicates how the increased availability of music has ... led to a reduction in the value placed on it by listeners',[11] concluding that our relationship to music in the digital age 'is not necessarily characterised by deep emotional investment'.[12] One example of this in reflected is our impatience with the album experience of ten or twelve songs sequenced to tell a particular story or sustain a certain mood[13] which has given way to the quick musical fix of cherry-picking the album's hit songs since, as industry commentator Bob Lefsetz wrote, 'No one's got the time to sit and hear your hour plus statement.'[14] Yet music demands emotional investment to realise its potential, so if we become more aware of the benefits of listening well and knowing *why* this is worth achieving, we'll be taking a vital step towards getting more out of our listening experiences.

We all come to music with a certain amount of baggage – what we prefer to listen to, how we like to listen to it, when we like to listen to it, where we like to listen to it and what we expect of it. Clearly there isn't a 'correct' way to listen and engage with music because it's such a subjective and personal experience. Everybody's different, but there seems no virtue in assuming the relativist position that everyone's way of listening to music is equally valid, because if all perspectives have equal validity then a limitless plurality of values is indistinguishable from no values at all. This may mean acknowledging some music is not intended for, or indeed suited to, secondary listening and demands active or engaged, rather than passive, listening. Don't forget, a perpetual background of music to which little serious attention is paid can have the effect of actually diminishing the listening experience, so the more you put into listening to jazz when it's the sole focus of your attention, the quicker you're likely to get into it.

As we listen, certain musical characteristics are subconsciously stored in our long-term memory as schema – think of them as 'templates' of previous listening experiences. The more a piece of music conforms to the templates of music we've previously enjoyed, the more we're inclined to like it and correspondingly, the more a performance conforms to templates of music we haven't liked, then the more we're likely to give it a miss. As the cognitive psychologist and neuroscientist Daniel Levitin has pointed out, 'Our ability to make sense of music depends on experience, and on neural structures that can learn and modify themselves with each new song we hear, and with each new listening to a new song.'[15]

Encountering a new piece of music is analogous to meeting a new colleague at work; in both instances increased familiarity often brings greater understanding; for example, 'X is a much nicer and more interesting person than I first thought'. The key, of course, is taking the time and trouble to get to know someone; indeed, studies by Jay Dowling and his colleagues[16] demonstrate how our memory for music develops over time – initially we get an overall picture of the song and with more exposure, more and more details are subconsciously filled in on our musical template. Sometimes it takes a while to build a good musical memory of a piece, but once it's done it can be strong and long-lasting. The key factor here is that with repetition comes familiarity. It's perhaps no coincidence that in sport, business, religion and philosophical disciplines, goals are often achieved by repetitive affirmation.

Yet whatever realm of music we choose to listen to, there will be certain performances we simply don't get, even after repeated listening. We shouldn't be put off by this; it's making the effort that counts, because quite often a strange thing happens. That same piece of music you were trying to make sense of can come back and bite you a few months, or even a few years, later. Sometimes a chance encounter – via the radio, TV, at a party, in a wine bar or any number of social settings – suddenly makes perfect sense in a way that it had not in the past. When this happens it can be a pretty powerful experience and is often explained by the slow but sure process of broadening your listening experiences – as you expand your musical memory with more and more templates, what seemed like a formidable challenge a month, six months or a year ago suddenly becomes today's essential listening.

All this, of course, requires a bit of patience, time and effort that involves the old-fashioned notion of delayed gratification, which is setting longer-term, rather than short-term, goals to produce rewards. This may sound a bit much in the consumerist age of instant gratification, but how many times do you fall in love at first sight? Once in a lifetime? Usually the deepest relationships are forged over time and take a bit of effort, and it's just the same with jazz.

1

Setting the Scene

What does Jazz Actually Mean?

Although jazz has been around for over a hundred years it's never been satisfactorily defined, posing the inevitable question: 'Well if you can't define it, how do you know it's jazz?' This curious paradox dates back to the music's origins when, in early 1917, a group of five young musicians from New Orleans calling themselves The Original Dixieland Jazz Band recorded 'Livery Stable Blues' for the Victor Talking Machine Company, which quickly became one of its earliest million-selling recordings. Compared with other popular musical styles, jazz sounded brash, loud and abrasive, yet there was widespread interest and curiosity in this new, unruly music, its uptempo abandon coinciding with a craze for social dancing that took off immediately following the industrialized death and destruction of World War I. As R.W. S. Mendl later wrote, 'Jazz is the product of a restless age; an age in which the fever of war is only now beginning to abate its fury; when men and women, after their efforts in the great struggle, are still too much disturbed to be content with a tranquil existence.'[17]

For a traumatized generation of young people who had survived the conflict and wanted to forget the past and ignore the future, jazz was more than a musical style: it was the style of the times. This was the so-called 'Jazz Age' of novelist F. Scott Fitzgerald, whose *Tales of the Jazz Age*, a collection of eleven short stories published in 1922, gave its name to an era. Jazz music quickly became associated with youth, energy and a revolt against convention. For those with money in their pockets wanting to shake up the stifling social conventions of the time, the intersection of alcohol, jazz and dance had a liberating and dizzyingly dangerous aura.

Today Scott Fitzgerald is regarded as one of the greatest American writers of the twentieth century, but when he paused in 1931, after a decade of booze and partying that had only been cut short by the stock market crash of 1929, to reflect on the origins of the Jazz Age he explained that jazz music, 'first meant sex, then dancing, then music'.[18] By then, the word jazz had passed into common usage as an all-purpose adjective that was applied to almost anything from clashing colours to clothing with loud patterns. But jazz music was something else – 'to jazz' was to dance in a frenzied fashion, while to 'jazz something up' meant to give it a bit of pep and energy.

Almost a hundred years later, the word jazz invokes equally vague connotations. For most, jazz is music we take to be jazz, and although it has acquired the requisite gravitas due an important musical genre, in practice it's an umbrella term covering a multitude of subgenres, any one of which might represent jazz in the public's mind, which is why this book is content to go along with an open definition of jazz.

However, things are not quite such plain sailing in the land of its birth, the United States, where there's a more rigid understanding of what jazz should be. In the 1980s, a line of reasoning was adopted by some that for jazz to be 'jazz', it must possess certain elements that were present when jazz was a social and cultural expression of urban black America between the turn of the twentieth century and the 1950s. It was a period when swing and a feeling for the blues were central to the music's expressionism, and these elements were retrospectively claimed as benchmarks to define what jazz was. However, the very act of defining jazz in terms of what it used to be had the effect of narrowcasting the music and setting in train a perception among the American people that jazz was now more about the past than the present. 'The real jazz' was deemed to be music that touched base with the jazz from its Golden Years, and more experimental forms of the music were not considered by some to be jazz at all.

This prescriptivist view of jazz overlooked the radical processes of evolution which jazz had undergone in both a national and global context, and does not appear to acknowledge how any art form inevitably grows beyond its roots and as it does so evolves and changes. Today, for example, opera is making considerable inroads in China, a development composer and musicologist Howard Goodall reminds us 'is likely to have an impact on opera itself within a generation or two. Each culture that has embraced it has played a part in its development and mutation.'[19] No art form, not even opera – or jazz – remains pure when it goes out into the world and rubs up against the conventions of other cultures.

Thus many people might raise their eyebrows that in an age of globalization, the Internet, 4G mobile telecommunications technology and cheap air travel, some American jazz academics, ideologues and assorted camp followers argue that for jazz to be jazz it must reflect a specific Afro-American identity. This may have something to do with what Milan Kundera called 'the parochialism of large nations', meaning they do not look beyond their borders since all their perceived needs can be found within them, so making them surprisingly naive about what is happening in the rest of the world.[20] Outside the United States jazz has taken on a life of its own, where, after a century of assimilation and emulation, a reconceptualization of the music has occurred, often with 'local' musicians developing ways of playing jazz that do not necessarily conform to the way jazz is played in America. This has tended to happen at a local level where American jazz has been reinterpreted, recast and transformed as part of a local cultural repertoire in a way that gives it meaning and relevance to its local community. This is hardly unique to jazz. In the world of classical music, for example, the interface between the global and the local was highlighted by a performance of the São Paolo Symphony Orchestra during London's Henry Wood concert season of 2016, the *Daily Telegraph* noting, '[They] want to be taken seriously on the international stage, which means playing the core classics to a high standard, yet to ignore their own music would be perverse … so the São Paolo honoured both.'[21] So Kabbalah, by the Brazilian composer Marlos Nobre was a combination of the global, western classical music, and the local, 'Brazilian percussion.' Similarly, it would be equally perverse if Brazilian jazz musicians wanted their music to sound like the product of urban Black America when they have the whole rich musical heritage of their own country to draw upon by adding elements from the samba, the bossa nova and other Brazilian rhythms into the jazz mix. Today, if we only listened to American jazz we would certainly be impoverished, yet the joy of listening to Brazilian jazz is just one example of the richness and diversity to be found in the global jazz scene. Clearly, then, jazz is many things to many people. It is, after all, an art form still in flux, still growing and developing with all the twists and surprising turns this implies, and at this point in the twenty-first century it has become a bewilderingly pluralistic music.

Using Playlists

Clearly it would take something of a Luddite – a term describing those opposed to, or slow to adopt, change in their lifestyle – to ignore the changes in how we now consume recorded music in a book such as this. So from now on, each chapter is followed by a recommended playlist and a song-by-song listening guide that's something akin to the old album liner notes of years ago. The idea is that you have the detailed overview of the subject at hand in the body of the chapter and a more informal discussion of the music that relates to it in the listening guide. Each playlist can be easily sourced and downloaded from the Internet and either stored on your iPod or on Compact Disc. I should stress that they are not intended to be condensed 'histories of jazz' or, in the case of the next chapter, a condensed 'history of the blues'. Equally, these playlists are not intended in aggregate to represent the 'best 250' or so jazz recordings and nor should they be construed as such. They are simply a means of illustrating each chapter in as interesting a way as possible. The whole idea is to try and avoid what is known in radio and television as the 'tune-out factor' by including tracks that are likely to put the listener off – jazz is, after all, something to be enjoyed rather than endured. Try and stay with the playlist for each chapter for as long as you can before moving on to build up your templates of listening experiences – with jazz it really is a case of familiarity breeding content.

2

The Blues

Recognizing the Structure

The vast majority of compositions, or songs, used in jazz have an underlying structure known as a song form which is always adhered to when the song is performed. These song forms, which vary from composition to composition, can be broken down into three broad categories – the blues, the American Popular Song (or Standard) and the original composition. Free jazz is less concerned with fixed forms, often favouring different organizing principles which we won't concern ourselves with at this point. Recognizing a song form and knowing a bit about how they work is a very useful aid in understanding jazz, so in the next couple of chapters we're going to look at each of the three categories, since together they cover a vast swathe of recorded jazz, and then in Chapter 4 we'll see how this information can be used to get more out of listening to an improvised jazz solo.

You can Hear an Awful Lot Just by Listening

When we listen to music, our ears are drawn naturally towards the melody, or the words and melody if it's a vocal performance. Some people think of the melody in 'horizontal' terms, meaning the twists and turns it takes as it seems to unfurl from left to right, or across the horizon. Underneath is the harmony, which is often thought of as 'vertical'. These are blocks of notes piled one on top of another that, when sounded together, is called a chord. A succession of chords is called a chord sequence – sometimes called a chord progression, chord changes or simply the 'changes' – and whether these changes are simple or complex, they nevertheless give a song its sense of direction.

The chord sequence, then, is what's going on beneath the melody of a song. One complete playing of a song's chord sequence is known as a chorus and with every subsequent chorus, the sequence of chords is retained in precisely the same order no matter how long the song lasts. A song form, or 'the form of a song' or simply 'the form' is just a term for a container that preserves a particular sequence of chords in a particular order. For example, every time you open the container labelled 'The Batman Theme' – which incidentally is a 12-bar blues – you'll find the same sequence of chords that are played in exactly the same way every time the tune is played. As the American jazz pianist Uri Cane observed, 'I would say that for a lot of people, when they hear jazz, they're not really hearing what the underlying structure is. Especially if they're used to hearing songs in forms which are much more simple [than jazz]. They hear someone playing for 30 minutes and think, "What's going on here?" But once you understand the underlying principle of what's going on … then you start to hear what's going on.'[22] What Cane is referring to is the underlying chord sequence, and once you've heard a song a few times and can hum or whistle along with it and know what's coming next, you have already grasped something of its structure or form. It's that easy.

The Blues Form

Chances are you will have heard the blues a million times before you bought this book, since they are just as much a

staple of rock and pop as they are of jazz – if you've heard
the Elvis Presley single 'Hound Dog', Chuck Berry's 'Johnny
B. Goode', Little Richard's 'Tutti Frutti', The Rolling Stones'
'Little Red Rooster', Tracy Chapman's 'Give Me One Reason',
ZZ Top's 'Tush', Eric Clapton's 'Sweet Home Chicago' or James
Brown's 'I Got You (I Feel So Good)', then you'll have heard a
12-bar blues. What this chapter does is look at how jazz musicians make use of the idiom. This is better understood when
you're listening to the music. Each time you tap your foot to
the rhythm, it's a beat. Four beats equals a bar. In their most
typical form the blues lasts for 12 bars and if you were to count
those 12 bars it would be: **1**-2-3-4, **2**-2-3-4, **3**-2-3-4, **4**-2-3-4
and so on until **12**-2-3-4, when the twelfth bar is reached and
the whole sequence is repeated over and over until the end
of the performance. Our brains tend to make sense out of the
blues by 'hearing' them as 3 lots of 4 bars – but you need the
music playing to hear what I mean. Here the blues lyrics help –
a phrase of 4 bars is followed by a similar phrase of 4 bars and
then resolved by a third 4-bar phrase. By listening to the lyrics
in conjunction with the chord changes, you get a better sense
of these 4-bar units. Go to the playlist that follows, and the first
song by Elmore James. Keep listening to the lyrics until you
can sing along with them. Note how each word is placed in
relation to the blues changes being played on his guitar. Now
sing the lyrics below – 'The Beginner's Guide Blues'[23]— in the
style you've picked up from Elmore James. Then play the 'The
Sun Is Shining' and when Elmore James starts singing, sing 'The
Beginner's Guide Blues' lyrics in the style of Elmore James *over*
his vocal. You'll soon get the hang of it, and once you do, you'll
realize that what sounds easy isn't quite as easy as you might
have first thought, and on top of that you'll have deepened your
understanding of the blues form in a way that will last you a
lifetime.

Readin' a Beginner's Guide, gotta chapter on the blues
    1 – 2 – 3 – 4, 2 – 2 – 3   4, 3 – 2 – 3 – 4, 4 – 2 – 3 – 4 (4 bars)
    Readin' a Beginner's Guide, I said it's got a chapter on the blues
    5 – 2 – 3 – 4, 6 – 2 – 3 – 4, 7 – 2 – 3 – 4, 8 – 2 – 3 – 4 (4 bars)
    Jus'gimme one more hour' an, I'll be an expert on the news (pronounce: nooze)
    9 – 2 – 3 – 4, 10 – 2 – 3 – 4, 11 – 2 – 3 – 4, 12 – 2 – 3 – 4 (4 bars)

Counting the number of bars as they go by during a performance is a simple skill that's easy to master and is a valuable tool to help you understand the more complicated forms that are outlined in the next chapter. Somehow we're all hardwired to understand the blues; it's both a simple and a profound idiom and is better heard than written about. The relatively short cycle of 12 bars means you hear the blues chord changes several times during one performance, so you soon become very familiar with the blues form. On an instrumental blues like 'Chitlins Con Carne' by Kenny Burrell,[24] which is well worth downloading, the first beat of each 12-bar cycle is 'marked' by the drummer on the 'One' of the 1-2-3-4 sequence that starts the 12-bar cycle. This is a useful aid to keeping your bearings during the performance.

As a listener, it's worth spending time with the blues playlist until you're familiar with where the chords change in real time, since hearing and feeling the blues changes is an important step towards understanding form. It also provides a valuable means of hearing how a solo relates to the chord sequence underneath it and you will also begin to get a sense of the soloist's expressive coherence within the form since he or she has a certain number of notes that fit each given chord at any given moment. The trick is to juxtapose the notes that fit each chord to maximum expressive effect to tell a musical story. Since, in its basic form, the blues only involves three chords, most jazz musicians have learned several classic blues solos note-for-note to better understand the rules of the game in the same way English literature students learn the great sonnets to better understand the work of the great poets.

One way of 'hearing' the blues changes more clearly is to think of each chord change as a musical colour. To help you do this the blues changes are shown below in graphic form with underlying chord movement of the blues depicted in black, grey and white. These are not very exciting colours, I grant you, so in your mind's eye I suggest you picture them in more vivid hues. The blues usually starts in the home key (we'll be here all day if we start listing exceptions) which is shown in black, and lasts for 4 bars (or 4 units of 1-2-3-4). The home key, incidentally, is like the home key on the computer keyboard which returns you to the beginning of the document. In music it's the chord the composition began in.

The first 4 bars of a 12-bar blues

1-2-3-4, 2-2-3-4, 3-2-3-4, 4-2-3-4

The next chord movement goes up four notes to grey. This new chord lasts for 2 bars.

The first 6 bars of a 12-bar blues

1-2-3-4, 2-2-3-4, 3-2-3-4, 4-2-3-4, **5**-2-3-4, **6**-2-3-4

The next chord movement is down again to black, or the home key, for another 2 bars.

The first 8 bars of a 12-bar blues

1-2-3-4, 2-2-3-4, 3-2-3-4, 4-2-3-4, 5-2-3-4, 6-2-3-4, **7**-2-3-4, **8**-2-3-4

The next chord change is up five notes, to white, for 1 bar only.

The first 9 bars of a 12-bar blues

1-2-3-4, 2-2-3-4, 3-2-3-4, 4-2-3-4, 5-2-3-4, 6-2-3-4, 7-2-3-4, 8-2-3-4, **9**-2-3-4

The blues then resolves, first by going down one step to grey for one bar.

The first 10 bars of a 12-bar blues

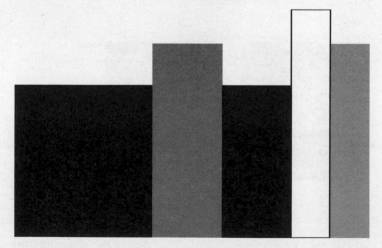

1-2-3-4, 2-2-3-4, 3-2-3-4, 4-2-3-4, 5-2-3-4, 6-2-3-4, 7-2-3-4, 8-2-3-4, 9-2-3-4, **10**-2-3-4

Finally, the blues returns to the home key of black for the final 2 bars.

The complete 12-bar blues in graphic form

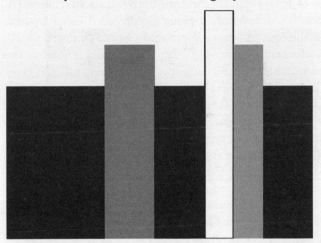

Count:

1-2-3-4, 2-2-3-4, 3-2-3-4, 4-2-3-4/ 5-2-3-4, 6-2-3-4/ 7-2-3-4, 8-2-3-4/ 9-2-3-4/ 10-2-3-4/ **11**-2-3-4, **12**-2-3-4

This complete chord sequence is then repeated over and over for the duration of the performance.

Try and hear the chord changes as changes of vivid musical colour at bars 5 (grey), 7 (black), 9 (white), 10 (grey) and back down to the home key (black) at 11.

The Blues in Different Guises

The blues can have lyrics, be fast or slow, happy or sad and there are even occasional examples where the 12-bar blues form has been incorporated lock, stock and barrel into a larger song and mixed with sections that are not blues at all, for example, 'Blues in the Night' comprises 54 bars (12 + 12 + 18 + 12). Here the 18-bar section is not the blues at all, and appears as the song's 'bridge'; 'Black Coffee', made famous by an album of the same name by singer Peggy Lee, comprises 44 bars (12 + 12 + 8 + 12). Here the 8-bar section is not a blues; 'Locomotion' from the album *Blue Train* by saxophonist John Coltrane also follows the previous 44-bar format, but this time the 8-bar chord sequence in the middle is pinched from George Gershwin's 'I Got Rhythm', while in the case of Jerome Kern and Oscar Hammerstein II's 'Can't Help Lovin' That Man', the 12-bar blues is used as the verse (or introduction) to a song that's not a blues at all. On Dave Brubeck's 'Blue Rondo à la Turk', a 12-bar blues acts as a contrast to the distinctive 'Blue Rondo' theme in 9/8, by providing the underlying chord sequence in 4/4 for solos. Finally, it perhaps goes without saying that there are countless examples of the blues that don't have blues in their title, such as Miles Davis's 'Freddie Freeloader', Charlie Parker's 'Now's the Time' and 'Cheryl', Bill Haley's 'Rock Around the Clock', Booker T. and the MG's 'Green Onions', Duke Ellington's 'Things Ain't What They Used to Be', The Modern Jazz Quartet's 'Bag's Groove', Lee Morgan's 'Sidewinder' – which is actually a 24-bar blues, with each of the black, grey and white sections lasting twice as long as a 12-bar blues – while 'Watermelon Man' is often called a 16-bar blues.

Note that not all tunes with 'blues' in their title are 12-bar blues, or even a blues at all – Richard Rodgers' 'Little Girl Blue' is an AB tune of two chord sequences that each last 12 bars, neither of which are blues chord changes, while 'Sugar Blues' is a non-blues 18-bar form. 'Birth of the Blues' uses a 32-bar AABA form and 'Bye Bye Blues' is a 32-bar ABAC form, which you will quickly spot once you're familiar with the 12-bar blues form and have read the next chapter.

The Blues Playlist

For our first playlist it will be necessary to download the following tunes:

1. Elmore James: 'The Sun Is Shining' from the album *History of the Blues.*
2. Sidney Bechet: 'Blue Horizon' from *Jazz Classics Vol. 1.*
3. Sammy Price: 'Jonah Whales Again' from *Mid Century Jazz* (originally released as *Barrelhouse and Blues*).
4. Count Basie: 'Boogie Woogie (I May Be Wrong)' from the album *Count Basie at Newport.*
5. Donald Byrd: 'Funky Mama' from *Fuego.*
6. Charlie Parker: 'K.C. Blues' from *The Complete Charlie Parker on Verve* and various Parker compilations.
7. Jimmy Smith: 'Organ Grinder Swing' from *Organ Grinder's Swing.*
8. Buddy Rich: 'Big Swing Face' from *Big Swing Face.*
9. Modern Jazz Quartet: 'Bags Groove' from *The Complete Last Concert.*
10. Stan Getz and Cal Tjader: 'Crows Nest' from *Cal Tjader/Stan Getz.*
11. Oscar Peterson Trio: 'Sandy's Blues' from *The Way I Really Play Vol. 3.*
12. Gil Evans: 'Las Vegas Tango' from *The Individualism of Gil Evans.*
13. Dave Brubeck: 'Blue Rondo à la Turk' from *Time Out.*
14. Monty Alexander: 'Bluesology' from *The Way It Is.*

The idea of this playlist is threefold – (i) to create a playlist you can actually enjoy *and* learn from; (ii) to get used to some of the sounds of jazz using the 12-bar form and (iii) to illustrate some of the many guises the 12-bar blues form can pop up in. It is worth emphasizing again that this is not a history of the blues in fourteen songs. The key point about these examples is that the chord changes (from black to grey and back again to black, and so on) ring through loud and clear. Once you're familiar with these changes, you'll hear them crop up in all sorts of musical situations, including pop music and soundtrack music for films and television. When listening to each playlist, focus on the music, the sound and the rhythm. Allow the music to wash over you and release you from the stress of the day. Listen for the feelings that the music expresses (happy? sad? grooving?). Let yourself engage with those feelings, and notice how your body also responds to the music – is your foot tapping in time to the music? The composer and pianist Stephen Halpern has researched the ways in which different musical vibrations affect various parts of the body – high frequencies are felt in the head while lower frequencies are felt in the throat, chest and abdomen. It's interesting to see what notes register where in your body. Identifying the emotional and physical aspects of this music allows your body as well as your mind to respond to it, and helps you engage with the music at a deeper level than superficial listening and heightens your involvement with it. Finally, why not try applying Halpern's principles to each playlist as you listen to them as a way to trying to get a bit more out of them?

Listening Notes for the Blues Playlist

1. Elmore James: 'The Sun Is Shining' from *History of the Blues*

Here is a classic blues performance by Elmore James (1918–63) that captures the flavour of the early itinerant blues singers that could be heard on many a street corner, courthouse square or plantation cabin in America's deep south as the nineteenth century gave way to the twentieth, when the blues emerged as the voice of the disenfranchised black community. A performance such as this is profoundly moving and seems to bypass a lot of cultural information – James was one of the survivors from the early decades of the blues; he's raw and uncompromising but also profoundly moving, his music influencing seminal pop figures such as Jimi Hendrix, Eric Clapton, the Beatles and more. This, then, is the blues at its most primal, using the classic 12-bar blues form.

2. Sidney Bechet: 'Blue Horizon' from *Jazz Classics Vol. 1*

On this December 1944 performance of 'Blue Horizon', Bechet plays clarinet and his sumptuous sound on the instrument was highly distinctive and instantly recognizable. Individuality such as this was accorded high status among the early jazz musicians. Another characteristic of the early jazzmen was how they tended to frame their improvisation within 12-bar units (note the short pause at the end of each chorus). Bechet takes six choruses; note how closely he follows the blues changes. The strength of this performance is how he conveys the 'blues feeling' in a way that is both intense and expressive.

3. Sammy Price and his Jaycee Stompers: 'Jonah Whales Again' from *Mid Century Jazz* (originally released as *Barrelhouse and Blues*)

It was inevitable that the blues should make the transition from the streets and into the saloons, bars and brothels of America's Southwest where entertainment was often provided by pianists. Pianists in America's Southwest devised a style of playing known as 'Fast Western' or 'Texas Piano', a style we now recognize as boogie-woogie. It was well suited to the upright pianos found in the bars and clubs since its highly percussive style could rise above the background noise and get everyone onto the dance floor – however small. This performance touches base with those early days of jazz when the band would ramp up the excitement and get the dancers crawling up the walls. Opening with a call to arms from trumpeter Jonah Jones, each soloist is a master of the 12-bar blues form, yet their approach is very personal – Pete Brown on alto saxophone, who follows Jones, is oblique and economical, trombonist Vic Dickenson is measured and elegant while Sammy Price on piano – no shrinking violet – let rip boogie-woogie style.

4. Count Basie: 'Boogie Woogie (I May Be Wrong)' from *Count Basie at Newport*

Although pianist Count Basie came from Red Bank, New Jersey, he ended up in Kansas City in America's Southwest in the late 1920s, where he quickly absorbed the boogie-woogie style. The leader of a big band for over fifty years, he's caught in fine form at the 1957 Newport Jazz Festival with his big band, combining boogie-woogie with a blues vocal by the great Jimmy Rushing (note the classic blues stanza of three lines, with the third line rhyming in resolution). The tenor saxophone break is by Lester Young, who fashions a solo of passion and elegance despite the rising tide of excitement around him that is a stone's throw from early rock 'n' roll. Note Young's distinctive tone on tenor saxophone and his laid-back way of playing that, as we'll see later, was widely imitated.

5. Donald Byrd: 'Funky Mama' from *Fuego*

Picture a jazz club at 2 a.m. The band is playing their last set for the few remaining customers. The bandleader calls for a slow blues. The performance is a series of solos all made up on the spot, first by the bassist Doug Watkins, the next by pianist Duke Pearson, then the solo by alto saxophonist Jackie McLean catches our ear; imbued with the blues feeling, it's a minor classic. Listen to the drive, energy and passion of his playing, even at a slow tempo, which he climaxes by moving into 'double time', or doubling the tempo, at the end. Pearson comes back in on piano, returning to the original tempo, cleverly sustaining the early hours mood. Listen to how he hands trumpeter Donald Byrd a springboard into his solo. Note how, like the preceding soloists, Byrd builds his solo before gradually bringing us back to earth and winding up the performance.

6. Charlie Parker: 'K.C. Blues' from *The Complete Charlie Parker on Verve*

'K.C. Blues' is a good example of Parker's mature style. He enters after Walter Bishop Jr's 4-bar piano introduction and states the theme, following it with two powerful, cogently constructed choruses, a flow of dramatic, interlocking ideas that grow into an enduring statement in the blues form. Such is the emotional force of Parker's solo that it eclipses those by a young Miles Davis on trumpet and Bishop on piano that follow, before he returns with another improvised chorus at the end. In the 1970s Parker's first two improvised choruses were harmonized across the brass and saxophone sections of the Don Ellis big band (available as an iTunes download as Don Ellis/'K.C. Blues'), the musical integrity of Parker's solo standing firm even when orchestrated and performed against rock rhythms.

7. Jimmy Smith: 'Organ Grinder Swing' from *Organ Grinder Swing*

Hammond B-3 organist Jimmy Smith frequently appeared in the lower reaches of the *Billboard Best Selling Pop Singles Chart* in the 1960s with a series of singles, first on the Blue Note label, then on the Verve label. 'Organ Grinder Swing' is a typical example, reaching No. 51 in April 1966. Smith grabs your attention from the first 'shout chord' – a loud chord intended to get our attention – and holds it throughout. Accompanied by Kenny Burrell on guitar and Grady Tate on drums, don't worry if you can't understand Smith's brief, half spoken, half mumbled vocal interpolations that occur twice in this performance – you're not supposed to. They just add a little spice to what is already a commanding performance, but in the last of the mumbled episodes, the reference to the police is clear since, then as now, their impartiality when policing black neighbourhoods continues to be a cause for concern.

8. Buddy Rich: 'Big Swing Face' from *Big Swing Face*

At the Newport Jazz Festival of 1965, some of jazz's greatest drummers were gathered on stage to show off their prowess – Elvin Jones, Art Blakey, Louie Bellson and Buddy Rich. When it came to Rich's solo, Dan Morgenstern, internationally acknowledged as perhaps the greatest authority on jazz, observed, 'If nothing else of value happened at Newport, to witness Rich would have made it all worthwhile. The audience's standing ovation seemed a modest tribute … [he is] without a doubt, the greatest drummer who ever lived.'[25] Buddy Rich's speed and precision was the stuff of legend, but his great gift was the ability to make a big band 'swing'. However, nailing down a definition of 'swing' is just as fraught as nailing down a definition of jazz. It's something that's 'felt' by both performers and audience, rather than something that can be written down or rehearsed. It's a feeling that readily communicates, usually in terms of a feel-good factor that seems to demand a physical response in return – tapping your foot, snapping your fingers, and so on. 'Big Swing Face' is a classic Rich big band performance that includes a masterfully swinging yet understated piano solo by Ray Starling; an alto solo by Ernie Watts that shows great fluency and ease in the blues idiom; a saxophone *soli* – two choruses of the blues written to sound like a single saxophone solo to 'show off' the whole saxophone section – followed by a parabolic trumpet solo by Bobby Shew.

9. Modern Jazz Quartet: 'Bags Groove' from *The Complete Last Concert*

By the time this recording was made, the Modern Jazz Quartet had become one of the most popular groups in jazz following their first regular engagement at the New York jazz club Birdland on 5 August 1954. Comprising John Lewis on piano, Milt Jackson on vibraphone, Percy Heath on bass and Connie Kay on drums, their mission was to move jazz out of the smoky nightclub and onto the concert stage. Despite such high aspirations, they succeeded. Immaculately attired in evening dress and black bow ties, they were quiet experimenters, most notably incorporating the influence of Bach and Baroque music into jazz. But they were never happier than when they stepped outside the genteel and cultivated personas they created for themselves to indulge in some heartily swinging jazz. Vibraphonist Milt Jackson was a consummate master of the blues form with a seemingly endless fund of ideas, the fluency of his playing concealing an intensity of the don't-mess-with-me kind. He is followed by the leader, John Lewis, who refined the less-is-more ethic into a personal style that perfectly contrasted Jackson's.

10. Stan Getz and Cal Tjader: 'Crows Nest' from *Cal Tjader/Stan Getz*

Here's a 12-bar blues that doesn't immediately sound like a 12-bar blues, but most assuredly is, as becomes clear when saxophonist Stan Getz, vibist Cal Tjader, guitarist Eddie Duran and pianist Vince Guaraldi take their solos; what emerges is five young men in fine form enjoying themselves in the shared language of the blues. Recorded in February 1958, the easy optimism of this performance illustrates the distance the blues had travelled since the turn of the century, when the blues was the language of the itinerant musicians in America's deep south. Note how Getz's tenor saxophone sound is inspired by Lester Young, a deceptively laid-back style that conceals the acute musical mind behind it. The driving bass player is Scott LaFaro and the drummer is Billy Higgins.

11. Oscar Peterson: 'Sandy's Blues' from *The Way I Really Play Vol. 3*

'Sandy's Blues' is a masterful performance of the blues by the piano virtuoso Oscar Peterson. Here the blues becomes a tour de force that moves through a series of tempo changes until the final climax. Notice how Peterson creates excitement by the use of 'question–and–answer riffs' – a brief, repeated chorded motif 'answered' by a fingered response. This dates back to the big bands of the 1930s and 1940s that Peterson heard on the radio as he was growing up. There was only one pianist in the world, then and now, who could have pulled off an astonishing performance like this, and that was Oscar Peterson.

12. Gil Evans: 'Las Vegas Tango' from *The Individualism of Gil Evans*

Here is an atmospheric, moody conceptualization of a 12-bar blues in a minor key by arranger Gil Evans. Notice how the burden of complexity has been reversed from the performance by the Buddy Rich band where the trumpets, trombones and saxophones did all the fancy, complex stuff, while Rich's role was essentially that of keeping time underneath. In contrast, the role of the trumpets, trombones and saxophones in 'Las Vegas Tango' is confined to simple long notes and later, trumpet stabs to mark out the blues changes while the drummer, Elvin Jones, is responsible for the complex stuff, laying down a polyrhythmic carpet in compound time – instead of counting 1–2–3–4, 2–2–3–4 and so on, you count 1–2–3, 2–2–3, 3–2–3, etc. The striking trombone solo is by Jimmy Cleveland.

13. Dave Brubeck: 'Blue Rondo à la Turk' from *Time Out*

It's not often that a jazz single got onto to *Billboard's Hot 100*, but pianist Dave Brubeck's 'Take Five' reached No. 25 on the chart on 9 October 1961, going on to become the bestselling jazz single of all time (and helping the Brubeck quartet become the most popular group in jazz during the 1960s). The flip side was Brubeck's 'Blue Rondo à la Turk', which is an example of a 12-bar blues coming packaged in a larger form. The blues section emerges after the rumbustious 'Blue Rondo' theme is stated in 9/8 when Paul Desmond's sax solo emerges swinging sublimely in 4/4, hitting the right mood from the very first note.

14. Monty Alexander: 'Bluesology' from *The Way It Is*

In 1976 Alexander formed a trio with John Clayton on bass and Jeff Hamilton on drums, and in 1979 he recorded 'Bluesology', a 12-bar blues that builds and builds with irrepressible swing and a genuine blues feeling. It presents an appropriate climax to a playlist that seeks to show what a remarkably malleable and flexible form the blues is. And by the way, jazz was once dubbed 'The Sound of Surprise', for reasons you'll discover here.

3

The American Popular Song

Setting Standards

Listening to jazz, either on record or in live performance, can be construed as cultural consumption. The thing about cultural consumption is that the more knowledge you have of what is being consumed, the more you're likely to get out of the experience. This differs from material consumption, when goods are consumed without any prior knowledge or apprehension of their meanings. Knowledge of how a bottle of lemonade is made, for example, is not going to enhance your enjoyment of it one way or the other, when you're knocking it back on a hot day. When it comes to 'culturally consuming' jazz, a basic understanding of the various ways American Popular Songs, or Standards as they're more commonly called, are constructed – in other words, how composers bolt together different chord sequences to create a songform – can work wonders in speeding up our appreciation of what jazz musicians are up to when we hear them play a standard.

The American Popular Song is the term used to describe vintage American pop songs from the Golden Age of Songwriting, which runs, from 1900 to about 1955, most of which appeared in Broadway musicals. From around the late 1920s, jazz

musicians and popular singers began adding them to their repertoire, so giving them a second life beyond the Broadway stage.
The very best – by composers such as George Gershwin, Jerome
Kern, Cole Porter, Harold Arlen, Richard Rodgers, Vincent
Youmans, Irving Berlin and others – were a marriage of words
and music where the words seemed to give greater meaning to
the melody and the melody seemed to give greater meaning to
the words. They're little gems of musical genius capable of bearing rigorous musical analysis, as Alec Wilder's classic study *American Popular Song* (1972) demonstrated. Audiences, critics and
musicians quickly acknowledged that the best of these songs set
the standard in Popular Music, hence the term Standards.

What is interesting about these songs is that they possessed
a certain autonomy so that there's no single, definitive version
of any of them – they are seemingly capable of withstand-
ing endless interpretation. For example, even though singers
of the stature of Bing Crosby, Ella Fitzgerald and Billie Holiday all covered the 48-bar 'Night and Day' by Cole Porter (an
ABABCB form with each strain of 8 bars – I'll explain about
this alphabetic stuff in just a minute), it was never a 'Crosby
song', or a 'Fitzgerald song' or even a 'Billie Holiday song' in
the way pop songs today are inextricably linked to a performer's
single, memorable recorded performance of it. Instead, 'Night
and Day' remained a 'Cole Porter song' with an independent
life of its own, recorded by a wide range of artists that include
Frank Sinatra, Fred Astaire, Doris Day, Tony Bennett, Eartha
Kitt, Deanna Durbin, Shirley Bassey, Dionne Warwick, Etta
James, Jamie Cullum and even U2. When Alec Wilder spoke
of Cole Porter bringing 'a certain theatrical elegance, as well as
interest and sophistication, wit and musical complexity to the
popular song form',[26] he was also implying a corollary value
judgement that doesn't just apply to Porter but to the best of
the Great American Songbook as well.

AABA – a Swedish Pop Group?

The majority of Standards – most estimates agree on around sixty percent – tend to use an AABA form over which the melody is written. 'Yes' I hear you saying, 'Do I really need to know this?' Well, everyone has heard any number of AABA songs on the radio; here's a couple of examples – 'Will You Still Love Me Tomorrow?', 'Just the Way You Are' (with a great alto saxophone solo by Phil Woods on the Billy Joel version), 'Yesterday', 'Great Balls of Fire', 'Hey Jude' and of course, the 'Christmas Song' – you know, where the lyrics go: 'Chestnuts roasting on an open fire …'[27]

Simply put, the 32-bar AABA song breaks down into four sections of eight bars each. On the first two sections the melody remains largely the same, but lyrics continue the song's story. Then there's a contrasting section of 8 bars called the 'middle eight', 'the bridge' or 'the release', then we're back to the melody we started with for the final 8 bars. If we call the 8-bar sections that are identical in melodic/harmonic content 'A' and the contrasting 8-bar section 'B',[28] then we might say a song with this particular construction is a 32-bar AABA song.

> ### A BASIC SONGFORM: AABA
>
> A – Exposition of the Melody
> A – The melody is repeated to increase our familiarity with it
> B – A contrasting melody is introduced
> A —The initial melody is repeated

To get some hands-on experience of this form, go to the playlist at the end of this chapter and listen to the John Coltrane/Johnny Hartman version of 'They Say It's Wonderful'. Allow the selection to play through until Johnny Hartman's vocal: in practice, it's pretty easy to follow the AABA construction. If you're in any doubt, just count the bars 1-2-3-4, 2-2-3-4 and so on behind the vocal until 8-2-3-4 and the second A section begins. The B section is easy to recognize – a beautifully written melody that perfectly contrasts the two A sections that preceded it – and finally the chorus ends with a return to the A section.

At this stage you're probably thinking, well, that was pretty simple, what's all the fuss about? But take away the lyrics and melody and you have the basic materials a jazz improviser works with – the rhythm and harmonic structure. It's up to the improviser to provide his or her melody that fits that selfsame chord sequence in the form of an improvisation. So why not try this. Once you're familiar with the melody and lyrics of an AABA song, try singing them quietly to yourself *behind* a jazz improvisation on that tune. It may take a bit of concentration at first, but you'll quickly realize how both the song you're singing and the notes the improviser is playing both 'fit' the harmonies of the song, which are repeated over and over – AABA, AABA, AABA and so on – until the end of the performance. This simple exercise will help you better appreciate the jazz improviser's art.

Not All Standards Come in the AABA Format

While the 32-bar AABA form accounts for the majority of Standards, there is a significant minority that do not fall into this basic scheme. Some composers take delight in varying the AABA set-up in order to make life interesting. For example, 'Don't Know Why', sung by Norah Jones, and 'Every Breath' by The Police are AABABA songs – in other words, they are AABA songs plus a BA section tagged on at the end for extra interest. 'How High the Moon' juxtaposes the A and B sections as ABAB. If we say the A and B sections represent two different strains, we should also be aware that other composers like to keep us on our toes by slipping in an alternative 8-bar strain within the 32-bar form. For example, 'Autumn Leaves' includes a third C strain, making it an AABC song, while 'My Romance', 'Embraceable You', 'Out of Nowhere', 'Stardust', 'Sweet Georgia Brown', 'On Green Dolphin Street' and 'Indiana' juxtapose the three strains as ABAC. Interestingly, the enduring Standard 'Summertime' also uses the ABAC form, but it's only 16 bars long with each section 4 bars long instead of the usual 8.

Standards can also exceed 32 bars in length and can be virtually any length a composer wants, within musical reason. For example, 'Girl from Ipanema' may be 40 bars long but settles for the AABA form (the A sections remain the usual 8 bars while the B section is 16 bars). However, most of the longer standards have what might be described as ad hoc forms: 'Begin the Beguine', for example, is 108 bars long (!), and uses an A-A-B-A-C1-C2 form with the A, B and C1 sections 16 bars long, and a C2 section of 16 bars plus 12 bars – that additional 12 bars at the end providing a neat sense of resolution. Other examples might include the 48-bar 'I'll Remember April', which has an ABCDAB form (each strain is 8 bars in length) while the 56-bar 'I've Got You Under My Skin' has an ABACDEF form (each strain is 8 bars long).

Generally speaking, the infinite number of melodies dreamt up by songwriters usually came with a bespoke set of chords although it's worth noting that it's not unknown for a composer to pinch a chord sequence from another song and write their own melody on top. For example, George Gershwin's 'I Got Rhythm' (a 32-bar AABA song) famously provided the chord sequence for the theme tune of the Hanna-Barbera cartoon series *The Flintstones* and umpteen other jazz Standards.[29] Staying with TV themes for a moment, 'The Muppet Show Theme' is also an AABA song where the A section uses the 'I Got Rhythm' chords while the B section uses an original chord sequence.

During the Big Band Era, running roughly from 1935–45, any number of songs were based on the chords of 'I Got Rhythm' and 'Honeysuckle Rose' (both 32-bar AABA songs) – for example, these chord sequences and the 12-bar blues provided the core repertoire of the early Count Basie band – while Duke Ellington's theme tune 'Take the A Train' was loosely based on the harmonic grid of 'Exactly Like You'. From 1945 the net was widened to include the chords of more sophisticated Standards – Thelonious Monk's 'Hackensack' was based on the chords of 'Lady Be Good', 'In Walked Bud' was based on 'Blue Skies' while in '52nd Street Theme' the A sections came from 'I Got Rhythm' and the B section from 'Honeysuckle Rose'. In fact, it's hard to think of an original jazz composition from this period that was not based on the chords of some other tune. For example, 'Bird of Paradise' and 'Prince Albert' were based on the chords of 'All the Things You Are', 'Hot House' and 'Wham Bam Thank You Ma'am' on 'What is This Thing Called Love?'; 'Bongo Bop' was based on 'When I Grow Too Old to Dream', and so on. Songs such as these, that use a new melody over a pre-existing chord sequence, are known as contrafacts.

As Standards come with so many different melodic schemes and chord progressions, it's clearly not possible to illustrate them graphically in the same way as we did for the blues. However, the principle of *listening* is just the same as with the blues, and that is to try and picture the shifting harmonic movement – the chord changes – under the melody in terms of colours. The difference with Standards is that usually the chords, or colours, change with much greater frequency than the blues. By following the often ingenious ways in which the chords move underneath the melody and the way they return 'home' at the end of each section for a pleasing sense of resolution, you will be getting a sense of the song's form.

The Standards Playlist

For our second playlist we will call on the services of the jazz vocalists, since knowledge of the lyrics is a useful aid to help remember both melody and form. Indeed, some of the finest improvising jazz musicians insist on learning the lyrics of a song in addition to its melody and accompanying harmonies before embarking on an improvisation. Among those who have adopted this technique are pianist Keith Jarrett in contemporary times, while further back in history saxophonists Dexter Gordon and Lester Young were both well-known advocates of learning the lyrics – indeed, Dexter Gordon even liked to recite the lyrics of a song he was about to play as part of his (often humorous) stage patter. Some musicians say knowledge of the lyrics helps them relate to the song's emotional content (pianist Keith Jarrett, for example).[30]

Once you've heard this playlist a few times, you'll discover the lyrics and melodies start to stick in your memory without any apparent effort; think of the number of times you join in with pop songs on the radio without having made any conscious attempt to remember the words – 'Hi Ho Silver Lining' by Jeff Beck, anybody? Becoming familiar with the words and melodies of the songs on this playlist will be enormously useful when you get to Chapter 5, which deals with the improvised jazz solo. Here you will discover exactly the same playlist in exactly the same order, only this time in instrumental versions. So the more time you spend getting to know the vocal versions of these songs, the less time it will take you to unlock the mysteries of the instrumental versions. For our second session, the playlist consists of the following tunes:

1. John Coltrane and Johnny Hartman: 'They Say It's Wonderful'.
2. Billie Holiday: 'Good Morning Heartache' from *Billie Holiday: The Complete Original American Decca Recordings*.

3. Anita O'Day: 'Sweet Georgia Brown' from *Jazz on a Summer's Day*.
4. Billie Holiday: 'I Loves You Porgy' from *Billie Holiday: The Complete Original American Decca Recordings*.
5. Ella Fitzgerald: 'Moonlight in Vermont' from *Ella Fitzgerald at the Opera House*.
6. Sarah Vaughan: 'On Green Dolphin Street' from *Sassy Swings the Tivoli*.
7. Ella Fitzgerald: 'Love for Sale' from *Ella in Berlin*.
8. Sarah Vaughan: 'There Will Never Be Another You' from *Live at the 1971 Monterey Jazz Festival*.
9. Mel Tormé: 'Isn't It Romantic' from *Mel Tormé and Friends*.
10. Ella Fitzgerald: 'Mack the Knife' from *Ella in Berlin*.
11. Sarah Vaughan: 'What Is This Thing Called Love' from *Sassy Swings the Tivoli*.
12. Betty Carter: 'My Favourite Things' from *The Audience and Betty Carter*.

Listening Notes for the Standards Playlist

1. John Coltrane and Johnny Hartman: 'They Say It's Wonderful'

When Coltrane's record producer Bob Thiele wanted to reveal the lyrical side of Coltrane's art for record buyers and in March 1963, the elegant voice of Jonny Hartman was added to Coltrane's regular working quartet, the saxophonist having admired Hartman's singing since the 1950s.[31] In the event, on *Johnny Hartman and John Coltrane*, Coltrane emerged as a subtle foil for Hartman, both artists rising to the challenge of creating a unified artistic statement.

2. Billie Holiday: 'Good Morning Heartache' from *Billie Holiday: The Complete Original American Decca Recordings*

During her early career, Billie Holiday sang from the perspective of a woman unlucky in love, but as an older woman never far from the clamour of the tabloid headlines, she sang from the perspective of a woman unlucky in life, frequently choosing songs in the first person that put her at the centre of the action where her life experiences appeared to be mirrored in the lyrics of her songs. A good example is 'Good Morning Heartache'. Here she sings about unrequited love, and there's a wonderful *film noir* sound quality about this performance, very much of its time – 1946 – yet with a depth and universality that transcends its era. Especially written for Holiday by Irene Higginbotham, the former wife of the celebrated Swing Era pianist Teddy Wilson, 'Good Morning Heartache' uses a 32-bar AABA form but, because of the slow tempo, the second chorus is truncated to just BA since the old 78 rpm recordings had a time limit of around three minutes and couldn't accommodate two complete AABA choruses.

3. Anita O'Day: 'Sweet Georgia Brown' from *Jazz on a Summer's Day*

A 1949 version of this song by Brother Bones was adopted by the Harlem Globetrotters as their theme song in 1950 and today it is inextricably linked with them. However, in jazz the definitive performance of 'Sweet Georgia Brown' must surely belong to Anita O'Day. This version is taken from the soundtrack of the film *Jazz on a Summer's Day*, which documents some of the best performances at the 1958 Newport Jazz Festival. Available on DVD, be sure to get it since there's not a dull moment on this beautifully photographed 85-minute film. Here is jazz as performance art with Miss O'Day's subtle choreography at the microphone lending both drama and humour to her performance. Miss O'Day never lacked chutzpah, and the way she won over her sceptical audience with her performance here was a film highlight. To say that 'Sweet Georgia Brown' has a 32-bar ABAC form scarcely does justice to Miss O'Day's rendition. As a singer she had a small vocal range – not much more than an octave – yet the listener is never conscious of this because of the way in which she cleverly marshals her vocal resources by avoiding any notes beyond her range – clever stuff. What emerges is a sort of quasi-instrumental expressionism, with syllables articulated to enhance the rhythmic impetus of the lyrics, since the one thing Miss O'Day could do was swing. The long, drawn-out introduction to drum accompaniment serves to heighten the tension until the dramatic release when the song bursts into a grooving swing tempo and then, when the tempo unexpectedly doubles in the next chorus, the audience is won over.

4. Billie Holiday: 'I Loves You Porgy' from *Billie Holiday: The Complete Original American Decca Recordings*

'I Loves You Porgy' comes from George Gershwin's musical/ opera *Porgy and Bess* (Gershwin called it a folk opera) that was first produced on Broadway in 1935. Opera critics dismissed it, and it lost a lot of money. Then in 1942, five years after Gershwin's death, it reopened at the Majestic Theatre, again on Broadway, in edited form and was acclaimed by the critics and public alike. Six years later, on Friday 10 December 1948, Billie Holiday introduced the tune to the jazz repertoire. As originally written, the song was a duet between Porgy and Bess, but here Holiday sings Bess's stanzas, albeit discarding the first stanza and modifying some of the 'Aunt Jemimaisms' in the original lyrics. The performance was worked up in the studio with Holiday a little worse for wear either through drink or drugs, or both, and capable of only one take, but that was enough to capture this profound and affecting interpretation of the song that became a benchmark for jazz vocalists who subsequently recorded it.

5. Ella Fitzgerald: 'Moonlight in Vermont' from *Ella Fitzgerald at the Opera House*

'Moonlight in Vermont' is one of the better ballads, a well-conceived melody that falls into the familiar AABA form, but watch the A sections: they are only 6 bars in length, as 6+6+8+6. Listen closely as Ella Fitzgerald sings the lyrics – interestingly they do not rhyme, which is unusual for a Standard, since each verse (A sections) is a haiku.[32] Recorded during the 1957 Jazz at the Philharmonic tour of the USA when they played Chicago, Ella has Rolls-Royce accompaniment in Oscar Peterson on piano, Herb Ellis on guitar, Ray Brown on bass and Jo Jones on drums.

6. Sarah Vaughan: 'On Green Dolphin Street' from *Sassy Swings the Tivoli*

'On Green Dolphin Street', from the 1947 movie of the same name written by Bronislau Kaper, was perhaps surprisingly not the hit everyone had expected, since quite apart from its haunting melody, it had a lot going for it. Basically it's a 32-bar ABAC form, with a melodic line that many vocalists find difficult to sing in tune, so is usually performed as an instrumental, but for a singer of Sarah Vaughan's ability (she had perfect pitch) it's meat and potatoes. Note how, in the first chorus, the Latin and swing sections neatly demarcate the A from the B sections. The opening 8-bars have a Latin feel which had become common performance practice, followed by the first 8-bar A section that begins 'Lover, one lovely day'. Listen how, in this section, the Latin feel continues. This is contrasted by a swinging 8-bar B section that begins 'Green Dolphin Street supplied the setting'. The bass returns to the light Latin feel for the next 8-bar A section, which is again contrasted by the swinging 7-bar C section. Then comes a return of the 8-bar introduction that leads into the second chorus and revisits the A-B-A-C form, but this time Vaughan and her accompanists swing throughout in 4/4, Vaughan adopting a more expansive tone to explore the feeling of freedom from the alternating Latin and swing sections.

7. Ella Fitzgerald: 'Love for Sale' from *Ella in Berlin*

Cole Porter, famous for brilliantly satirical lyrics, left nothing to the imagination with his down-to-earth handling of sex in the lyrics of 'Love for Sale', a song of a prostitute advertising her wares. Written for the musical production *The New Yorkers* that opened on Broadway on 8 December 1930, it caused a sensation and was quickly banned from radio airplay. But when Walter Winchell championed it in his syndicated newspaper column he created enough curiosity to ensure the success of vocalist Libby Holman's recording, which rocketed to No. 5 on the Hit Parade in 1931. Because of the subject matter, vocalists are usually tempted to be somewhat overly theatrical, wringing every drop of pathos they can from it. Not so Miss Fitzgerald; she lets the lyrics and the alternating major/minor tonality of the piece do their work. The song, like so many Standards, has an AABA form, but it is twice the length of a usual Standard – 64 bars. Miss Fitzgerald is accompanied here by Paul Smith on piano, Jim Hall on guitar, Wilfred Middlebrooks on bass and Gus Johnson on drums.

8. Sarah Vaughan: 'There Will Never Be Another You' from *Live at the 1971 Monterey Jazz Festival*

This is Sarah Vaughan eight years after her Tivoli concert, and it's immediately clear the timbre of her voice has darkened with age (she was then forty-seven) as her artistry deepened. The tempo is brisk, posing a challenge for the vocalist to articulate the lyrics properly and so give them expressive meaning – you only have to read something aloud extremely quickly to see how the nuances of speech become progressively more difficult the faster you talk. Needless to say Miss Vaughan makes light of the challenge, imparting a real swing feeling to each word, despite the tempo. When a singer is swinging, as Miss Vaughan is here, the song seems to take flight. Note how she caps off this bravura perfor-mance with a remarkable excursion into her altissimo register with a high-note glissando that leaps into a range best appreci-ated by Labradors. The casualness with which this remarkable feat is tossed off belies the vocal technique needed to achieve it with such perfect intonation. Composed by Harry Warren with lyrics by Mack Gordon, this 32-bar ABAB song was first published in 1942, and has always been popular among jazz musicians because of its appealing melody – one of the best by Warren – and its equally appealing harmonies.

9. Mel Tormé: 'Isn't It Romantic' from *Mel Tormé and Friends*

This Richard Rodgers song is a top-drawer Standard that's pretty close to songwriting perfection.[33] Mel Tormé had previously recorded this song back in 1955, but on this live version, with Mike Renzie on piano, Jay Leonhart on bass and Donny Osborn on drums, he makes it appear as if the song had been written especially for him. By the time he came to make this recording, at Marty's in New York City in 1981, Tormé had been around the block and then some in a career that stretched back to the 1920s. This 32-bar song has an ABAC form; Tormé's diction, the effortless way he has with both melody and lyrics, negotiating the tricky minor-seventh interval between the last note of the 15th bar and the first note of 16th bar (at the end of B) with throwa-way ease, creates a perfect match between singer and song.

10. Ella Fitzgerald: 'Mack the Knife' from *Ella in Berlin*

Having stated the case for hearing the lyrics of a Standard as a means of getting to know it better, it may seem a bit strange to pick a tune where the singer actually forgets her lines in the heat of performance. However, this does not phase Miss Fitzgerald in the slightest, despite performing in front of an audience of 12,000 people – in fact, she finds it amusing, making up her own lyrics on the spot that add to the charm of this performance. When it was released as a 45 rpm single in the spring of 1960 it went on the *Billboard Best Selling Pop Singles* chart in May that year at No. 27, remaining there for a total of 14 weeks. It also earned Ella a Grammy Award for *Best Song by a Female Vocalist* while the album from which it was taken, *Ella in Berlin*, also won a Grammy for *Best Album by a Female Singer*. This concert, in Berlin's huge Deutschlandhalle, was the first stop for the 1960 Jazz at the Philharmonic tour of Europe which Miss Fitzgerald headlined. No doubt she included the number with her German audience in mind, since she says the song is new to her as she introduces it. In the event the German audience was hugely appreciative of her inclusion of this Kurt Weill song from *The Threepenny Opera*. It's worth dwelling on her forgetting the lyrics for a moment since her 'improvisation with words' effectively substitutes her lyrics made up on the spot for the lyrics of the song. The next logical step is 'improvising with the melody' by creating a wordless variation of the melody on the spot that fits the harmonies of the song. It's known as scat singing, and is explored in the final two tracks of this playlist.

11. Sarah Vaughan: 'What Is This Thing Called Love' from *Sassy Swings the Tivoli*

The younger Sarah Vaughan again, and another Cole Porter classic with an alternating major/minor feel. A 32-bar AABA tune, note the standpoint from which Miss Vaughan sings the lyrics – she really wants to know what this thing called love is, because when we get to the middle 8, all is answered: she saw him there 'one wonderful day', and he took her heart '*and cast it away*' – note the change to a bittersweet tone reflecting love found and lost before demanding to know WHAT IS this thing called love? The second chorus begins with an episode of scat singing for the duration of the AA section of this AABA song. Normally, unless the singer is exceptional, this is the time to head to the bar, but not with Miss Vaughan. Scat is vocal improvisation using phonetic sounds traditionally (but not always) similar to the instrumental sounds of jazz. The sound of scat is a mixture of consonants and vowels and most scat lines have a preponderance of phonetic consonants, usually words that begin with 'b' or 'd'. In this example of scat, Miss Vaughan favours words beginning with 's', 'b' and 'd' while her improvised line remains firmly in her middle register (mezzo-soprano). During this short 16-bar episode, it is easy to imagine Miss Vaughan's scat being played by a trumpet or saxophone. She returns to the lyrics of the song for the B section and final A section to complete the second chorus. During the third and final chorus, listen to how she *demands* to know *What Is This Thing Called Love?* emphasizing each word of the question, and then asking, little-girl-like, 'Why should it make a fool of me?' As the song reaches its climax, note the key change which adds to the excitement; it's a performance that lasts just two minutes and four seconds, yet Miss Vaughan succeeds in cramming a remarkable amount of detail into a short space of time.

12. Betty Carter: 'My Favourite Things' from *The Audience and Betty Carter*

Miss Carter's version of 'My Favourite Things' is somewhat different to the Julie Andrews performance in the film version of the Rodgers and Hammerstein musical *The Sound of Music*. Here,

Miss Cater sings lyrics of 'My Favourite Things' but often improvises the melody and, together with pianist John Hicks, lifts this performance into the realms of the truly exceptional. Listen also to the power of Curtis Lundy's bass line and Kenny Washington's whiplash drumming and the way Hicks' accompaniment gradually blossoms into a counter-line to Miss Carter's repeated 'And then ...' towards the end – who can say which of the two lines predominate? To say this is among the finest jazz vocal performances on record is limiting because it is also one of the great performances of contemporary jazz on record.

4

The Original Composition

What is an Original?

As we have seen, the vast majority of recorded jazz is based on some kind of organizing principle, most commonly songforms: the blues and the Standard (or American Popular Song), and this largely holds true for the original composition as well. Just as Standards come in almost any sensible length, so too the original composition. As we saw in Chapter 3, some original jazz compositions can comprise an original melody line based on a pre-existing set of chords – a good example of this is the seemingly endless list of compositions based on the chords of George Gershwin's 'I Got Rhythm'. Some original melodies were even based on the chord sequence of an A section from one tune mixed and matched with a B section from another tune, such as Charlie Parker's 'Scrapple from the Apple', which uses the A section of 'Honeysuckle Rose' and the B section of 'I Got Rhythm'. Then there is the original composition in the true sense of the word: an original set of chord changes plus an original melody to go with it, such as John Lewis' classic 'Django'.

From the 1960s, originals appeared which incorporated elements of free jazz within compositional structures, where a skeletal theme (sometimes written, sometimes improvised) exists to establish the key and tempo but chord changes are abandoned, leaving the improviser free to create his own melody line and leave it to the rhythm section to provide harmonic correlation, a principle known as 'time, no changes' which we explore in greater detail in Chapter 8. Here, the rhythmic pulse – or groove – is retained and the convention was to improvise around the home key or related keys, giving the illusion of preset chord changes. These techniques inform the Miles Davis 1967 album *Sorcerer*, for example, while on his 1967 album *Nefertiti* the composition 'Prince of Darkness' is a 16-bar form with very few pre-arranged harmonies where the improviser is expected to join up the spaces between the written harmonies with improvisation. In short, with the original composition, form, chord sequences and melodies could be permutated in endless ways to produce compositions that covered the whole spectrum, from the banal to the beautiful.

Two Days in 1959

Some of the most enduring, and beautiful, original compositions in jazz can be found on the Miles Davis album *Kind of Blue*, the biggest-selling album in jazz history. For this reason I have chosen it to illustrate the sort of ingenious twists and turns original compositions in jazz can take, but also as a means for us to get to know one of the truly great jazz albums of all time in the process. It was ranked No. 12 in *Rolling Stone* magazine's list of the 500 greatest albums of all time in 2003, and frequently turns up at the top, or near the top, of similar listings around the world, such as *the Independent*'s '50 Best Recordings of the 20th Century'[34] in 1999 or *the Guardian*'s '1000 Albums to Hear Before You Die'.[35] For the purposes of this book it provides a perfect illustration of jazz's core values, which it conveys in a subtle, easily digestible form – the smooth, elegant rhythmic propulsion known as swing, and hummable original themes with a subtle mood of melancholy we associate with the blues. 'If we keep listening to it, again and again, throughout a life-time, well, maybe that's because we sense there's still something more, something not yet heard', wrote Robert Palmer in the liner notes of the CD reissue.[36] It is a point well made. While it's by no means representative of every possible permutation original songforms can take, it does at least illustrate how some jazz musicians were thinking beyond the structures of the blues and Standard songforms to frame their improvisations in more challenging and/or interesting structures.

Recorded in two sessions at Columbia's 30th Street Studio, New York City on 2 March and 22 April 1959, the chord changes on *Kind of Blue* are replaced by modes on all the compositions except 'Freddie Freeloader' and 'All Blues', which are both 12-bar blues. Modes go back into early music history (and I do mean early – like the early Greek civilization of Aristotle and Plato), but suffice to say the best way to think of a mode is as a tonal centre. Modes are best heard rather than spoken about, since as long as one mode is sustained there is no change of key, thus harmonic movement is said to be static. Modes are a specific sequence of notes which provide the chord with a certain 'flavour', but we don't want to get too complicated here. Although the use of modes in jazz had occurred before *Kind of Blue*, the popularity of this album sped their use into common jazz practice. However, it would be wrong to say modal jazz was born with *Kind of Blue* as is often claimed.[37] George Russell was experimenting with modal ideas in the late 1940s and Shorty Rogers and Duane Tatro in the early 1950s. George Russell's Smalltet recording *The Jazz Workshop* from 1956 included several modal pieces, while pianist Bill Evans had impressed the jazz world with his modal solo on 'All About Rosie' (recorded with George Russell) in 1957. Davis himself had been dabbling with static harmony/modal concepts on *Ascenseur pour L'échafaud*

(1957) and *Porgy and Bess* (1958) prior to the modal 'Milestones' from his album of the same name (1958), recorded a year before *Kind of Blue*. *Kind of Blue* made modes fashionable in jazz, and within months of the album's release on 17 August 1959, countless jazz musicians around the world were experimenting with them. It was that influential.

The Original Composition Playlist

These listening notes are based on the CD Miles Davis *Kind of Blue* (Columbia/Legacy CK64935). Try and source this particular CD issue, or download the music from it, rather than one of the several *Kind of Blue* reissues that have appeared over the years since it's pretty much the definitive digital version: the recorded sound is exceptionally good thanks to a new remix and 20-Bit remastering. The pitch irregularities have been corrected from earlier issues (two tunes were recorded at the wrong speed on the original vinyl and early CD reissues) and the tune designations corrected (original vinyl issues and early CD reissues had two tracks in the wrong order). Even though this album was made in 1959 it is exceptionally well recorded[38] so there is considerable detail in both the background (the rhythm section of piano, bass and drums) and the foreground (the ensemble and the soloist), so be aware that a typical MP3 file will not do *Kind of Blue* justice as the frequency range has to be compressed to fit into sound files which can mean a loss of up to seventy-five percent of audio information. Bear in mind *Kind of Blue* is best heard how Miles Davis and his record producer Irving Townsend intended, as an album-length statement. You should try and allow time to listen to this album right through as many times as you can in order that your mind is able to make the connections it needs to really get into this music. For our third playlist session it will be necessary to create a playlist by down-loading the following tunes:

1. 'So What' from Miles Davis *Kind of Blue* (Columbia/Legacy CK64935).
2. 'Freddie Freeloader' from Miles Davis *Kind of Blue* (Columbia/Legacy CK64935).
3. 'Blue in Green' from Miles Davis *Kind of Blue* (Columbia/Legacy CK64935).
4. 'All Blues' from Miles Davis *Kind of Blue* (Columbia/Legacy CK64935).
5. 'Flamenco Sketches' from Miles Davis *Kind of Blue* (Columbia/Legacy CK64935).

Listening Notes for the Original Compositions Playlist

Personnel: Miles Davis (trumpet); Julian 'Cannonball' Adderley (alto saxophone); John Coltrane (tenor saxophone); Bill Evans (piano) – replaced by Wynton Kelly on 'Freddie Freeloader' only; Paul Chambers (bass); Jimmy Cobb (drums).

1. Miles Davis 'So What'

'So What' is for me the quintessential modal tune and comprises just two chords – one for the A section and one for the B section. As it's a 32-bar AABA composition, you will notice the slight gear change at B as the second chord makes its appearance, and you will hear it change down a gear after 8 bars, when it goes back to A and the home key. After the introduction, which is not in strict tempo, a straightforward 32-bar AABA form emerges with the bass playing a series of questions which the piano answers for the duration of the first A section. The second A section has the bass again asking the questions, but this time the whole ensemble answers. On the B section the bass and ensemble continue their question-and-answer routine, followed by the final A section for another 8 bars. The first solo is by Miles Davis. It is one of the most famous in jazz. It sounds like a composition in its own right. A compelling aspect of his solo is his use of space where he actually seems to 'play' silence so that it becomes an integral part of the solo, leaving windows through which we can enter his musical world.

2. Miles Davis 'Freddie Freeloader'

This song is a 12-bar blues with an original melody. Remember how the 12-bar form neatly divides itself into 3 units of 4 bars, the first 2 units of 4 bars closely related while the final 4 bars provide resolution. See if you notice the drummer subtly mark the beginning of each 12-bar chorus. Bill Evans is not the pianist on this selection; it's Wynton Kelly, who is making his only appearance on the album, playing in a forthright style not normally associated with Evans at this time. Listen to Miles Davis's solo – once again he is very lyrical, yet there's great poise and assurance in what he plays. Once again a feature of his playing is his use of silence that seems to frame each note and give it greater impact. Note the rhythmic drive and intensity in John Coltrane's solo, and how during the first 12 bars of his solo he clearly outlines the 12-bar blues harmonies. Remember, try and think of these harmonies in terms of colours. Equally, the accompaniment of Wynton Kelly continually outlines the 12-bar blues form so that you should soon be able to tell where you are in the 12-bar blues cycle. Finally, note the contrasting yet complementary style of Cannonball Adderley – his playing is more conversational than Coltrane and there are more 'bluesy' phrases in his solo than Coltrane's.

3. Miles Davis 'Blue in Green'

This theme is 10 bars long, which is unusual in jazz. You can count the number of bars it lasts as **1**-2-3-4, **2**-2-3-4, **3**-2-3-4, and so on up to **10**-2-3-4, when the cycle repeats itself. During each solo, the improviser is allowed to double or halve the chord sequence and use that as the basis of his improvisation. This is clever stuff, and is revealing of the increasing sophistication of modern jazz in the hands of master musicians like Davis and his colleagues. Don't try and fathom all this out – just enjoy how the solos are framed to fit the overall mood of the piece, and be aware that with original compositions this kind of variation to the norm is possible. Note that Davis solos using a harmon mute[39] with adjustable central shank removed to produce his signature sound.

4. Miles Davis 'All Blues'

'All Blues' – as the name implies – is a 12-bar blues, but this time it is in 6/8, which gives it a lilting feel and is counted **1**-2-3-4-5-6, **2**-2-3-4-5-6, **3**-2-3-4-5-6 and so on. Note the calm, hypnotic, swaying feel of the **1**-2-3-4-5-6 rhythm. Davis plays the theme of 'All Blues' with his signature harmon-muted trumpet, but solos on 'open', or un-muted, trumpet. When you hear the sound of a harmon muted trumpet on the soundtrack music of a film or TV programme it will often be in the kind of moody musical context associated with Davis's music, indicative of the trumpeter's influence beyond jazz. Note that at the beginning, the rhythm section plays a 4-bar introduction – a rolling piano feel with bass and drums that lasts for **1**-2-3-4-5-6, **2**-2-3-4-5-6, **3**-2-3-4-5-6, **4**-2-3-4-5-6 (or 4-bars) before the saxophones enter. Note how this 4-bar figure, or vamp, is used as a brief interlude between solos, which adds to the atmospheric feel of the piece. Interestingly, the simple but insinuating 6/8 theme of 'All Blues' played by the saxophones was used by the folk group Pentangle on their composition 'I've Got a Feeling' sung by vocalist Jacqui McShee on their 1968 album *Sweet Child*, which speaks of the universality of this music.

5. Miles Davis 'Flamenco Sketches'

This selection has its genesis in an introduction pianist Bill Evans worked out for the composition 'Some Other Time', recorded with his own trio on the album *Everybody Digs Bill Evans*. It was further developed into Evans' composition 'Peace Piece' on the same album, and here it surfaces again as the opening of 'Flamenco Sketches' by way of a 4-bar introduction. Evans is, of course, the pianist here, and in the liner notes to the original vinyl issue of *Kind of Blue* he wrote, '["Flamenco Sketches"] is a series of five scales, each to be played for as long as the soloist wishes until he has completed the series.'[40] In practice, the soloists opted to stay on each scale for either 8 or 4 bar lengths (except Miles Davis, who ends his *second* solo on the fifth and final scale using 2 bars). Davis takes two solos, the first opening the solo sequence where he is followed by John Coltrane, Cannonball Adderley and Bill Evans and then he returns once more at the end. Davis wanted the improvisers to reflect the flavour of each scale or mode. For example, the fourth scale (or mode) in the five-scale sequence has a Spanish feel to it, which Davis makes maximum use of during his first solo. He had already shown an affinity for Spanish themes on 'Blues for Pablo' on the album *Miles Ahead* from 1957, and in November 1959 he immersed himself in Spanish music for the jazz classic *Sketches of Spain*. On 'Flamenco Sketches' he creates an exceptionally lyrical solo with an unmistakably Spanish flavour. By listening carefully to the soloist and the bassist you might hear how the bassist signals the new tonality as each soloist moves through the five scales or modes.

5

The Instrumental Solo

Engaging with the Improviser's Art

Coming to terms with the jazz solo may, on the face of it, appear to be the big challenge in getting into jazz. After all, instrumental solos have steadily lost ground in pop music since the Punk era, when they were roundly condemned for being too clever by half. Gone are the days when an instrumental pop band like the Ventures could chart 38 albums and sell over 100 million records. There are, no doubt, countless reasons for this, not least the much-reported drop in attention spans – humans now have a shorter attention span than a goldfish, according to a report in *Time* magazine[41] – and the trend in pop music, as musician and author Ted Gioia points out, towards 'simple songs, without harmonic modulations and built on repeated note melodies',[42] has not done instrumental music any favours. Yet as we have seen, untrained listeners come to music with an impressive array of instinctual skills in music cognition. What this chapter seeks to do is to build on this and the previous chapters to better appreciate the jazz improviser's art.

As we have already discovered, the more we listen to music, the more templates of previous listening experiences we accumulate, which in turn helps guide our understanding of what we hear. In the case of the jazz solo, the more of them we hear the more we become aware of how a song's form and chord sequence influences what the musician is playing. The blues form has a fairly slow harmonic rhythm (the speed at which the chords pass by); for example, the first 8 bars of the blues retain the same, or related, harmony,[43] enabling the improviser to think in melodic terms, since, speaking generally, the absence of harmonic complexity permits a certain creative freedom that favours melodic development.

In contrast, Standards (or the American Popular Song) typically have a faster harmonic rhythm (chords come and go much quicker), forcing the improviser to concentrate more on the chord changes – or the changing musical colours – as he or she develops their solo. In other words, reaching back to a term we used in Chapter 2, the improviser must now think more vertically and be aware of how the notes that comprise each chord must relate to what is being played.

In an AABA song form, the transition from the first A section to the next A section in an AABA song is straightforward enough, but the transition to the B section (or bridge) often means moving to a different key (or a different harmonic colour). A good improviser can capitalize on the bridge's inherent capacity to provide contrast to advantage. Also, notice how drummers often mark the point where each 8-bar section turns around into the next, often paying special attention to the B section by giving the soloist a bit of oomph as they enter it. This marking of each section by the drummer (and often the pianist and bassist, too, working in conjunction with the drummer) is useful if you are not sure where the improviser is during his solo. However, once you are able to identify the bridge, or B section, in an AABA song, you will have recovered your bearings. Often, arrangers in more orchestrated forms of jazz will use the bridge as a window for a solo in an ensemble passage, while another common practice is to leave the final middle 8 empty, allowing the drummer to climax a performance with a solo, the band returning for the final A section and what they hope will be a standing ovation.

In the 1920s and 1930s, improvisers tended to think in 8-bar units that coincided with the construction of the AABA song-form, often leaving a brief silence, or small pause, at the end of each A or B section. This was also true of their approach to the 12-bar blues, briefly pausing before the end of bar 12 before they started again on the next chorus – we heard Sidney Bechet do this on 'Blue Horizon' from the blues playlist, for example. Bechet was by no means alone; this was pretty much common practice as jazz emerged from the 1920s into the 1930s. As musicians became theoretically and technically more adept during the 1940s, bright young minds sought to sustain the momentum of their improvised line into the next section (or, in the case of the 12-bar blues, the next chorus). Since the final 2 bars of the A and B sections of Standards and the final 2 bars of the blues were usually in the tonic or home key, they came up with idea of substituting a couple of interesting chords in their place at the end of an A section (or the end of a 12-bar sequence) to help the improviser play through into the next section or chorus without interrupting his or her flow of ideas. These 2-bar (sometimes 4-bar) chord progressions, substituted at the end of an A or B section, or the end of a 12-bar blues, are known as turnarounds. These can sometimes be a bit confusing when first listening to contemporary jazz improvisation if you're also trying to follow the song's underlying form, but often, and by no means always, the drummer tends to mark out each chorus and, in the case of an AABA tune, the bridge, so listen out to get your bearings.

The Importance of the Instrumental Ballad Performance

The composition 'They Say It's Wonderful' that opens both the Standards playlist and the Instrumental Solo playlist is performed as a ballad, played at a slow or slow/medium tempo. The great

improving masters of jazz history seemed to sense the importance of a ballad as a vehicle to distinguish themselves – after
all, they reasoned, if you can't improvise around an attractive
melodic line and its rich underlying harmonies, then something
is missing; maybe maturity or experience. By listening carefully
to George Coleman's performance of 'They Say It's Wonderful', you are hearing one of the commanding ballad players in
jazz at work, a master of the little techniques that evoke specific
emotional responses from the listener so that by the end you feel
as if you have been on a very real musical journey. Because of
the inherent spontaneity of jazz, many listeners imagine that the
subjective feelings an improvisation can arouse have been created
equally spontaneously, since most jazz commentary excludes the
possibility of jazz musicians using certain musical techniques to
arouse certain emotions, although this is well enough known in
classical music and occupied the great classical composers for
centuries. Understanding how such musical devices work, and
knowing how audiences responded to them, were part of the
great composers' stock-in-trade, and it's perhaps not surprising,
therefore, that the best jazz improvisers, in their own modest
way, should also take account of certain techniques to arouse
their audience's emotions during an improvisation. When Paul F.
Berliner interviewed pianist Kenny Barron for his monumental
Thinking in Jazz: The Infinite Art of Improvisation, the pianist advo-
cated starting a solo simply, 'in a way that is sparse and low key' so
'the solo has somewhere in which it can build' – in other words,
you don't play all your cards at once – suggesting that an appropriate moment to begin to build a solo was when 'a tune became
more interesting harmonically'.[44] This might seem like a simple
aesthetic, but in the hands of a master improviser like Barron it is
a remarkably effective technique. Other devices improvisers often
draw on include creating the archetypical sensation of tension
and release by utilizing a rising line, often by gradually moving
from lower to higher notes; using notes outside the underlying

harmonies to create tension (know as sideslipping) or simply doubling the tempo of their improvisation while the rhythm section retains the original tempo to achieve tension and heightened expectation. Coleman's performance is interesting for the structured way he deploys such techniques, building his improvisation stage by stage in a way that takes his listeners with him.

Mastering ballad playing like George Coleman takes a lifetime of study and remains one of the great challenges in jazz. At a slower tempo, every note becomes available for microscopic scrutiny, since short notes become long notes and long notes become even longer. This can often reveal deficiencies in tone, technique, breath control and musical invention that do not reveal themselves at faster tempi which is why some musicians steer clear of ballads since they have no desire to expose any weakness in the playing. For example, some may find it difficult to control their tone evenly through all registers of their instrument in an expressive or meaningful way at slower tempos; others simply find it difficult to relax at a slow tempo, wanting to return to their comfort zone of faster tempos by playing in double time (playing twice as fast as the underlying ground beat), while still others falter in their melodic inventiveness, which becomes exposed at slower tempi, and so lose sight of the storytelling privilege that is at the heart of a great ballad performance. It is no coincidence, then, that all the great jazz improvisers were also masters of the ballad performance.

What do Soloists Actually Play When They Improvise?

This is an interesting question. In the past, there have been examples of auto didactical jazz musicians who have had no formal music training, yet have reached the top of their profession, such as drummer Buddy Rich, pianist Erroll Garner or trumpeter Chet Baker, none of whom could read music, but these tend to be rare exceptions. Today, I cannot think of any contemporary jazz musician who has not had some degree of formal music education. Thus it's possible to say jazz improvisation derives from a combination of formal musical knowledge and practical skill – and inspiration! Formal music knowledge and practical skills are dealt with by two types of brain function: one for storing facts and the other for encoding actions. Facts are stored in the declarative (or descriptive) memory, which is associated with the medial temporal lobe and the temporal and frontal cortices. Actions acquired through practice (often unconsciously) are associated with procedural memory and are encoded in a loop that includes the cerebellum and the basal ganglia. Highly developed motor skills are an important element in playing a musical instrument and are developed by motor learning, the repeating of a sequence of movements over and over again until all of the relevant neural systems work together to produce smooth, efficient actions automatically. For a sequence of movements to become so ingrained that it requires no thought takes hours of daily practice, yet jazz improvisation requires musicians to develop an array of motor skills across a wide range of actions in order to improvise effortlessly. It is often called developing muscle memory as the muscles seem to take over from the brain and appear to fulfil the sequence of movements without conscious thought. Motor skills such as these are separated from factual memory because the brain treats these functions in different ways. Declarative memory is conscious knowledge while procedural memory – the motor or movement-based aspect of memory – is optimized for rapid reflexes that are not necessarily accessible to the conscious mind. Jazz improvisation is a blend of the two and most jazz musicians find it difficult to articulate this aspect of the improvisational process. For example, one quote, often attributed to saxophonist Charlie Parker in the 1950s, went something like, 'You've got to learn everything, then, when you finally get up on the bandstand, you forget it all.' At the time it seemed puzzling, yet is a surprisingly apt statement in the light of what we now know about memory function. However, knowing jazz improvisation combines both the declarative and procedural memories is one thing; understanding the mysteries of how they interact is quite another. Not a great deal is known about what happens when a skill moves from making great demands on our attention – such as the skills required to ride a bike, drive a motor car or perform a complicated piece of music – to becoming automatic and not appearing to require conscious thought. In a 2009 interview, saxophone legend Sonny Rollins, frequently cited as jazz's greatest living improviser, enlarged on what the improvisation process meant for him: 'When I am working with a piece of music, I will study the music and learn the melody and the chord progression in preparation for my instrumental improvisation. Now, when I improvise after formally learning these things, I forget them. I don't go up on the stage and think of them, I forget them and that's where the creativity comes in. That little area is quite mysterious. Music is magical, we all know that, and that area where you create and your subconscious is at work, you don't know what you're playing. Often I play things, if I'm in the right groove, I'll play things that I surprise myself with, those are things that are deep in my subconscious and they come out during my improvisation, but they are not things I went into the song thinking about. And this is why in improvisation it is so top of the field when it comes to artistic expression, to me, because there is so much skill involved in playing music, and yet it has got to be free and loose – the skill is there, you learn the skill and you forget it. In a way improvisation is making the mind blank, when I'm playing I'm just in a trance. So that's what I have learned about music, about improvisation, and it's beautiful.'[45]

The Instrumental Solo Playlist

It is worth bearing in mind that the solos you are about to hear require an attentive mode of listening to get the most out of them. There is no shortage of scientific studies that reveal how attention spans have decreased over the decades, and several that suggest how the influence of the Internet has contributed to speeding up this process.[46] So bear in mind that the majority of great recorded jazz comes from a time when attention spans were longer than they are today – but always remember that you can't get more out of listening to a piece of music than you are prepared to put into it.

1. George Coleman: 'They Say It's Wonderful' from *George Coleman At Yoshi's*.
2. George Coleman: 'Good Morning Heartache' from *George Coleman At Yoshi's*.
3. Terry Gibbs: 'Sweet Georgia Brown' from *Terry Gibbs Dream Band Vol. 4 Main Stem*.
4. Miles Davis: 'I Loves You Porgy' from *Porgy and Bess*.
5. Johnny Smith and Stan Getz: 'Moonlight in Vermont' from *Moonlight in Vermont*.
6. Miles Davis: 'On Green Dolphin Street' from *58 Sessions Featuring Stella by Starlight*.
7. Buddy Rich: 'Love for Sale' from *Big Swing Face*.
8. Stan Getz: 'There Will Never Be Another You' from *The Steamer*.
9. Bill Evans: 'Isn't It Romantic' from *The Bill Evans Trio at Shelly's Manne Hole*.
10. Erroll Garner: 'Mack the Knife' from *Dreamstreet/One World Concert*.
11. The Dave Brubeck Quartet: 'What Is This Thing Called Love' from *Plays Cole Porter*.
12. John Coltrane: 'My Favourite Things' from *My Favourite Things*.

Listening Notes for the Instrumental Solo Playlist

1. George Coleman: 'They Say It's Wonderful' from *George Coleman At Yoshi's*

Although under-appreciated in jazz, George Coleman is a jazz master – *The New Yorker* once noting, 'Coleman is a marvel; there isn't a sax player who knows his instrument better, or one who imparts so much knowledge in every marathon solo.'[47] 'They Say It's Wonderful' uses a 32-bar AABA form and after pianist Harold Mabern sets the tempo and mood with his introduction, Coleman begins with an exposition of the melody (that begins with the lyrics 'They say that falling in love is wonderful'), embellishing it en route in a way that suggests its rich potential for improvisation. Note how sensitive his tone is at this point in the song – soft and breathy, it's known as sub-tone – note too the ease of his control, especially at the end of the second A section when he reaches into the lower register of his instrument – known as bell-tones. The bassist is playing the second and fourth beats of the bar (as in 1-**2**-3-**4**, 2-**2**-3-**4**, and so on), known as playing in two, albeit decoratively. As we enter the second chorus the drummer continues to play a discreet role in accompaniment as Coleman works his way into the improvisation while keeping his audience in touch with the melody. As he enters the third chorus, Coleman's tone gets steelier as he prepares to engage more deeply with his improvisation. Note that the drummer is now playing a more proactive role in accompaniment and how the rhythmic tension is temporarily released by moving into four beats to the bar, but as Coleman begins to soar, bassist Ray Drummond hints at returning to two, continuing this feeling of rhythmic tension since the B section (or middle eight) mixes a two-and a four-metre feel. In the final A section, Coleman makes use of the rising line, using high notes beyond the usual range of the instrument, but are integrated into the overall contour of the improvisation. Coleman enters the fourth chorus by increasing the sense of drama he created during the third – this is powerful stuff, the drummer now making himself felt, as Coleman's playing reaches the climax of his improvisation. You should recognize when he reaches the B section of this chorus since he uses it to lower us back to earth and lead into a recapitulation of the melody in the final A section, expressed in the sub-tone we heard during his original exposition of the melody to create a pleasing sense of symmetry and resolution. Bassist Drummond takes over for the sixth chorus, his improvisation keeping us in touch with the melody, while the seventh, and final, chorus sees Coleman winding the song up by returning to the melody. But there is a surprise at the B section when Mabern introduces a Latin feel; and in the final A section Coleman gracefully brings the song to a modest conclusion.

2. George Coleman: 'Good Morning Heartache' from *George Coleman At Yoshi's*

George Coleman entered jazz in the 1950s, at a time when all the great players were expected to 'tell a story' in their improvisations. 'Good Morning Heartache' is a well-constructed 32-bar AABA song from both a melodic and harmonic standpoint with a pleasing major/minor ambivalence. It's perhaps surprisingly written in a major key since the feeling of love lost or yearning is usually exploited in a minor key. Coleman presents an exposition of the melody after he has been set up with a tasteful piano introduction by Harold Mabern, and behind him the pianist provides a rhapsodic backdrop with bass and drums playing in a discreet two. Coleman begins his improvisation on the second chorus with Mabern laying out for 16 bars (the first two AA sections), rejoining Coleman at the B section (or middle eight), but now Coleman, the bassist and drummer are teasing the listener by implying a four feel, so increasing the rhythmic tension. When the quartet do break into four at the beginning of the third chorus, the effect is electric as Coleman steadily builds the intensity of his solo through the use of a rising line, and at the end of the chorus he inserts a 16-bar transition (a brief interlude inserted between two AABA choruses) comprising a repeated figure that gradually appears to gather momentum and intensity as it rises in pitch with Coleman using circular breathing, a technique that allows him play and play without appearing to pause for breath. This interlude provides a dramatic means of changing key and launching into two further choruses of powerful melodic improvisation that range from deep bell-tones to a high-note climax beyond the normal range of the saxophone. Towards the end of the majestic fourth chorus, he brings us back to earth with strong suggestions of the original melody and by moving from a metre of four to two. He then winds up this remarkable performance by playing just 8 bars of A that lead to a rubato (a fluctuation of tempo) finish to complete a remarkable saxophone tour de force.

3. Terry Gibbs: 'Sweet Georgia Brown' from *Terry Gibbs Dream Band Vol. 4 Main Stem*

That the arranger could be as much a creative force in jazz as the improviser is apparent in this big band version of 'Sweet Georgia Brown' – remember this is a 32-bar ABAC form. It opens with a 4-bar introduction that uses a specific riff that goes on to provide the counterpoint to the first 16 bars of the 'Sweet Georgia Brown' melody (the AB bit) played by Gibbs on vibraphone. This is answered with a variation of the melody by the band for the next 16 bars – the AC bit – but note the introductory riff remains underneath. That same riff continues as a 4-bar transition to form a springboard for Gibbs's 32-bar improvisation on the ABAC form that follows. After Gibbs, the arranger as soloist takes over (the arranger is Manny Albam) and what follows is a virtual fantasia on

'Sweet Georgia Brown'; you can sense the enjoyment the band are getting from playing this by the sheer elan of their playing. Each succeeding passage seems to build on the previous one – note the perfect phrasing of the brass (trumpets and trombones) and saxophones that make the written sound improvised, and don't miss the very swinging rhythm section headed by Mel Lewis on drums.

4. Miles Davis: 'I Loves You Porgy' from *Porgy and Bess*

Is it possible for time in music to appear to stand still? The opening moments on this recording, featuring Miles Davis with an orchestra arranged and conducted by Gil Evans, come pretty close. A dither of brooding, atmospheric instrumental colour immediately captures our attention, yet there is nothing here that we can tap our foot or snap our fingers to. The sound is detailed, yet unusual, Evans using combinations of woodwinds and brass to unique effect. Our sense of time is temporarily suspended until the entrance of Miles Davis on a harmon-muted trumpet. The harmon mute is used here with the central shank removed, producing a distinctive metallic sound that has come to be associated with Davis. The first 8 bars of the solo is used to outline Gershwin's distinctive melody, so establishing a sense of tempo, which is answered by 8 bars where the French horns take the lead (you don't often encounter French horns in jazz) before Davis re-enters with a melodic solo that circles the song's melody without actually stating it, the expressive force of Davis's trumpet propelling this performance into our memories.

5. Johnny Smith and Stan Getz: 'Moonlight in Vermont' from *Moonlight in Vermont*

'Moonlight in Vermont' is the title track of an album that marked Johnny Smith's first session as a leader. It was an instant bestseller and was voted Jazz Record of the Year for 1952 by the influential *Downbeat* magazine. Now recognized as a jazz classic,[48] 'Moonlight in Vermont' sounds deceptively simple, displaying Smith's legato technique of melody/chord playing for the first AABA chorus (remember on this tune the A sections are 6 bars and the B section 8 bars), which should be easy to follow at the relaxed tempo Smith chooses. On the second chorus, saxophonist Stan Getz, who has been playing a background obligato role during the previous chorus, emerges into the spotlight to take the first solo on the first A section. Smith solos on the second A section, and notice the effortless command of his instrument, opening with one of his trademark lightning-fast runs; the 8-bar B section is given to bassist Eddie Safranski and those high-pitched pings by the guitar that seem to fall amid his solo like snowflakes are called harmonics, difficult to master yet here effortlessly executed, while the final A section includes a brief arranged passage for guitar and saxophone to bring the performance to its conclusion. Much has been written about this widely admired performance, which lasts just 3 minutes 13 seconds, but in its brevity and its less-is-more ethic it succeeds in saying all that needs be said.

6. Miles Davis: 'On Green Dolphin Street' from *58 Sessions Featuring Stella by Starlight*

This version of 'On Green Dolphin Street' by a sextet with Davis on trumpet, Julian 'Cannonball' Adderley on alto saxophone, John Coltrane on tenor saxophone, Bill Evans on piano, Paul Chambers on bass and Jimmy Cobb on drums, is effectively a prelude to Davis's *Kind of Blue*, widely regarded as the finest jazz album ever made, that was recorded just ten months later. A song with a 32-bar ABAC form, after the introduction you can distinguish the A and B sections by the Latin bass feel of the A sections that contrasts with the two or four feel of the B section. Note also that as Davis ends both his statement of the theme and his solo by replacing the last 4 bars of the final C section with a transition that comprises 8 bars to introduce the next solo, leaving the 8th bar of this transition silent, called a break, which is used as a pickup for the next soloist that leads into the A section of the subsequent chorus. Note this 8-bar transition is only used at the end of each solo, and following Davis comes Coltrane (listen to how Cobb marks the beginning of each new A and B sections), Adderley and Evans. They all use this 8-bar transition at the end of their solo to hand over to the next soloist with Davis returning at the end with a recapitulation of the theme. After Davis's version of the song, it became something of a tradition when performing this song to incorporate this transition to lead into solos from the statement of the original theme and hand over the solo spot to the next man.

7. Buddy Rich: 'Love for Sale' from *Big Swing Face*

'Love for Sale' is an AABA form, but it is twice the length of a usual Standard – 64 bars. Rich's performance is not intended to reflect the song's lyrics, but is an example of how an attractive chord sequence and melody can develop into a compelling jazz performance. Opening with a simple statement of Cole Porter's melody introduced by unison trombones that exploit the major/minor feel of this piece, the swinging intention of the band is immediately made clear. A well-constructed solo by Ernie Watts on alto saxophone is followed by an ensemble interlude and a fine solo by trumpeter Chuck Findley – just twenty years of age at the time – then a brief ensemble interlude leads into an elegant tenor saxophone solo from Jay Corre, who provides the momentum that links the written with the improvised. As his solo distances itself from the theme, you are able to keep your bearings within the song through the backing figures played by the rest of the band. The ensemble then takes over, gathering momentum like a rock tumbling downhill, leading the listener towards the climax, a startling drum solo by the leader that's an explosion of speed and precision. Rich clearly had well developed slow twitch (type I) muscles (the muscle type that helps athletes run marathons or cyclists compete for hours in events like the Tour de France) which enabled him to maintain a high energy level through a two-hour plus concert. Remarkably, he also possessed well-developed fast twitch (type II) muscle fibres that fire more rapidly than any other muscles and are an asset to athletes such as sprinters who need to generate power as soon as the starting gun fires. As trumpeter Dean Pratt, who played in his band between 1976–8, has written: 'A talent like Buddy's is a rare gift and one that graces our profession once in a lifetime.'[49]

8. Stan Getz: 'There Will Never Be Another You' from *The Steamer*

Tenor saxophonist Stan Getz tended to play with a deceptively laid-back feel. Accompanied by Lou Levy on piano, Leroy Vinegar on bass and Stan Levey on drums, Getz's solo on this 32-bar ABAB song is very melodic and his ideas so organic they seem to flow effortlessly from his saxophone. The tempo is such that it gives you an opportunity to follow the melodic arc of his solo, since his articulation – the musical equivalent of diction in spoken language – was unsurpassed and his saxophone technique so accomplished even the most intricate phrases are tossed off effortlessly. Listen also to the tonal shading he uses during his solo that adds an emotional edge to his playing.

9. Bill Evans: 'Isn't It Romantic' from *The Bill Evans Trio at Shelly's Manne Hole*

Throughout his life, pianist Bill Evans dedicated himself to what he called 'the science of building a line' during his improvisations. The clarity of expression Evans achieves is such that every note seems to have its place in the overall architecture of this solo – nothing can be added or taken away without destroying the symmetry and balance of his improvised line that throughout possesses the integrity of melodic beauty. A 32-bar song with an ABAC form, the song's melody seems to shimmer beneath the surface of Evans's improvisation that, while never losing a feeling of the spontaneously conceived, has great structural unity throughout.

10. Erroll Garner: 'Mack the Knife' from *Dreamstreet/One World Concert*

Pianist Erroll Garner, like Buddy Rich, couldn't read a note of music. Not that it affected either man's career a jot, since both were virtuoso musicians. Garner was able to play thousands of songs by ear and composed many originals, including his enduring ballad 'Misty'. Garner liked to devise introductions that were completely out of left field and here, with allusions to Beethoven's 'Moonlight Sonata' (*Piano Sonata No. 14 in C sharp minor*), he keeps the audience guessing until Kurt Weill's memorable theme explodes into view. There is something compelling and hypnotic about Garner's playing – even his exposition of the 'Mack the Knife' theme vibrates with energy and is followed by a joyous roller-coaster ride through variations of, and extemporizations on, 'Mack the Knife'. This performance contains all the hallmarks of Garner's style – his ability to play on top of the beat, his exuberance, a wonderful sense of melodicism that never distanced him from his audience and above all, a compelling, foot-tapping sense of swing. With good reason a profile of Garner on America's National Public Radio was called 'The Joy of a Genius'.[50]

11. The Dave Brubeck Quartet: 'What Is This Thing Called Love' from *Plays Cole Porter*

This is a very different version of Cole Porter's 32-bar AABA song to Sarah Vaughan's memorable performance. Here, the tempo is dramatically slowed down, which has the effect of altering the mood of the song, and showcases another great lyrical improviser in alto saxophonist Paul Desmond. Desmond's preference was for less interaction from other members of the group during his solo than was the norm in jazz, arguing that it interfered with his concentration, and fellow quartet members duly obliged. Desmond enters after Brubeck's short solo with a perfectly judged phrase that grabs your attention and his delicately crafted solo weaves an air of questioning melancholy that perfectly echoes the song's lyric. Throughout, you get the feeling that Desmond's solo is more like an intimate conversation which he spices with a mischievous or unexpected melodic twist or turn. (As an aside, Desmond had the reputation of being an extremely witty and erudite conversationalist.) Brubeck continues in similar mood, perfectly complementing Desmond's elegant craftsmanship.

12. John Coltrane: 'My Favourite Things' from *My Favourite Things*

Recorded with his newly formed quartet of McCoy Tyner on piano, Steve Davis on bass and Elvin Jones on drums, Coltrane uses a soprano saxophone (he also poses with it on the cover since very few jazz fans at the time knew what one looked like).

'My Favourite Things' became something of a signature in live performance – he was even performing the song on his last-known live recording three months before he died (*The Olatunji Concert*), despite the fact that his music had taken on the characteristics of free jazz. Played as a medium-tempo waltz, this is an AAB form, but Coltrane initially plays the A sections only, assigning the B section to function as a coda.[51] After a fanfare-like introduction on piano, Coltrane plays the familiar melody, but note that his solo is not based on the chords of 'My Favourite Things' but a sustained vamp (or repeated chord) that together with a swaying 3/4 rhythm lent a mysterious, incantatory quality to his playing – note the rootless chords of pianist McCoy Tyner. Rootless means the anchoring element of the chord, the root, or bottom note of the chord – is missing, giving it a floating or harmonically ambivalent feel. Coltrane re-enters with a recapitulation of the theme and a further solo before an exposition of the contrastingly bright (major tonality) feel of the B section, lending a pleasing sense of resolution to a powerful musical experience.

6

From Forms to Styles

Underneath the Jazz Umbrella

As we've seen in the last few chapters, an understanding of form and structure is a very useful aid when listening to jazz, since it provides us listeners with a sort of road map to guide us through what we're hearing. This knowledge is particularly helpful when we look underneath the jazz umbrella at the various styles of jazz gathered there since even though one style of jazz may *sound* quite different to another, the good news is that usually the basic organizing principles of form and structure, as well as the relationship of the jazz solo to them, largely remain the same (you'll recall free jazz usually uses different organizing principles). Since many different styles of playing jazz have evolved over time, the best way of getting to know them is to lay them all out end to end in chronological order and work through them one by one. This way, we can see how one style mutated into the next until we arrive at the present. En route we'll discover what changed and what remained the same, so that by the time we reach the present day, we can see how contemporary jazz vibrates with meanings from both the past and the present.

Brass Bands Spread Music Across America

As the popular saying goes, if you want to understand the end then you have to go back to the beginning, so in the case of jazz we return to the *fin de siècle* of the nineteenth century, a time when America was beginning to find its feet as a nation. With industrialization came regular working hours, a weekly pay packet, the increasing availability of leisure time and the growth of a leisure industry. It was a rich and colourful period in American history, when brass band music was enjoying considerable popularity across America. These bands performed regularly before the public, often in outdoor entertainment parks that were then a feature of American public life, performing polkas, quadrilles, waltzes, a selection of light classics (such as overtures by Verdi or Rossini) as well as marches, mainly written by American composers. The most popular bands of the day were those led by Patrick Gilmore, the Italian Giuseppe Creatore and John Philip Sousa, known as the March King for his role in popularizing military marches. One of Sousa's most successful march pieces was 'The Liberty Bell', which the whole world now knows as the Monty Python theme tune. Bizarre as it might seem today, there was a vogue for dancing to marches at this time and many of Sousa's compositions, most famously 'The Washington Post March' also functioned as dance music since, as Peter van der Merwe points out, 'some bands played for dances as well as marches, and in any case the two streams of dance and march music came together at the end of the [nineteenth] century in ragtime'.[52]

The Ragtime Craze

Ragtime began as a piano-based music whose rhythmic oompah beat was ideally suited for dancing the two-step and the cakewalk, the two most popular dances of the day. Its genesis seems to have been through the interface of American march music and the Afro-American dance called the jig.[53] Ragtime was initially centred around the fairly small geographical area of Missouri, where the cities of Sedalia, Carthage and St Louis saw the emergence of a number of talented ragtime pianists and composers including the most talented pianist and composer of them all, Scott Joplin. A good example of Joplin's genius is his 1902 composition 'The Entertainer', one of the classics of the Ragtime era. It enjoyed a revival in 1970 when pianist Joshua Rifkin released *Scott Joplin: Piano Rags* on the Nonesuch label that promptly became the label's first million-selling record. 'The Entertainer' was also chosen as the theme music for the 1973 Oscar-winning Hollywood film *The Sting*, starring Robert Redford and Paul Newman. On 18 May 1974, pianist Marvin Hamlisch, who was responsible for the film's soundtrack adaptations of Joplin's music, reached No. 3 on the *Billboard Hot 100* chart with his version of 'The Entertainer' from the soundtrack. You will find this is the first selection on the playlist and it's as good a working definition of ragtime as any – in other words, the ragtime style is so distinctive that once you have heard 'The Entertainer' you will immediately recognize the ragtime style the next time you hear it.

The early popularity of ragtime in the Afro-American communities of Missouri quickly spilled out across the rest of the United States, hitting New York in 1896, when a young southerner, Ben Harney, introduced the music there to considerable celebrity. To this northern, big-city public, ragtime seemed far more exciting than any other popular music of the day and having conquered New York, it swept through Europe, the *San Francisco Chronicle* headlining 'Paris Has Gone Rag Time Wild'[54] in 1900.

By 1910, ragtime was at the peak of its popularity and even top society bands at plush New York venues like the Ritz-Carlton, the Waldorf-Astoria, Delmonico's and the Hotel Astor were playing ragtime hits. The most popular rag of the day, 'Maple Leaf Rag', written by Scott Joplin, sold over a million copies of piano sheet music (the measure of a song's popularity in this pre-gramophone era) and used an AABBACCDD form, which was common to many rags at the time and a 'direct continuation of march forms'."[55] What is perhaps overlooked in jazz histories is the extent to which different genres of popular music during this period overlapped. For example, the composition 'A Warm Up In Dixie' came with the instruction that it could be played as a march, a cakewalk or a two-step (since in terms of dance steps there wasn't that much difference between the cakewalk and the two-step, which shared the same syncopated oompah rhythm). Equally, the demarcation between ragtime and marching songs could also be hazy, especially since many published rags came with the instruction that they should be played in march tempo or *tempo di marcia*. Arthur Pryor's 1909 recording of 'The African 400 (An Educated Rag)', for example, sounds as much a march as it does a rag (Pryor had been an arranger for John Philip Sousa in the 1890s). This dualism between march and rag resulted in a popular practice of 'ragging' the final chorus of marches, a synco-pated effect that distantly anticipated the sounds of early jazz.

The Musical Dark Ages

In the years immediately prior to World War I, ragtime's popu-larity began to wane but as music historian Larry Gushee has noted, 'The period from the decline of ragtime to the beginnings of real jazz has been in critical limbo, a kind of musical Dark Ages in miniature.'[56] What we do know is that it was in New Orleans that the transition from ragtime to what we now recog-nize as jazz occurred. Perhaps surprisingly, cornet player Buddy Bolden gets the lion's share of credit for this, even though we have no recorded evidence of his playing. His band was a cause célèbre in New Orleans between 1900 and 1905 although he 'apparently did not improvise melodies freely in the manner of later jazz musicians, but found ingenious ways of ornamenting existing melodies'.[57] In 1906, he showed distinct signs of violent mental derangement culminating in his institutionalization with acute schizophrenia in 1907, his troubled life eventually ending in 1931. More compelling are the claims of pianist Ferdinand 'Jelly Roll' Morton, interviewed by musicologist Alan Lomax at the Library of Congress in May 1938[58] and subsequently published in the book *Mr. Jelly Lord*. Morton was a prime witness to the New Orleans music scene at the beginning of the twentieth century – his recollection of Bolden was as a 'great ragtime trumpet man' – and while it seems fair to say Morton was a colourful character – he was variously attributed with being a pool shark, a pimp, a hustler, a braggart and a womanizer – he was also a genius.

FERDINAND JOSEPH 'JELLY ROLL' MORTON (C. 1890–1941)

Morton was brought up in New Orleans, learning piano from an early age. An accomplished pianist by his early teens, he began work as a pianist in the bordellos of the Storyville district of New Orleans, possibly from the age of 14. When his churchgoing great-grandmother, with whom he lived, discovered what he was up to (he said he was a night watchman in a factory), he was kicked out of her house, adopting a peripatetic lifestyle that included touring in the American South, Chicago, New York City and the West Coast. During this period he composed several enduring early jazz classics, including 'Jelly Roll Blues', possibly the first jazz composition ever published (1915) while 'King Porter Stomp' also comes from this early period. In 1922–3, he settled in Chicago, where his 'Wolverine Blues' became a hit.

Jazz – the Eureka Moment?

Morton emerges from the Library of Congress recordings as a credible and knowledgeable witness despite a reputation for hyperbole. As musicologist Gunther Schuller has noted, 'He had a total conception of jazz that transcended the external details of style … [yet] very few understood Morton's fine qualitative distinctions. For Morton was the first theorist, the first intellectual, that jazz ever produced.'[59] The key moment on these recordings comes when Morton demonstrated an interpretation of 'Maple Leaf Rag' in the stiff, formal manner of ragtime (similar to Marvin Hamlisch's performance of 'The Entertainer' from the film soundtrack of *The Sting*). He then plays the piece again, this time giving it the characteristics we would now call 'swing' by ironing out the rigid oompah feel of ragtime. The effect is electric. The more you listen, the more you realize how profound this apparently simple step was. Morton's swing feel is the basic ingredient that separates one version of 'Maple Leaf Rag' from the other: this could well have been the Eureka moment when jazz was born and, as Schuller notes, was 'a radical innovation, one that even the early ragtime instrumentalists like Bolden and Bunk Johnson never adopted in quite that way',[60] concluding, 'Morton's claims to have invented jazz no longer seem quite so rash.'[61]

At the turn of the twentieth century, the New Orleans marching band repertoire was full of ragtime tunes that included James Scott's 'Grace and Beauty', Charles Daniels' 'Hiawatha', Abe Holzmann's 'Smokey Mokes', plus 'High Society', 'Fidgety Feet', 'Chattanooga Stomp', 'Buddy's Habits' and others, with the early jazz staple 'Tiger Rag' coming out of this tradition. As Morton demonstrated on 'Maple Leaf Rag', the transition between ragtime and jazz was subtle, historian Ted Gioia pointing out that, 'In the early days of New Orleans jazz, the line between ragtime and a jazz performance was so fine that the two terms were used interchangeably.'[62] Interestingly, the surviving New Orleans musicians who were around in the late nineteenth and early twentieth centuries always referred to their music as 'ragtime', not jazz, when interviewed by historians in the late 1930s and 1940s. In the event it was the dance floor that proved to be the compelling agency of rhythmic change that speeded up this transition. From around 1918, the two-beat oompah feel of the ragtime sound had given way to the more evenly accented swing feel we associate with early jazz as the two-step gave way in popularity to the fox-trot.

Blues – The Crucial Ingredient

Although early jazz primarily evolved from marches and ragtime, other elements went into the mix such as hymns and bits and pieces from classical music; but perhaps the most crucial ingredient was on its doorstep – the blues – which came out of the deep south. For the dancers, its most popular early manifestation was the 'Funky Butt' or the 'Slow Drag' as it was later called, that had its origins as a ragtime dance but was later adapted to the blues, so changing its rhythmic feel. As a dance it was fairly minimal, described as 'hanging on each other and barely moving'[63] and was much in demand in the bars, clubs, bordellos and whorehouses because of the bodily contact it permitted. As Larry Gushee notes: 'The rougher the environment, the raunchier and bluer the music … the small bands developed a way of playing the blues that had little to do with marching but much with rough and dirty dancing.'[64] Playing the Slow Drag was apparently a speciality of Buddy Bolden, and we can get an idea of what this style was like from Jelly Roll Morton's recording of 'I Thought I Heard Buddy Bolden Say', from September 1939. Morton sings the lyrics, but skirts possible censorship issues by giving the 'Funky Butt' refrain to the band to play.

Jazz Moves Out of New Orleans

Itinerant musicians such as Jelly Roll Morton and bands out of New Orleans, such as the Original Creole Band (with trumpeter

Freddie Keppard, whom Morton rated highly), blazed a trail for this new ragtime-into-jazz style in the northern cities of the United States. Between 1911 and 1917 the Original Creole Band were instrumental in opening up a market for jazz in Chicago for New Orleans musicians. They also travelled extensively across America and were offered a recording contract in 1916 by the Victor Talking Machine Company in New York, but trumpeter Freddie Keppard turned down the offer because, he reasoned, once his musical style was captured on record, others would 'steal my stuff'. Thus we are deprived of a crucial piece of the ragtime-into-jazz puzzle since Keppard was a player whose reputation has often been conflated with that of Buddy Bolden. Keppard is the one who got away, a trumpeter at the head of a then-leading New Orleans band who could have cast valuable light onto what was going on musically at the time. He would finally record in 1924, but by then history had passed him by. His subsequent sessions were scanty and on some it's hard to identify conclusively his playing, while the quality of recorded sound of some recordings were often acoustically catastrophic. Add the deterioration of his health through alcoholism and we have a set of circumstances that do not exactly conspire to illustrate the high regard in which he was held by his contemporaries as a younger man.

Ragtime into Jazz New York Style

The transition from ragtime to jazz was less advanced in America's northern cities if the example of 'Castle House Rag',[65] recorded in New York in February 1914 by one of the leading black bands of the city, James Reece Europe, is anything to go by. To modern ears 'Castle House Rag' sounds unusual with a combination of cornet, clarinet, cellos, piano, banjos, mandolins and drums. Initially they follow the somewhat stiff ragtime syncopation of the day before cutting loose towards the end, prompting Larry

Gushee to write, 'Europe may have let his band loose for three choruses of ad-hoc basic rag, accidentally transmitting to us the only example from its time of orchestral ragtime extemporisation.'[66] In fact, the banjos actually get into a groove that would resurface over a decade later in Morton's 'Black Bottom Stomp', suggesting that a desire to push on from ragtime towards something else was in the air – even up north in New York.

Another interesting example from the ragtime-into-jazz period again comes from James Reece Europe, this time from five years later with his 369th US Infantry Hellfighters Band. When Europe recorded 'Castle House Rag' in 1914, he was New York's leading society orchestra bandleader. In 1917, he volunteered for war service, becoming leader of the 369th US Infantry band, deemed to be the finest of its kind. Today, Europe is an obscure, shadowy figure seldom mentioned in jazz history, yet he was a significant pre-jazz figure and the most important African-American musical leader at a time when ragtime was on the wane but before the emergence of figures such as Joe 'King' Oliver and Louis Armstrong. Europe made twenty-four recordings for the Pathé label between March and May 1919, but it was not until 1996, when they were transferred to CD, that their importance was revealed. Europe's recording of 'Memphis Blues'[67] merits special attention since the piece was originally written as a rag that included a section of 12-bar blues. Clearly this performance retains the oompah feel of ragtime, yet it sounds remarkably jazzy with exuberant instrumental breaks for trumpet, trombone and clarinet. This recording shows that, just like Hegel's Beach that was neither land nor sea, this is not quite ragtime, although it contains characteristics we associate with ragtime, but neither is it quite jazz, although it contains properties we associate with early jazz.

By the early 1920s, ragtime had all but run its course, but its ethos would live on in New York through a style that became known as 'Stride Piano' developed in and around Harlem during the 1910s, its leading composers and performers including James P. Johnson, Thomas 'Fats' Waller and C. Luckyeth 'Lucky' Roberts.

The Original Dixieland Jazz Band Conundrum

When the Original Creole Band declined the opportunity to record with the Victor Talking Machine Company, it was to the Original Dixieland Jazz Band the Victor company turned, who promptly provided them with one of their earliest million-selling records. History has not treated this band too kindly, as historian Catherine Parsonage has pointed out, 'The implication is that because the group was white and commercially successful this somehow diminishes their authenticity as a jazz band and their importance in jazz history.'[68] So perhaps we should stand back and actually listen to what's going on here. For a start the ODJB's recordings for Victor between February 1917 and July 1918, especially pieces like 'Tiger Rag' and 'Clarinet Marmalade', are competently performed, and well recorded in the context of their time, have good group cohesion and possess a sense of swing we identify with jazz (although Nick La Rocca's trumpet lead often evokes the rhythmic phrasing of ragtime). The ODJB was a band that had paid their dues in cheap, tough dance halls, cabarets and saloons and knew what they were about; they created excitement, first in Chicago, then in New York prior to recording for Victor. Yes, there are novelty effects, but that is consistent with what many New Orleans bands were doing; the legendary trumpet player Joe 'King' Oliver, for example, had a repertoire of tricks using mutes of all shapes and sizes while Jelly Roll Morton's recording of 'New Crawley Blues' includes a laughing clarinet and a crying trumpet.

As Randall Sandke has pointed out, the ODJB emerged from 'an already well-established tradition' of white jazz musicians in

New Orleans.[69] The sheer number of white musicians on the scene at the time seems to have presented a problem to some jazz scholars, who have airbrushed them out of the script, though it is clear 'white and black bands did have numerous opportunities to absorb influences from each other'[70] – indeed, the ODJB clarinettist Larry Shields lived just two doors away from Buddy Bolden.[71] It may be an inconvenient truth, but the ODJB are the only window we have into the New Orleans jazz of the period. But whatever verdict posterity ultimately visits on them, their brash, polyphonic group improvisation not only presented a model of jazz that was widely influential among a subsequent generation of young musicians – including cornetist Bix Beiderbecke[72] and clarinettist Benny Goodman[73] – but their influence also extended internationally, playing in London in 1919–20. Here, they caused a sensation when they played the Savoy restaurant's Victory Ball in June 1919 in the presence of the king and queen and various other dignitaries; in October they took up a six-month residency at London's Hammersmith Palais de Danse. As Catherine Pasonage notes, 'The fact that the ODJB played the newest and largest dance venue from its opening night for six months is significant, as their version of "jazz" was widely disseminated and firmly established as the new dance music in Britain.'[74] Although not widely known, the Swedish jazz historian Lars Westin[75] has pointed out that the ODJB's influence extended at one remove into Sweden, via early broadcasts in the 1920s on shortwave radio from London hotels by ODJB-influenced bands, prompting the formation of similar-style bands in Stockholm, in restaurants, hotels and dance venues.

Jazz in Chicago

The first two decades of the twentieth century saw Chicago establishing itself as a huge industrial hub, presenting employment opportunities that attracted a labour force from the more economically deprived southern states, including New Orleans. Here the better standard of living meant there was disposable income left over at the end of the week for entertainment, and Chicago at the time was buzzing. The success of the Original Creole Band in Chicago between 1911 and 1917 was such that other ambitious musicians felt inclined to try their hand there. Trumpeter Joe 'King' Oliver was one such and in 1922, billed as King Oliver's Creole Jazz Band, appeared at the Lincoln Gardens dance hall and wrote himself into jazz history. The acclaim his band received made it hard for recording companies to ignore but the significance the thirty-seven recordings they made between April and December 1923 lay in the inclusion of trumpeter Louis Armstrong in the band's line-up. Although faithful to the early ensemble style of New Orleans jazz with its dense and some-what rigid improvised counterpoint, one important element of the band's performances was how they had moved beyond the rhythmic implications of ragtime to the kind of swing feel we now associate with jazz. This was due in part because jazz was now played for an audience that wanted to dance to the fox-trot, which had begun to replace the two-step in popularity by 1920, as a feature in *Talking Machine World*, headlined 'Why the Fox-Trot Flourishes' made clear: 'It was not long ago that the fox-trot was an unknown quantity … but today it seems to have monopolised the dance field.'[76]

Jelly Roll Morton and his Red Hot Peppers

In 1922–3, Jelly Roll Morton, now at the zenith of his abilities, also settled in Chicago. In 1926 he secured a recording contract from the Victor Talking Machine Company and over the next nine months he recorded seventeen songs with his band the Red Hot Peppers.

These recordings are marvels of recording fidelity, speaking to us down the ages clearly and powerfully, since they used Victor's latest electronic recording equipment, the new Bell-Western 'electric' process. The Peppers were not a regular working group like Oliver's Creole Band but assembled especially for each recording session. Morton carefully rehearsed them at his home and while 'punctilious with respect to all ensemble passages and as well as introductions, transitions and endings, was happy to receive suggestions from his players as well as allowing them freedom in their solos'.[77] The musicians did not play from written music, but were taught their parts individually by Morton. This was a time-consuming business, especially on a piece with a complicated structure like 'Black Bottom Stomp', whose form owed much to ragtime. Yet this remarkable performance has such a compelling rhythmic feel that the complexities of its construction recede beneath the exuberance of the performance; we are swept on from one musical event to the next – ensemble passages, riffs, breaks and bittersweet solos – until we reach the stirring climax. Here was a multi-thematic composition where a lot of ideas and detailed musical organization were crammed into a small space of just under three minutes, or one side of a 78 rpm recording, that reveals Morton's genius in full flower.

Louis Armstrong Takes Centre Stage

The recordings trumpeter Louis Armstrong made with his Hot Five in Chicago from November 1925 were a seismic event in the evolution of jazz, and after them the music world would never be the same again.

If Armstrong's contribution to jazz had been his stop-time cornet breaks on 'Potato Head Blues' (actually with his Hot Seven) or his opening cadenza on 'West End Blues', his place in the pantheon would surely have been secure, but there was so much more he recorded during this astonishingly creative

LOUIS 'SATCHMO' ARMSTRONG (1901–71)

Born in New Orleans and raised in dire poverty, Louis Armstrong's introduction to music was singing on street corners for dimes. An act of delinquency resulted in his detention at the Home for Colored Waifs. Here he was given a cornet which cemented his determination to become a musician. By 1918 he was a member of the leading band in New Orleans led by Kid Ory prior to moving to Chicago in 1922 under the mentorship of Joe 'King' Oliver. In autumn 1924 he joined the Fletcher Henderson Orchestra in New York, then the leading black band in the city. When he returned to Chicago in 1925 he recorded more than sixty performances with his Hot Five and Hot Seven that were to transform jazz. In 1932 he headlined at the London Palladium, and in 1936 he appeared with Bing Crosby in the movie *Pennies from Heaven* that saw the beginning of his transition to personality-entertainer and that subsequently saw him recording with jazz bands, vocal groups, pop singers and even with Hawaiian orchestras. In 1947 he formed a jazz sextet which was an immediate success, and became the setting in which he would see out the latter part of his career, billed as Louis Armstrong and his All Stars. He appeared with his band in a number of movies in the 1950s and 1960s – in all he appeared in almost fifty films during his lifetime – most notably in *High Society*, where he and his All Stars were joined by Bing Crosby for 'Now You Has Jazz', which became an enduring memento of his singing and playing during this latter period of his career. He also undertook a number of international tours under the auspices of the US State Department, his genial and affable personality projecting a favourable image of the United States during the Cold War. Despite numerous health scares, Armstrong kept going until the end, and even though in later years he could no longer play his inimitable trumpet, he rode high in the pop charts displacing bands like the Beatles with vocal singles such as 'What a Wonderful World' and 'We've Got All the Time in the World'.

period that it's literally littered with jazz classics. The Hot Five and Hot Seven were studio bands assembled to feature Armstrong's talents – 'Heebie Jeebies' introduced his vocal and scatting skills while numbers like 'Cornet Chop Suey', 'Struttin' With Some Barbecue' and 'Basin Street Blues' not only display his trumpet virtuosity but also exude joy and warmth. The verbal exchanges between Armstrong and saxophonist Don Redman on 'Tight Like This' are a reminder of 'the music's role in night-time rites of revelry and bawdy cheer. The comedy here, from variety house stages of the period, also reflects a dimension of the music that has been diminished as it has been formally institutionalised.'[78] A pertinent observation indeed. Perhaps the most enduring of the Hot Five's numbers was the recording on 28 June 1928 of 'West End Blues', whose clarion unaccompanied trumpet introduction became part of Armstrong's live shows at the time and was guaranteed a standing ovation. It is of course a blues, and comes with a wordless Armstrong vocal and a stunning trumpet climax at the end whose audacity must have stunned audiences (not to say fellow jazz musicians). Almost twenty years later Armstrong featured the song again in the Hollywood motion picture *New Orleans* (1947) that also starred singer Billie Holiday.

The New Orleans Revival in America

By the end of the 1920s, big bands had virtually eclipsed the New Orleans ensemble, but a modified, adrenalized form of New Orleans jazz enjoyed a second life in the late 1920s and '30s played by brash young white musicians from Chicago. Their style – perhaps unsurprisingly dubbed Chicago Jazz – became largely associated with a coterie of musicians who subsequently gravitated to the ensembles led by bandleader Eddie Condon, including Jimmy McPartland, Pee Wee Russell, Bud Freeman, George Brunies and George Wettling. By the 1930s they could be found in the clubs on 52nd Street in New York City before they took up residence in Condon's in Greenwich Village. In 1939, the trumpet player Muggsy Spanier formed a band he called, perhaps tellingly, his Ragtimers. They enjoyed considerable initial success at Chicago's Hotel Sherman before moving to Nick's Club in New York City for a brief run, when the band was promptly wound up. They left behind a series of recordings dubbed 'The Great Sixteen' that were purposely and solidly retrospective, including numbers made famous by the Original Dixieland Jazz Band, Louis Armstrong, King Oliver and Bix Beiderbecke, plus some early jazz staples like 'Someday Sweetheart', 'I Wish I Could Shimmy Like My Sister Kate' and 'Mandy, Make Up Your Mind'. They were interpreted with audible glee by the Ragtimers, a band greater than the sum of its component parts. Recorded at the height of the Big Band era, they brought a foretaste of a New Orleans revival championing a return to the traditional values of New Orleans jazz. This trend was given momentum in 1939 by two influential books, Wilder Hobson's *American Jazz Music* and Frederic Ramsey Jr and Charles Edward Smith's *Jazzmen* that explored – some say romanticized – early jazz. The authors of the latter had interviewed some of the original musicians around at the dawn of jazz, including trumpeter Bunk Johnson, who had played alongside Buddy Bolden. Johnson was persuaded (with the promise of a new set of false teeth) to come out of retirement,[79] and other old timers followed suit, including trombonist Kid Ory, and a jazz revival was under way: 'Ory seemed as good as [he'd] ever been. Bunk was on occasions quite magnificent, the combination of what he was trying to play and the overwhelming feeling of nostalgia and romance was enough to make it quite clear that this particular noble experiment had been a most valuable one.'[80] The authenticity these old timers brought to the New Orleans revival should not, however, be overshadowed by bands like the Dukes of Dixieland, The Firehouse Five Plus Two and The Dixieland Rhythm Kings that sprung up, playing a commercial form of Dixieland of the sort that could be heard at Republican and Democratic party conventions when the balloons were released from the ceiling.

The Trad Boom – the New Orleans Revival in Britain

In the mid–1940s a traditional jazz revival also got under way in the United Kingdom, but it owed little to events in America from which it was effectively cut off for all but essential wartime supplies. However, it did share one thing in its genesis, and that was the view held by dedicated record collectors and fans that New Orleans jazz was the source and the essence of the music. In both instances, in America and the United Kingdom, the New Orleans revival was not a part of the natural evolution of the music, nor was it linked to commercial ends. Instead, it arose from an almost idealistic pursuit of jazz in what was considered its purest form. Some took their fanship a stage further by teaching themselves to play in order to indulge their passion for the music. In wartime Britain in 1943, a band comprising mainly factory workers assembled in the garden basement of The Red Barn public house in Barnehurst, Kent. A more unlikely venue for the start of a jazz revival boom could not be imagined, set in the heart of London's suburbia, a half-hour train journey from Charing Cross station. George Webb's Dixielands were not the only band of do-it-yourself revivalists, but they emerged as the most significant, attributed to the authenticity and sheer energy their music managed to generate. Their growing popularity helped spearhead a movement that was to alter the popular music industry in the United Kingdom in the 1950s. In a grey, post-war Britain with food rationing, power cuts, a general shortage of just about everything useful and nothing much more to look forward to than the next Benjamin Britten opera, Traditional Jazz – or Trad Jazz or just Trad as it became dubbed – struck a chord with Britain's young people. Here was a happy noise that you could tap your foot to, dance to and, since the venues of choice for Trad were usually pubs, make merry to. Very quickly, like-minded bands sprang up around the country, taking their inspiration less from the New Orleans masters, and more from the popular Trad bands of the day led by Humphrey Lyttelton, Chris Barber, Acker Bilk and Kenny Ball, all of whom figured at various times in the British pop charts. The popularity of Trad saw it become, to all intents and purposes, the jazz mainstream in the UK with, somewhat ironically, modern jazz the supporting attraction. British Trad Jazz undoubtedly had a sound of its own, and often provided the soundtrack for meetings and events held by the Campaign for Nuclear Disarmament (CND), most notably their annual London to Aldermaston march (the location of the Atomic Weapons Research Establishment) at Easter where several bands paraded in the marching band style of the New Orleans bands along with the demonstrators, presenting the interesting irony of a British-i-fied version of American jazz being used as a music of protest against American nuclear values. The popularity of British Trad spread to Europe, with bands like the Dutch Swing College in Holland, Claude Luter's band in France and several German Trad bands in the then British occupied zone of West Germany, influenced by British Trad bands playing for UK troops garrisoned there. Interestingly, there are German bands modelled on Chris Barber – who was hugely popular in Germany in the 1950s – still to this day in the former British occupied zone. Eventually the Trad boom was undone by the emergence of the Beatles and other like-minded 'beat' groups in the 1960s, whose British invasion of the States was to about change the face of pop music.

New Orleans Jazz Today

New Orleans musicians tenaciously hung onto their home-grown style of jazz, especially the marching band tradition, despite the winds of change that blew through jazz. At its heart was Preservation Hall, established in 1961 as a music centre presenting New Orleans jazz 350 nights a year. Marching bands continued to give the Gulf City its unique musical character that was so appealing to its tourist trade. In the late 1970s and during the 1980s, bands like the Dirty Dozen Brass Band, the Soul Rebels Brass Band and the Rebirth Brass Band started adding new flavours to the traditional marching band sound such as funk, hiphop and bebop that reflected the desire of younger musicians to stamp their authority on the music. These bands quickly graduated from playing the parades and clubs in the French Quarter to festivals and stages around the world, a tradition that continues to this day.

Early Jazz Playlist

1. 'The Entertainer' *The Sting/Soundtrack Version/Piano Version* from *The Sting*.
2. 'Maple Leaf Rag' St Louis Style/'Maple Leaf Rag New Orleans Style' from *Jelly Roll Morton: The Complete Library of Congress Recordings* track 3, CD3 (Rounder).
3. 'Blackbottom Stomp' by Jelly Roll Morton from *Birth of the Hot*.
4. 'Doctor Jazz' by Jelly Roll Morton from *Birth of the Hot*.
5. Original Dixieland Jazzband: 'Tiger Rag' from *The Complete Original Dixieland Jazzband* (Jazz Tribune).
6. King Oliver with Louis Armstrong: 'Dippermouth Blues' from *Louis Armstrong and King Oliver*.
7. Louis Armstrong: 'West End Blues' from *The Complete Hot 5 and Hot 7 Recordings*.
8. Louis Armstrong: 'Potatohead Blues' from *The Complete Hot 5 and Hot 7 Recordings*.
9. Bix Beiderbecke: 'Singin' the Blues' from *Bix Beiderbecke Vol. 1: Singin' the Blues*.
10. Muggsy Spanier: 'That Da Da Strain' from *The Great 16*.

11. Chris Barber and his band: 'Ice Cream' from *Barber in Berlin*.
12. Dirty Dozen Brass Band: 'I Ate Up the Apple Tree' from *My Feet Can't Fail Me Now.*

Listening Notes for the Early Jazz Playlist

1. 'The Entertainer' *The Sting/Soundtrack Version/ Piano Version from The Sting*

On 7 June 1903, the *St. Louis Globe-Democrat* proclaimed 'The Entertainer' was 'The best and most euphonious' of Joplin's compositions. This performance by Marvin Hamlisch comes from the soundtrack album of the motion picture *The Sting*. The album topped *Billboard's 200* chart between May and June 1974 and the single 'The Entertainer' taken from it reached No. 3 on *the Billboard Hot 100* singles chart. It showed how ragtime's innocent charm still had the power to appeal to audiences in the rock age. It's interesting to note that in 1970, Joshua Rifkin released the album *Scott Joplin Piano Rags* on the Nonesuch label, selling 100,000 copies in the first year and going on to become the label's first million-selling record (and this on a label that had signed The Doors).

2. 'Maple Leaf Rag' St Louis Style/'Maple Leaf Rag' New Orleans Style from *Jelly Roll Morton: The Complete Library of Congress Recordings* track 3, CD 3 (Rounder)

Here pianist Jelly Roll Morton plays 'Maple Leaf Rag' in a formal manner, similar to Marvin Hamlisch's performance of 'The Entertainer'. He then plays it New Orleans style, and the difference is best heard rather than spoken about. If, as he claims, he was doing this around 1903, or even later, it could well be the moment when ragtime's oompah feel was replaced by a swing feel that we associate with early jazz. It all seems so simple now, but back then it would have been a radical change that flew in the face of a musical craze reaching its height.

3. 'Blackbottom Stomp' by Jelly Roll Morton from *Birth of the Hot*

This is a bona fide jazz classic. A lot happens in a short space of time. Ensemble densities are constantly shifting, soloists are very aware that they must serve the needs of the song and all the time the sheer energy and ebullience of the rhythm sweeps the band and listener along to the climax. Above all else, the piece is masterfully constructed, and as one musical event leads into the next the listener's curiosity is constantly aroused – where is all this heading? What's going to happen next?

4. 'Doctor Jazz' by Jelly Roll Morton from *Birth of the Hot*

This tune, recorded in the year it was written by Joe 'King' Oliver, is another exuberant performance by Morton, who here contributes the vocal. It also includes a fine example of collective New Orleans ensemble improvisation between cornet, trombone and clarinet contrasted by prearranged stop-time breaks and improvised solo passages. Throughout, Morton shows a degree of musical organization that sustains interest throughout the performance.

5. Original Dixieland Jazzband: 'Tiger Rag' from *The Complete Original Dixieland Jazzband*

First recorded by the Original Dixieland Jazz Band on 25 March 1918, the composer credit for 'Tiger Rag' was shared equally by each member of the band. It quickly became *the* jazz standard of the pre-bebop era recorded by just about everyone – or so it seemed – since at least 136 recordings of the song had been made by 1942,[81] while it had been featured in over thirty films and cartoon features. It uses a ragtime form – AABAACDEFFGGGGFFFF – and every self-respecting jazz musician prior to 1945 was expected to know it by heart. Note how Nick La Rocca on cornet plays the lead and Larry Shields on clarinet and Eddie Edwards on trombone improvise a rumbustious counterpoint around him – New Orleans jazz was about a polyphonic group sound in which each instrument was expected to perform a specific role.

6. King Oliver with Louis Armstrong: 'Dippermouth Blues' from *Louis Armstrong and King Oliver*

Once again the emphasis is on an ensemble sound and collective music-making, but clearly Oliver's ensemble was more nuanced than the ODJB. His band was a sensation in Chicago, prompting Oliver to call on Armstrong, still in New Orleans, to come and join his band. Armstrong's role was as second cornet, improvising a loose form of counterpoint around King Oliver's cornet lines, which he did with considerable skill. 'Dippermouth Blues', recorded in April 1923, has Oliver's most famous solo that was subsequently referenced by every trumpet player who played this jazz classic.

7. Louis Armstrong: 'West End Blues' from *The Complete Hot 5 and Hot 7 Recordings*

8. Louis Armstrong: 'Potato Head Blues' from *The Complete Hot 5 and Hot 7 Recordings*

The Hot 5 and Hot 7 recordings placed Armstrong-as-soloist at the centre of events, so moving the focus of jazz away from the ensemble to the individual virtuoso performer. Since these recordings are among the finest in jazz, everyone will have their favourites; here are two of mine and they're not short of highlights. 'West End Blues' still startles with its audacious opening cadenza, while Armstrong's solo after his wordless vocal seems to break free of the ground beat and dances to its own time above the ensemble. 'Potato Head Blues' is less pretentious, the focus of this performance the stop-time chorus and the seemingly effortless virtuosity that lies behind everything Armstrong did.

9. Bix Beiderbecke: 'Singin' the Blues' from *Bix Beiderbecke Vol. 1: Singin' the Blues*

On the face of it, the expansive style of Louis Armstrong might appear to put every other cornet or trumpet player of the day in the shade. Yet Beiderbecke's solo on 'Singin' the Blues', recorded on 4 February 1927 with Frankie Trumbauer and his Orchestra, and his solo on 'Way Down Yonder in New Orleans', recorded by the same ensemble four days later, have been described as 'two of the most exquisite solos ever recorded by a jazz musician'.[82] Certainly, Beiderbecke's solo on 'Singing the Blues' is one of the most celebrated of his career and was the first ballad interpretation in recorded jazz.[83] His solo, spontaneously conceived, hangs together like a composition in its own right – indeed, it was played note for note by the Fletcher Henderson Orchestra in their 1931 recording of this tune. High praise indeed from one of the leading big bands of the day.

10. Muggsy Spanier: 'That Da Da Strain' from *The Great 16*

By the early 1920s, reports of Dadaism had appeared in the American press, possibly prompting songwriters Edgar Dowell, Spencer Williams, Babe Thompson and Bob Schafer to come up with the title 'That Da Da Strain' in 1922. Muggsy Spanier's ensemble lines up in the manner of a New Orleans band with trumpet, trombone, clarinet, piano, guitar (rather than banjo), bass and drums but with the addition of a tenor saxophone. This is hardly Dixieland, but among the finest examples of hard swinging Chicago Jazz – there are also moments of freewheeling New Orleans polyphony, but the accent is on arranged passages that give this band its relaxed cohesion. Led from the front by Spanier's trumpet, his drive and infectious sense of swing seems to lift the whole band.

11. Chris Barber and his band: 'Ice Cream' from *Barber in Berlin*

Trombonist Chris Barber was at the forefront of the British Trad Jazz revival, becoming one of Europe's most successful traditional jazz bands. 'Ice Cream' was recorded live at the Deutschlandhalle, Berlin on 23 May 1959. A massive auditorium that seats 12,000 people, it was sold out in advance. 'Ice Cream' is a powerful yet relaxed performance that – as you will hear – raised the roof a year before Ella Fitzgerald recorded her Grammy-winning *Ella in Berlin* there. There are enthusiastic solos by Barber, clarinettist Monty Sunshine and trumpet Pat Halcox, who here has one of his finest moments on record. Although 'When The Saints Go Marching In' quickly became a cliché of Trad Jazz, you won't hear a better, or more rousing version, than the one that climaxes this performance as the audience of 12,000 people go stark staring mad.

12. Dirty Dozen Brass Band: 'I Ate Up the Apple Tree' from *My Feet Can't Fail Me Now*

Jazz is as much a part of the DNA of New Orleans as it is an essential component of its tourist trade, with marching bands on hand for parades, funerals, picnics and other events. An influx of younger musicians in the 1970s prompted a renaissance of the New Orleans brass band tradition. Their bread and butter came from playing nightly in the clubs and bars of New Orleans for dancers, who demanded something more than the traditional standards their parents and grandparents had danced to, so the younger musicians started adding elements from bop, funk and hiphop to their music. One of the most popular of this younger breed of brass marching bands was the Dirty Dozen, whose rhythmic drive owed much to the agile bass lines played by Kirk Joseph on tuba who steals the show on this fine, danceable version of 'I Ate Up the Apple Tree'.

7

The Rise of the Big Bands

Thinking Big

In the decade that followed World War I, America set the pace on the global stage for social revolution and change. A post-war economic boom, triggered in part by the return of the troops from France in 1919, saw America's gross national product grow from $78 billion to $103 billion in one year. It meant Americans in 1920 had more money in their pockets than any previous generation and they flocked to leisure activities in increasing numbers. The rapid rise of dance halls meant a young generation now had a focal point to meet members of the opposite sex socially who did not live on the same street or in the same neighbourhood. Jazz musicians adapted to the changing times by expanding their ensembles to be heard more clearly in these huge dance palaces – the Palomar Ballroom in Los Angeles, for example, catered for a crowd of 20,000 on its opening night in 1925 – since electric public address systems would not arrive until the late 1920s. Clearly, some sort of organizing principle was required with more musicians on the bandstand; while the roles of musicians in typical New Orleans or Chicago ensembles were simple yet clear-cut, adding more instruments upset the balance of their freewheeling musical polyphony. The obvious answer was written arrangements which, in terms of evolution, was a massive change that occurred in a relatively short space of time. It had the effect of totally reinventing the sound of jazz from polyphony to antiphony with the traditional New Orleans style ensembles comprising trumpet, trombone and clarinet plus rhythm (piano, bass, banjo and drums) playing head arrangements, or arrangements committed to the 'head', or memory, swept aside by ensembles typically comprising three trumpets, two trombones, four saxophones plus rhythm playing sophisticated written arrangements. As trombonist Clyde Bernhardt recalled, 'If you didn't read [music] by 1927 or 1928, you got left out. No place for you in a quality band.'[84] It caused a massive dislocation with hitherto established jazz masters of the stature of Joe 'King' Oliver and Jelly Roll Morton forced into semi-retirement. Small wonder this polarized jazz debate at the time, with proponents of small-band New Orleans-inspired jazz claiming it was 'the real jazz' while the music of the big bands was considered something else.

As we saw in the previous chapter, New Orleans bands travelled as far as the West Coast of America, where several local bands copied their style, including one led by drummer Art Hickman, who landed a prestigious booking at the St Francis Hotel in San Francisco. Here the formal clientele demanded a little more from Hickman than a raggy version of New Orleans jazz. In 1914 Hickman invited Ferde Grofé, an exceptionally talented young pianist and arranger, to join his ensemble. Around the same time he also added Bert Ralton and Clyde Doerr, two talented saxophonists, to his band. Bear in mind the saxophone was something of a novelty instrument at the time, which Hickman hoped to exploit. However, Grofé was quick to seize their potential as a small choir within the overall ensemble, conceiving arrangements that divided the ensemble into separate brass and saxophone sections, an innovation that was an important early step in the development of big band jazz and dance music. Hickman was not the first bandleader to use saxophones in his ensemble, but it was the way in which Ralton and Doerr's strong musical personalities were integrated into an overall ensemble concept that caused a sensation.

Paul Whiteman – The King of Jazz?

In 1917, Grofé joined bandleader Paul Whiteman's Orchestra, where he was able to develop his ideas further for the 'modern dance ensemble'. In 1920, Calvin Child, director of Victor's Artists Bureau, brought Whiteman's then nine-piece Ambassador Orchestra into their Camden, New Jersey, recording studio. Their subdued and inoffensive reading of 'Whispering' (coupled with 'Japanese Sandman') was an enormous hit, selling more than two million copies, pushing Whiteman to the forefront of popular music, a position he did not relinquish for over a decade. Whiteman, through his arranger Ferde Grofé, played a pioneering role

PAUL WHITEMAN (1890–1967)

Whiteman played viola in the Denver Symphony Orchestra for seven years, but became captivated by the transition of ragtime into jazz, prompting him to organize a dance band in San Francisco in 1918. When he moved to New York he quickly became the best-known bandleader in America during the 1920s, touring the UK in 1923 and Europe in 1926. By the late 1920s he led his most jazz-orientated ensemble, going out of his way to feature the playing of Bix Beiderbecke, among others and, as musicologist Gunther Schuller has pointed out, 'there is no question that [the Whiteman band] was admired (and envied) by many musicians, both black and white ... [and] there is in the best Whiteman performances a feeling and sound unique in its way as Ellington or Basie'.[85] In a career that spanned sixty years, Whiteman changed the landscape of American music, with frequent appearances in the worlds of theatre, vaudeville, the concert hall, radio, motion pictures and finally television, winning accolades in all of them.

in 'restructuring the dance orchestra which continued (despite numerous modifications) to be fundamental for the next twenty-five years and persists even today. By intelligent scoring he managed to make saxophones and brass into principal voices in the dance orchestra . . . and incorporated into dance music many of the most interesting features of jazz.'[86]

It's often forgotten in jazz history books that Whiteman's success was played out against an extremely influential anti-jazz lobby in the aftermath of World War I, who saw jazz as a danger-ous musical subversion and an incitement to licentiousness, its vernacular origins as troubling to polite black society as they were to white. This powerful pressure group was as concerned to protect the morals of a nation as the anti-drink lobby, which had successfully lobbied for an alcohol and intoxicating beverages ban with the Volstead Act that came into force at midnight on 17 January 1920. The anti-jazz lobby wanted to do the same with jazz; the Superintendent of Schools in Kansas City proclaiming before an audience of a thousand school teachers, 'This nation has been fighting booze for a long time. I am just wondering whether jazz isn't going to have to be legislated against as well.'[87] It was a time when public bodies and institutions, govern-mental agencies, educational and religious leaders, periodicals, temperance organizations, Ivy League academics and prominent individuals in public life all seemed united in voicing anti-jazz sentiments. In New York, for example, the state legislature passed the Cotillo Bill to regulate where live music − jazz − could be played and when. Remarkably, the Victor Talking Machine Company, which had previously enjoyed a million-selling hit with the Original Dixieland Jazz Band's 'Livery Stable Blues', came under the sway of this powerful lobby and opted to set an example to the rest of the recording industry by announcing that it would henceforward concentrate on high-status singers, conductors and orchestras from the opera and classical worlds, according jazz low priority. 'Poor jazz!' said *Metronome* magazine in July 1922. 'It has been maligned in print and pulpit. All the sins of a wicked world have been traced directly and uncompromisingly to its door.'[88]

Interestingly, it would be Whiteman's non-jazz, classically orientated musical credentials that became the source of his legitimacy with the anti-jazz elites when he mounted a concert he called 'An Experiment in Modern Music' on 12 February 1924 at the Aeolian Hall in New York City. Here he debuted *Rhapsody in Blue*, a brand new composition by George Gershwin that caused a sensation. Much scholarly hot air has been expended on Whiteman's attempt to 'Make a Lady out of Jazz' at this concert, failing to contextualize jazz's equivocal status among the highly influential anti-jazz elites, especially during the run-up to the concert. Whiteman's concert was intended to take these powerful forces head on, and in this he was largely successful, since in its aftermath the one thing Whiteman had on his side was success, which has always been accorded the highest value in American life.[89]

By taking jazz and jazz-influenced music into the Aeolian Hall, New York's citadel of classical music, Whiteman turned the debate about the 'jazz problem' on its head. The concert was the major event in the New York music season that year, and in the audience were a host of A-list celebrities, attending at Whiteman's personal invitation. After performing a repertoire of popular American and jazz-influenced music culminating in *Rhapsody in Blue*, Whiteman then demonstrated that his musicians had the skills of classical musicians by concluding the concert with Edward Elgar's *Pomp and Circumstance* (March Number 1 in D major). Whiteman's orchestra clearly was not a European classical orchestra, although it could perform selections of classical music, so what was it? The answer was that it was an *American* orchestra playing music that was uniquely *American* and that included jazz. This had the effect of changing the nature of the argument, which was now about what constituted modern *American* music, so situating Whiteman's music within a broader debate about what constituted 'American-ness' in the arts and how this might be expressed in American national culture. It took a while, but as the dust began to settle after the 'Experiment in Modern Music' concert, the word 'jazz' in the 1920s and, 30s began to lose its connotation with the brothels and dives of New Orleans and, thanks to Whiteman, became seen as a native product unique to the United States of which Americans could be proud. Today, the Aeolian Hall concert is regarded as a defining event of the Jazz Age and of the cultural history of New York City.

After a tour of Europe in 1923 where his popularity skyrocketed, he was crowned 'The King of Jazz' as a publicity stunt on his return. The name stuck, much to the chagrin of the jazz purists who forget how his late-1920s ensemble represented a high point in early jazz, thanks to innovative arrangements from the likes of Bill Challis, Matty Malneck, Lennie Hayton, William Grant Still and Tom Satterfield that were 'complex, demanding scores that took everything [his] musicians could give';[90] they were not merely functional – music for dancing – but betrayed higher artistic ambition, revealing Whiteman's intent to broaden jazz's expressive resources through technically demanding yet sophisticated arrangements that helped set the pace for big band jazz in the late 1920s.

Whiteman went out of his way to feature cornetist Bix Beiderbecke, who at the age of twenty-four had accepted an invitation to join his orchestra as a featured soloist in 1927. A typical example is the Bill Challis arrangement of 'San', where Beiderbecke takes the opening solo chorus while the subsequent instrumental sections, first by the strings and then by the brass, are pure orchestrated Beiderbecke, as is the passage for trumpets on Matty Malneck's arrangement of 'From Monday On' (which also has a fine Beiderbecke solo), a measure of the high regard in which Beiderbecke was held in the Whiteman organization. Indeed, Whiteman's arrangers were taking account of this remarkable young man's creativity with orchestrated ensemble variations owing much to Beiderbecke's influence. On titles such as 'Changes', 'San', 'There Ain't No Sweet Man That's Worth the Salt of My Tears' and 'Dardanella', Beiderbecke's solos burst out of the ensemble with an elegance and poise that can still touch us today. Far from being the misunderstood genius driven to drink, Beiderbecke was greatly admired among musicians in the 1920s, as contemporaneous accounts attest. Although Beiderbecke died at the age of twenty-eight, virtually every recording on which he is featured is of interest today.

LEON BISMARK 'BIX' BEIDERBECKE (1903–31)

Beiderbecke was born in Davenport, Iowa with a prodigious gift for music. At the age of seven, the *Davenport Daily Democrat* reported that he was 'the most unusual and most remarkably talented child in music that there is in this city'. He learned the cornet by ear from recordings of The Original Dixieland Jazz Band, and at twenty was the star of the Wolverines, with whom he made his first recordings. After working and recording with the Jean Goldkette Orchestra, he joined Paul Whiteman in 1927. Recordings under his own name and with fellow Whiteman bandmate, saxophonist Frank Trumbauer, include 'Singing the Blues' and 'I'm Coming Virginia', both masterpieces of early jazz. In September 1929 he underwent a breakdown and returned to his parents in Davenport to recuperate. He never fully recovered, although he continued to play and record – his solo on 'Barnacle Bill the Sailor' is a gem from his twilight days – before death claimed him, aged twenty-eight, on 6 August 1931. It wasn't long before the Beiderbecke legend of a fallen angel who died young was under way. Dorothy Baker's 1938 novel *Young Man With a Horn*, inspired by Beiderbecke's life, prompted the 1950 Hollywood motion picture of the same name starring Kirk Douglas, Lauren Bacall and Doris Day. In 1985, ITV screened *The Beiderbecke Affair*, a series written by playwright Alan Plater, whose success spawned two sequels, *The Beiderbecke Tapes* and *The Beiderbecke Connection*. In 2012, the British Film Institute published a book about the series that acknowledged the cult status it had acquired – all three series available, by the way, on DVD.

Beiderbecke's tragic end was attributed to alcoholism, but musicologist Randall Sandke, while not denying Beiderbecke's drinking problem, points out that: 'Beiderbecke had sufficient self-control to hold down steady jobs, enjoy cordial and some-times close relationships with both men and women, pursue his passion for sports (mainly baseball, golf, swimming and tennis) not to mention performing brilliantly on scores of record-ings, particularly in the two years leading up to his physical and emotional breakdown.'[91] This occurred when he was twenty-five and a half, in September 1929, details of which are sketchy but which nevertheless prompted his rapid decline and left him with 'severe peripheral neuropathy affecting his legs and feet as well as chronic pneumonia (which would ultimately cause his death). His kidneys and liver didn't function properly. He appeared prema-turely aged …[and] had to use a cane to get around.'[92] Sandke points out that this attack was hardly consistent with prolonged use of alcohol, rather a sudden and acute poisoning – but with what? He reminds us that this was the Prohibition Era in the United States, and the Coolidge government was concerned at the vast amounts of illegal liquor flooding the market, including some 60 million gallons of ethyl alcohol that was stolen annu-ally to supply the country's drinkers illegally. The administra-tion's answer? Incredible though it may seem, they ordered that this alcohol be 'denatured' using poisonous methyl alcohol to render it undrinkable. The effects of drinking alcohol treated in this way were consistent with Beiderbecke's symptoms, resulting in 'an agonising two and a half years before his system finally gave out'[93] on 6 August 1931. Bix Beiderbecke, one of the most gifted musicians in the history of jazz, may well have died as a result of a lethal cocktail distributed by the US government as a means of deterring illegal sales of alcohol. As cultural historian Philipp Blom has noted, 'When the government began adding lethal methyl alcohol … people died [and] the authorities were accused of being complicit in murder.'[94]

Duke Ellington and his Famous Orchestra

The development of Ellington the composer, arranger, piano player and bandleader since his first recording with the Washingtonians in 1924 until his death in 1974 is unique in jazz. He followed his own path, not directly influencing the history of jazz as other major figures in the music have done, but creating a body of work universally acclaimed, both inside and outside jazz for its excellence. His first major job in New York City was at the Kentucky Club in February 1924. Here Ellington first encountered Paul Whiteman, whose influence would soon surface in his music, at one time billing himself as 'The Paul Whiteman of Harlem'.[95] Ellington's manager Irving Mills encouraged Ellington to adapt the extended format of Whiteman-style symphonic jazz to underline his credentials as a jazz composer. In his autobiography, Ellington's son Mercer confirms how Mills wanted Ellington to share with Whiteman the prestige of presenting an extended composition that occupied *both* sides of a ten-inch 78 rpm record: 'For a black band it was a major step forward,'[96] he said. Ellington's first extended arrangement was his version of the Original Dixieland Jazz Band's 'Tiger Rag', recorded in two parts, on 28 March 1929. Then came 'Creole Rhapsody', an original composition, again covering two sides of a 78 rpm, recorded on 14 May 1931 for Brunswick and on 11 June 1931 for RCA Victor. It's worth noting *Rhapsody in Blue* was actually a part of Ellington's repertoire in the 1930s (the instrumental parts arranged by Juan Tizol are now in the Ellington Collection at the Smithsonian Institution in Washington, D.C.) since this was the obvious model for 'Creole Rhapsody', albeit achieved in Ellington's very personal style. What distinguished Ellington from most of his contemporaries was that early on he was moving jazz beyond functional dance music into the realm of a large-scale work, something that would continue to absorb him throughout his life.

EDWARD KENNEDY 'DUKE' ELLINGTON (1899–1974)

The son of a butler, Ellington was born in Washington, D.C. and started learning the piano at the age of seven. Much influenced at the time by ragtime, his first composition was 'Soda Fountain Rag'. Initially he was a commercial artist by day and a bandleader by night, moving to New York to further his career in 1923 with Elmer Snowden's Washingtonians, which he took over, making his recording debut in 1924. Now known as Duke Ellington's Washingtonians, he steadily enlarged his ensemble to ten pieces while gradually evolving the signature sound of his band. When in 1927 he moved to Harlem's Cotton Club, he further enlarged his band, now known as Duke Ellington and his Famous Orchestra, where he quickly rose to become a leading figure in the world of jazz.

Some of Ellington's classics from this early period, such as 'East St. Louis Toodle-Oo', and 'Black and Tan Fantasy', are brought alive by the contributions of trumpeter Bubber Miley and trombonist Joe 'Tricky Sam' Nanton. Thereafter, Ellington's band would be built around strong musical personalities such as these with a very personal, individual sound, which Ellington exploited as strong musical flavours in his ensemble. It gave his band a sound and style quite unlike any other, and through his manager Irving Mills' advocacy, Ellington's band, now known as Duke Ellington and his Famous Orchestra, opened at the Cotton Club on 4 December 1927. This was a nightclub that seated 700 well-heeled patrons from show business celebrities to business tycoons, politicians to gangsters, sporting celebrities to film stars and more – in short, it was the place to be seen for New York's high rollers. Now Ellington had to contribute music for the floorshow, dancing and speciality acts and, more importantly, the music for each season's new revue. Ellington's striking accompaniment for these productions defined his great talent as a composer and arranger. Highlights from this period include

'Old Man Blues', 'The Mystery Song', 'Echoes of the Jungle', 'Harlem Speaks', 'Blue Harlem' and whether or not he borrowed the theme of Fauré's 'Sicilienne' from *Pelléas Et Melisande* Op. 80 for his 1932 hit 'It Don't Mean a Thing (If it Ain't Got That Swing)', the title was at least prophetic.

Ellington negotiated the 1930s with difficulties; the death of his mother on 25 May 1935 was a blow from which he took a long time to recover. His creativity took a nose dive, *Variety* noting that his 'discords have grown stale',[97] and – according to his son Mercer – it 'affected his musical output more than anything else that happened in his career'.[98] In 1935 came *Reminiscing in Tempo*, an extended suite spread over four sides of 78 rpm records whose sombre tonalities reflected his emotional disposition. As his creative drive began to return with pieces such as 'The Sergeant Was Shy', 'Braggin' In Brass', 'Tootin' Through the Roof' and 'Steppin' In To Swing Society', Ellington embarked on a twenty-eight-date concert tour of Europe, arriving in Le Havre on 30 March 1939. Its success, and particularly his reception in Sweden, lifted his creative spirit. On his return to the United States he broke ties with Irving Mills, his long-time manager, and made three important changes to his band: in mid-1939 he added Billy Strayhorn to his staff, an accomplished musician who would contribute compositions and arrangements that sounded like an extension of Ellington's own; at the end of 1939 he discovered Jimmy Blanton, then the finest bassist in jazz, and did away with the awkward two-bass set-up, so transforming his rhythm section at a stroke, and in January 1940 he hired tenor saxophonist Ben Webster, whose exciting solos added additional drama to his music. The scene was now set for what many consider his greatest musical triumphs.

In early 1940 Ellington left the Columbia record label and signed with RCA Victor, opening a new chapter in his discography on 6 March 1940 with two jazz classics, 'Jack the Bear', which includes a moment of jazz history actually being made as Jimmy Blanton showed the world his virtuoso pizzicato technique, and

'Ko Ko', which has been described as 'one of the monumental events in jazz music'. Throughout 1940, Ellington was producing two, sometimes three masterpieces every time he went into the recording studio, highlights including 'Conga Brava', 'Concerto for Cootie', 'Cottontail', 'Bojangles (A Portrait of Bill Robinson)', 'A Portrait of Bert Williams', 'Blue Goose', 'Harlem Air Shaft', 'Rumpus in Richmond', 'Sepia Panorama', 'In a Mellotone' and 'Across the Track Blues'. However, although the first recording session of 1941 produced yet another classic – Billy Strayhorn's 'Take the A Train'[99] that would become Ellington's theme song – a dispute over royalties between the American Society of Composers and Publishers (ASCAP) and the National Association of Broadcasters resulted in the latter banning ASCAP[100] songs from the airwaves. With Ellington engaged in writing the music for a new musical lampooning racial prejudice called *Jump for Joy*, Billy Strayhorn and his son Mercer had to quickly write new, non-ASCAP material in order to continue broadcasting. Of the twenty-two pieces Ellington recorded that year, only twelve had his involvement, and almost all lacked the riveting quality of his 1940 output. Even so, between February 1941 and July 1942 there were classics, such as 'Blue Serge', 'What Am I Here For?' 'I Don't Know What Kind of Blues I've Got', 'Mainstem', Strayhorn's 'Raincheck' and 'Chelsea Bridge', and two durable Standards in 'Perdido' and 'C Jam Blues'.

Almost half the material Ellington recorded for RCA Victor between March 1940 and July 1942, when the American Federation of Musicians foolishly imposed a recording ban, are bona fide jazz classics. The amount of orchestration plus the development of the written and improvised is remarkable – a lot happens in the 3 minutes available on a 10-inch 78 rpm recording. His use of highly individual, sometimes idiosyncratic, soloists in combination created great richness of tonal colour, what Strayhorn called 'The Ellington Effect', that set him apart from his contemporaries. When Ellington returned to the recording studio after the recording ban was lifted in 1944, there were some fine recordings, but what many regard as the highlight of Ellington's recording career was behind him. His career would see further creative peaks,[101] but for many he would never reach the heights of his great 1940–2 band.

Fletcher Henderson: The Musical Role Model

In the face of what Jeffrey Magee has called 'the power of the Paul Whiteman paradigm, which cannot be dismissed as merely a transient commercial alternative',[102] most bandleaders, both black and white, began to follow Whiteman's lead, *The New York Times Book Review & Magazine* pointing out, 'For a year now the dance orchestras of New York have been modelling themselves on the Whiteman plan.'[103] But it was not just in emulating Grofé's arranging methods; it was in sartorial elegance, too, with bandleaders conducting their orchestras in the Whiteman manner with a white baton (like a classical conductor). One of the first major American jazz ensembles to respond to Whiteman's influence was the black bandleader Fletcher Henderson, initially through his principal arranger and saxophonist Don Redman, whose association with the band lasted from 1923 to 1927. Redman's arranging style matured in a remarkably short space of time and gave force to the notion that the arranger could be as much a creative force in jazz as the composer or improviser.

Within four years Redman produced an arranger's tour de force (and jazz classic) with his treatment of Thomas 'Fats' Waller's 'Whiteman Stomp', recorded by both Henderson and Whiteman in 1927. Indeed, although jazz histories usually refrain from mentioning it, Redman would later provide Whiteman with several specially commissioned arrangements. However, perhaps Redman's most enduring work for the Henderson band was his

FLETCHER HENDERSON (1897–1952)

Born into a relatively well-to-do family, Henderson studied piano and European art music with his mother. On graduating from university with a degree in chemistry and mathematics in 1920, he moved to New York to pursue a career as a chemist, which proved impossible for a black person. He appears to have drifted into jazz, and by 1924 was leading a band at the Club Alabam on Broadway. Within a year he had moved to the Roseland Ballroom, the best-known dance hall in New York, which remained his base for ten years and provided his springboard to national fame.

1925 arrangement of 'Sugarfoot Stomp', a powerful rendering of King Oliver's 'Dippermouth Blues', which Henderson later cited as his favourite recording. Dubbed 'The Paul Whiteman of Race' by the French jazz writer Hugues Panassié, Henderson even included a version of *Rhapsody in Blue* in his repertoire during the winter of 1924–5. As Henderson biographer Jeffrey Magee explained: 'In the case of Henderson we have a black bandleader adapting songs . . . in a style suggestive of Paul Whiteman, the leading white . . . bandleader of the day. And . . . black critics were praising him for doing this.'[104]

With Redman's departure to form his own big band, Henderson took over the bulk of arranging duties, and while his approach may have initially taken inspiration from the Whiteman orchestra, he would actually render Whiteman's style old hat by the mid-1930s by creating a style of arranging that would become the blueprint for the Swing Era that was just around the corner. At the heart of his success was the logic of clear, uncluttered writing, as trombonist Dicky Wells, one of Henderson's sidemen, later observed: 'Fletcher had a way of writing so that the notes seemed to float along casually.'[105] If this all sounds simple, it wasn't. Henderson's style was remarkably sophisticated and a good example of his arranging style can be found in his arrangement of

'Down South Camp Meeting' which has its roots in the multiple strains of ragtime, yet updated to produce something memorable that seems to build and build throughout the performance. This sense of momentum owes much to the form, since none of the succeeding strains that comprise the song are repeated, we are always heading somewhere new, and as each section changes, so does the key, which heightens our sense of anticipation. En route there are question-and-answer passages and chains of syncopated accents that project a heightened feeling of swing. Another Henderson classic of the 1930s was 'Wrappin' It Up', based on a 32-bar ABAC form, with the climax coming on the third variation 'C', which might be described as an 'arranger's chorus'.

Benny Goodman and Swing (1935–45)

By the second half of the 1920s, the main jazz orientated big bands included Henderson, the Duke Ellington Orchestra, the Luis Russell Orchestra, the Jean Goldkette Orchestra, McKinney's Cotton Pickers, the Don Redman Orchestra and the Casa Loma Orchestra. However, when the bottom fell out of the entertainment business with the stock market crash of 24 October 1929, unemployment soared, peaking at 24.75% of the American labour force in 1933. Before the crash, record sales had been booming: in 1929 alone about 150 million recordings were sold in the United States. By 1933 sales had bottomed out at 34 million. Musicians, like the rest of the population, were forced to get by as best they could. But in March 1933, President Franklin Roosevelt was inaugurated, famously declaring, 'The only thing we have to fear is fear itself.' In his first ninety-nine days he proposed, and Congress swiftly enacted, an ambitious 'New Deal' to deliver relief, recovery and reform.

Gradually the American economy began to show signs of rallying and in 1934, a young 25-year-old clarinet player called

Benny Goodman decided to take the financial risk of forming his own big band. But his new band initially struggled. They were sacked from their first major job at Billy Rose's Music Hall in New York City, but then landed a regular spot on a national radio programme sponsored by the National Biscuit Company called *Let's Dance*.

BENNY GOODMAN (1909–86)

Born into a ghetto on Chicago's West Side, Benny's father earned less than $20 a week to support a family of twelve children. Occasionally out of work in bad seasons, he could only provide a precarious life for his wife and children. Benny's first professional job was at the age of twelve at the Central Park Theater. In 1923, he was playing in a band with Bix Beiderbecke and by 1925 he had left for Los Angeles to join bandleader Ben Pollack. By then he was providing for his whole family. In 1928 he was in New York, where he established himself as a leading freelance musician accompanying some of the brightest stars in the entertainment industry both on record and in live performance. A sought-after soloist by the major radio orchestras and bandleaders of the day from Paul Whiteman to Andre Kostelanetz, Benny also played on movie soundtracks, performed in the pit bands of some of the finest Broadway musicals of the day[106] and appeared on literally hundreds of recordings, including several jazz classics. He'd risen from poverty to become, in the eyes of many, the world's greatest jazz clarinettist.

Let's Dance was a three-hour radio 'dance party', Goodman landing the jazz band slot alternating with two other bands, a lush string orchestra directed by Kel Murray and a Latin band led by Xaiver Cugat. Crucially, the NBC contract also provided a budget for new arrangements to fill the time slot. This was a boon for a new band like Goodman's, who commissioned 156 arrangements during his six-month run from Glenn Miller, Arthur Schutt, Will Hudson, Jiggs Noble, Deane Kincade, George Bassman, Fud Livingstone, Gordon Jenkins, Edgar Sampson, Spud Murphy, Joe

Lippman and Benny Carter. Clearly Goodman had no particular band 'sound' or musical identity in mind for his band at this time. In fact, it was almost as an afterthought that John Hammond, Goodman's confidant (who would later become his brother-in-law) suggested he commission a few arrangements from Fletcher Henderson who, like many bandleaders following the stock market crash of 1929, was struggling financially. In the event, Goodman purchased thirty-six from him – most written for Henderson's own band and some even previously recorded by him – and it would be these arrangements that would shape the Goodman sound and with it, his destiny.

The first *Let's Dance* aired on 1 December 1934 and the welcome profile of a national radio show enabled Goodman to land a recording contract with RCA Victor, recording several pieces that would become staples of his repertoire including Henderson's arrangements of 'King Porter Stomp', 'Sometimes I'm Happy' and 'Blue Skies'. His final NBC broadcast was on 25 May 1935, and the band launched-out on a cross-country road tour that lasted some ten months, ending up on the West Coast. Some engagements were mildly successful, others were not, such as their three-week stint at Elitch's Gardens, Denver, Colorado, Goodman later describing it as 'the most humiliating experience of my life'.[107] Other dates on their long tour attracted only a handful of dancers. By the time they opened on 21 August 1935 at the Palomar Ballroom in Los Angeles, their final date before heading back to New York City, it was generally acknowledged the tour had been a flop.

Goodman began cautiously, but then a kind of 'let's-go-down-fighting' abandon overtook him: 'I decided the whole thing had gotten to a point where it was make or break. If we had to flop, at least we'd do it in my own way, playing the kind of music I wanted to … I called out some of our big Fletcher [Henderson] arrangements for the next set, and the boys seemed to get the idea. From the moment I kicked them off, they dug in with some of the best playing I'd heard since we left New York.'[108] They were greeted by a roar from the crowd that reverberated through the music business since the band was being broadcast coast-to-coast. Dancers gathered around the bandstand and screamed for more. Goodman, bespectacled and professorial-looking, was bewildered, but gave the crowd what it wanted. The band was a sensation, their booking extended for an additional three weeks, the crowds getting bigger and bigger every night, ending up breaking the ballroom's attendance record. If the Swing Era had a starting date then Goodman's opening at the Palomar was it.

Goodman's music was in tune with Roosevelt's New Deal optimism and was what teenage and college kids wanted – music that sounded fresh and exciting as America pulled itself out of the Depression. Within eighteen months Goodman was the biggest attraction in the music business. Henderson kept feeding Goodman new arrangements which came to define the band's sound – and the sound of the era – but credit must go to Goodman for what he described in his autobiography as going 'through [Henderson's] scores [to] dig the music out of them'[109] through meticulous, painstaking, rehearsal. There's an audible difference between Henderson's own band playing these arrangements and Goodman's versions. Through sheer hard work Goodman brought his band to a level of perfection that was widely admired in the music business. In 1937, the Harry James, Chris Griffin, Ziggy Elman trumpet section came together; 'Duke Ellington said it was the greatest trumpet section there's ever been,'[110] Griffin later recalled and even today their power, cohesion and effortless swing stand out in the history of big band jazz. Equally, Goodman's saxophone section was turning heads with their supple, seemingly effortless phrasing and precision. 'We set a standard for sax sections,' said lead alto saxophonist Hymie Schertzer. 'All of us interpreting the same, playing like one. And Benny as the leader, he set a fabulous example.'[111]

The recordings Goodman made with his band (and small groups) during the period 1935–9 divide themselves neatly into studio recordings for RCA Victor and live recordings. While the studio recordings reflect Goodman's relentless quest for perfection, they also reveal the tension he could create in the recording studio by rejecting take after take until he had what he considered to be the perfect master. As a result much of his studio output sounds stiff and cautious, with everyone careful not to incur their bandleader's wrath by making a mistake. The live recordings are a totally different kettle of fish; taken off the air from the band's weekly broadcasts from various locations around the USA, they capture the energy and spirit of the Swing Era in a way that no other recordings of the period do. Neither Goodman nor his band knew these radio broadcasts were being recorded, so they're relaxed, allowing the energy of the dancers and the enthusiasm of the crowd to lift their performances to a level that can only be described as inspired. Some of their best live performances from the 1937–8 period, when swing was at its zenith, were released in the 1950s and '60s as *Benny Goodman Jazz Concert No. 2* and the *Benny Goodman Treasure Chest*. Recorded off the air by Bill Savory (who later married Goodman's vocalist Helen Ward), they capture the spirit of the Swing Era in a way that no other recordings have done. While on the one hand swing was made popular by a dancing public who loved jitterbugging to the music – the athletic, acrobatic dance style that included whirling your partner in the air – on the other hand, many arrangements encouraged active listening, evidenced by the large crowds who gathered in front of the bandstand transfixed by the music. On, Roll 'Em', for example, Goodman gives his soloists their heads in a way that would be impossible in the studio because of the time constraints of the 78 rpm disc, and you can hear the listening audience applaud after each solo on what is maybe the first time this convention in jazz is captured live on record, and suggests this music was already being seen as something far more substantial than mere dance music.

All Goodman's big band performances during this period were interspersed with features for his trio, with pianist Teddy Wilson and drummer Gene Krupa and quartet, his trio plus vibist Lionel Hampton, that provided an ideal forum to let off creative steam. The trio's public performances began as early as 1935, while the quartet came into being a year later. Quite apart from their musical significance, the appearance of both black and white performers on the same stage was one of considerable socio-historical significance, something for which, perhaps surprisingly, Goodman has been given rather begrudging credit. His small-band music was not intended for dancing, but for listening, comprising, other than the theme at the beginning and end of each tune, entirely jazz improvisation. And audiences at the time were yelling for more. To get the full impact of the musical excitement these small groups created we again need to turn to the live recordings on *Benny Goodman Jazz Concert No. 2* for some fine examples of Goodman's work with a trio – 'Have You Met Miss Jones', 'Nice Work If You Can Get It' – and quartet – 'Benny Sent Me', 'Everybody Loves My Baby', 'Shine' and the remarkable 'Runnin' Wild'. In August 1939, John Hammond had the electric guitarist Charlie Christian audition for Goodman when he was playing the Victor Hugo Restaurant in Beverly Hills, California. Goodman was captivated by his playing and hired him on the spot and, with the addition of the bassist from the big band, the Benny Goodman Quartet became a Sextet. When Hampton left Goodman to form his own band, Goodman rejigged the combo with the addition of trumpet and tenor saxophone, which became perhaps the most successful – and exciting – small group in jazz of the period where technical virtuosity was at one with musical taste, a compelling duality.

Goodman's success triggered a big band boom, and pretty soon there were trumpet and trombone-playing leaders, reed-playing leaders, piano-playing leaders, violin-playing leaders, sweet bands and Mickey Mouse bands – all vying for national

WILLIAM 'COUNT' BASIE (1904–84)

Born in Red Bank, New Jersey, Basie was taught piano by his mother and Harlem Stride pianists but found himself stranded in Kansas City when touring the vaudeville circuit. Here he established himself with Kansas City bandleader Bennie Moten. Following Moten's unexpected death, Basie formed his own band, drawing largely on former Moten employees. Like all Kansas City bands, it was organized around a rhythm section that provided a foundation for the strong riff tradition of that city. This contrasted greatly with the more elaborate arrangements featured by Goodman and Ellington, but Basie always had outstanding soloists, initially in tenor saxists Lester Young and Herschel Evans, trombonists Dicky Wells and Benny Morten, and trumpeters Buck Clayton and Harry Edison. Many of his recordings between 1937 and 1941 for Decca and Vocalion are classics that capture the essence of this band – a fluid rhythm section, strong antiphonal riffs and excellent soloists. It's no secret that Goodman greatly admired Basie's approach to rhythm – he had Basie as a guest at his Carnegie Hall debut in 1938 and had him play on several of his sextet recordings for Columbia between 1940–1. Not generally known is that in October and November 1940, Goodman held a series of rehearsal sessions with Basie and his key band members; according to Goodman's biographer, Goodman was considering forming a fully integrated big band, but was persuaded against it by his booking office and press agent.[112] Basie's big band continued to be a major attraction in jazz up to his death in 1984, boasting a major fan in Frank Sinatra, who recorded *Sinatra at the Sands with Count Basie* and *It Might As Well Be Swing: Sinatra/Basie* on his own record label Reprise.

recognition. The 1930s was a decade when the arranger came of age, since he or she (yes, there were some fine female arrangers in the Swing Era, such as Mary Lou Williams and Marge Gibson) was responsible for developing a distinctive sound – or musical style – so essential for a band to differentiate itself from its competitors. By 1940, with countless bands copying the Fletcher Henderson arranging style, Goodman felt the need to tweak the sound of his band to keep ahead of the competition. To achieve this he turned to arranger Eddie Sauter, whose sixty or so arrangements between 1940 and 1942 included pieces such as 'Moonlight on the Ganges', 'La Rosita', 'Love Walked In', 'The Man I Love', 'How Deep Is the Ocean', 'My Old Flame', and 'More Than You Know', which even now sound strikingly modern. In fact they might be said to be modern jazz without being bebop. As Gunther Schuller has noted, during the early 1940s, both Goodman and his band 'played with a dazzling brilliance that was the envy of all the other bands. The emphasis was not on soloists – as with Basie, for example – but on the orchestra, and on jazz *as* arrangement and composition'.[113]

The End of an Era

When America entered World War II in December 1941, the musical and emotional climate began to change. The exuberance of big bands seemed somehow at odds with the climate of a nation at war, of soldiers, sailors and airmen being parted from their loved ones for combat overseas, from which many would never return. Singers seemed more in tune with the times; Helen Forrest's vocal 'You Made Me Love You' with the Harry James band or Billie Holiday's 'All of Me' were favourites of countless homesick GIs. When the American Federation of Musicians introduced a recording ban from July 1942, it effectively put several nails in the coffin of big bands, although union leader James Petrillo was too dim to see it. Singers, not considered musicians by the AFM, continued recording and when the ban was lifted in 1944, vocalists dominated popular music.

The extent to which vocalists had captured the public imagination is best summed up by the re-release in 1943 of 'All Or Nothing At All', originally recorded by trumpeter Harry James and his Orchestra for Columbia in August 1939 with a vocal chorus by a young, unknown singer called Frank Sinatra. It sold about 5,000 copies. When the record was re-released in 1943 (because of the ban, record companies were forced to re-release material made before it came into force to stay in business), Sinatra's popularity had skyrocketed so he was given top billing on the record label with 'Accompanied by Harry James and his Orchestra' in small print below. This time the record went straight into the pop charts, stayed there for 18 weeks and reached No. 2 on 2 June 1943. But there were also other factors that contributed to the decline of the big bands: the conscription of many young musicians who played in the bands left bandleaders struggling for adequate replacements; wartime gasoline rationing meant the curtailment of travelling by many touring bands, while the cost of moving fifteen or so musicians and their associated impedimenta around the country had simply become prohibitive. Even though the Woody Herman and Stan Kenton orchestras enjoyed their seasons in the sun in the late 1940s, the big band era was effectively was over.

But big bands did not disappear. Bandleaders such as Duke Ellington, Count Basie, Woody Herman, Les Brown, Lionel Hampton, Harry James and Stan Kenton continued successfully to lead bands into the 1970s and '80s. Benny Goodman tended to form bands for specific engagements, such as a residency at the World's Fair in Brussels in 1958 or tours in South America (1961), the USSR (1962) or Japan (1964). The Dorsey Brothers – Tommy and Jimmy – had a television show prior to their deaths in 1956 and 1957 respectively and in a sign of the changing times, presented a young guest artist called Elvis Presley. Yet big bands clung on – Terry Gibbs led a fine big band on the West Coast between 1958 and 1962, while the former Tommy Dorsey, Artie Shaw and Harry James drum star Buddy Rich formed a successful big band in 1966 that toured up until his death in 1987. Also in 1966, trumpeter Thad Jones and drummer Mel Lewis formed the Thad Jones/Mel Lewis Orchestra. It survived Jones's departure as the Mel Lewis Jazz Orchestra and on Lewis's death, it became the Jazz Orchestra that plays the Village Vanguard jazz club in

NewYork's GreenwichVillage to this day. In Europe, Britain'sTed Heath Orchestra,The Mike Westbrook Big Band and ensembles led by arranger Mike Gibbs have received worldwide acclaim, as has the Kurt Edelhagen Orchestra from Germany.Also based in Germany was the Kenny Clarke/Francy Boland Big Band, bankrolled by Gigi Campi, that comprised both European and American jazz stars and toured and recorded to considerable acclaim between 1961 and 1973.

Because a big band is an expensive item to present, a number of bands were formed for a brief tour, a residency or for record-ing purposes – so many, in fact, they are impossible to list here – but few became established as a regular performing entity. However, their potential as a training ground for young musi-cians was quickly seized upon by jazz educators, and today many schools, colleges and universities boast their own big band. In more recent times, Maria Schneider has crafted a distinguished career as a big band leader, composer and arranger following her recording debut in 1994 with *Evanescence*. In 2015 she released her eighth album, the Grammy-winning *The Thompson Fields* that was widely praised for her sensitive and imaginative writing. But don't be tempted to think big bands are more about the past than the present: they still have enormous relevance and pack a mighty punch – just listen to John Barry's memorable arrangement of Monty Norman's title theme for the James Bond movies, one of the most famous tunes in the consumerist world, to get an idea of their contemporary significance.

Big Band Playlist

In a book of this nature it is clearly impossible to document the mind-boggling number of bands that participated in the Swing Era.[114] Thus this text has tended to focus on 'jazz *as* arrangement and composition':[115] the Whiteman orchestra, which codified the instrumentation and arranging practices of the early big bands; the Fletcher Henderson orchestra, the main architect of the Swing Era; and the live recordings of 1937–8 Benny Goodman provide a summation of what the Swing Era was about. Most jazz histories have tended to overlook Goodman's early 1940s orchestra playing Eddie Sauter arrangements, even though they were widely regarded as a benchmark of music excellence at the time. Duke Ellington's magnificent 1940–1 orchestra was *sui generis*, his recordings an almost perfect realization of what the large ensemble in jazz can achieve. The playlist also attempts to point the reader in the direction of some of the more interesting performances from the Swing Era, in the hope that they will delve more deeply into this area of jazz, but makes no claim to completeness, rather an intention to provide a small window into a period of jazz when big bands provided the popular music of the day and to illustrate how the best transcended the functionality of a dance band by exploring the potential of the big band as a *jazz orchestra*. While this appears a long playlist, bear in mind most of the performances clock in at around three minutes because of the time restriction of the 10-inch 78 rpm recording, thus providing the opportunity of including more performances.

1. Paul Whiteman and his Orchestra: 'Changes' from *Paul Whiteman and his Dance Band Vol. 1*.
2. Fletcher Henderson and his Orchestra: 'Sugar Foot Stomp' from *Greatest Hits*.
3. Fletcher Henderson and his Orchestra: 'Down South Camp Meeting' from *Greatest Hits*.
4. Fletcher Henderson and his Orchestra: 'Wrappin' It Up' from *Greatest Hits*.
5. Benny Goodman and his Orchestra: 'Sugar Foot Stomp' from *Benny Goodman Jazz Concert No. 2 Live*.
6. Benny Goodman and his Orchestra: 'Down South Camp Meeting' from *Benny Goodman Jazz Concert No. 2 Live*.

7. Benny Goodman and his Orchestra: 'Roll 'Em' from *Benny Goodman Jazz Concert No. 2 Live*.

8. Benny Goodman and his Orchestra: 'Soft As Spring' from *The Very Best of Helen Forrest with Benny Goodman*.

9. Benny Goodman and his Orchestra: 'Clarinet a la King' from *Benny Goodman's Greatest Hits*.

10. Duke Ellington and his Famous Orchestra: 'Harlem Twist (East St. Louis Toodle-Oo)' from *The Okeh Ellington*.

11. Duke Ellington and his Famous Orchestra: 'Echoes of the Jungle' from *Daybreak Express*.

12. Duke Ellington and his Famous Orchestra: 'Jack the Bear' from *The Blanton-Webster Band*.

13. Duke Ellington and his Famous Orchestra: 'Ko-Ko' from *The Blanton-Webster Band*.

14. Duke Ellington and his Famous Orchestra: 'Concerto for Cootie' from *The Blanton-Webster Band*.

15. Duke Ellington and his Famous Orchestra: 'Harlem Air Shaft' from *The Blanton-Webster Band*.

16. Count Basie and his Orchestra: 'Harvard Blues' from *Blues by Basie*.

17. Count Basie and his Orchestra: 'Avenue C' from *Jazz the Essential Collection Vol. 3*.

18. Artie Shaw and his Orchestra: 'Stardust' from *The Essential Artie Shaw*.

19. Artie Shaw and his Orchestra: 'Suite No. 8' from *To a Broadway Rose (The Bluebird Recordings in Chronological Order)*.

20. Artie Shaw and his Orchestra: 'Summertime' from *The Very Best of Artie Shaw*.

21. Tommy Dorsey and his Orchestra: 'On the Sunny Side of the Street' from *Smash Hits of the 40s*.

22. Claude Thornhill and his Orchestra: 'Arab Dance' from *Snowfall*.

23. Woody Herman and his Orchestra: 'Apple Honey' from *Blowin' Up a Storm (The Columbia Years 1945–7)*.

Listening Notes for the Big Band Playlist

1. Paul Whiteman and his Orchestra: 'Changes' from *Paul Whiteman and his Dance Band Vol. 1*

While this has a vocal interlude that has a certain period charm – the harmony group is the Rhythm Boys and the solo vocal is by Bing Crosby – the centrepiece is the startling entry of Bix Beiderbecke, whose 16 bar solo is perfectly framed by this arrangement by Bill Challis. As Gunther Schuller has pointed out, 'The Whiteman sound, as fashioned by three of the greatest arrangers that ever worked in the field – Ferde Grofé, Bill Challis and the Dean of Black American composers, William Grant Still – is one of the half-a-dozen most original jazz sounds ever to have been created, and it provided the perfect setting and inspiration for Bix: like the jewel set perfectly in the centre of a crown. In its own way the Whiteman sound is as original and as beautiful as that of Duke Ellington's orchestra – very different, of course, but no less magical, no less inspired. And let no one forget that Ellington and the other great jazz orchestra leaders of the late twenties spent a great deal of time learning from the Whiteman "book" [of arrangements], emulating it and marvelling at its instrumental sophistication.'[116]

2. Fletcher Henderson and his Orchestra: 'Sugar Foot Stomp' from *Greatest Hits*

3. Fletcher Henderson and his Orchestra: 'Down South Camp Meeting' from *Greatest Hits*

4. Fletcher Henderson and his Orchestra: 'Wrappin' It Up' from *Greatest Hits*

The first arrangement, 'Sugar Foot Stomp' by Henderson's saxophonist Don Redman, is an update of King Oliver's 'Dippermouth

Blues' (included in the Chapter 7 playlist). Here was the blueprint of the Swing Era style of the 1930s, with the ensembles split between 'question and answer' passages between brass and saxes. 'Down South Camp Meeting' and 'Wrappin' It Up' are both discussed in the text.

5. Benny Goodman and his Orchestra: 'Sugar Foot Stomp' from *Benny Goodman Jazz Concert No. 2 Live*

6. Benny Goodman and his Orchestra: 'Down South Camp Meeting' from *Benny Goodman Jazz Concert No. 2 Live*

7. Benny Goodman and his Orchestra: 'Roll 'Em' from *Benny Goodman Jazz Concert No. 2 Live*

8. Benny Goodman and his Orchestra: 'Soft As Spring' from *The Very Best of Helen Forrest with Benny Goodman*

9.Benny Goodman and his Orchestra: 'Clarinet a la King' from *Benny Goodman's Greatest Hits*

The first three Goodman recordings are taken from *Benny Goodman Jazz Concert No. 2*. They are all recorded live and give a sense of what the Swing Era was about. Fletcher Henderson's arrangement of 'Sugar Foot Stomp' involves the kind of cohesion and precision between the sax and brass sections that no other band of the day matched, and even today remains a benchmark of excellence. Both this performance and 'Down South Camp Meeting' are well worth comparing to Henderson's versions to hear how Goodman realized their potential. 'Roll 'Em' is a 12-bar blues, boogie-woogie style, arranged by Mary Lou Williams, and if you listen carefully you can hear the

crowd applaud each solo and respond to the musical excitement the band begins to generate. The solo performances, by
Jess Stacy on piano, Goodman on clarinet and Harry James
on trumpet steer the band to its soaring climax in one of the
great performances of the Swing Era. The arrival of arranger
Eddie Sauter, whose advanced arranging style treated the big
band as a jazz orchestra, immediately set Goodman apart, with
startling introductions, interludes, modulations and codas that
even today sound imaginative and forward-looking. There was
simply no precedent in jazz for the opening and coda of 'Soft
as Spring' – listen to the piano in the opening passage: it doesn't
play a rhythmic role, but adds colour to the orchestrations with
arpeggiated figures that suggest a harp. Listen to the amount
of orchestration that goes on *behind* the vocalist and the subsequent ensembles that are written *across* the band (saxes and
brass in unusual combinations), which is diametrically opposed
to the Henderson style of writing by pitting the brass section
against the sax section in 'question and answer' riffs. Sauter
loved using advanced harmonies (for the time) and his writing
for Goodman was modern jazz in all but name. 'Clarinet a la
King' is a Sauter original that's effectively a miniature concerto
for clarinet with Goodman responding with some impassioned
playing. As Gunther Schuller has pointed out: 'During these
years of the early forties, the Goodman band – and Goodman
himself – played with a dazzling brilliance that was the envy
of all the other bands. The emphasis was not on soloists – as
with Basie, for example – but on the orchestra, and on *jazz as
arrangement and composition*'[117] (my italics, since this has guided
the selections in this playlist).

10. Duke Ellington and his Famous Orchestra: 'Harlem Twist (East St. Louis Toodle-Oo)' from *The Okeh Ellington*

11. Duke Ellington and his Famous Orchestra: 'Echoes of the Jungle' from *Daybreak Express*

12. Duke Ellington and his Famous Orchestra: 'Jack the Bear' from *The Blanton-Webster Band*

13. Duke Ellington and his Famous Orchestra: 'Ko-Ko' from *The Blanton-Webster Band*

14. Duke Ellington and his Famous Orchestra: 'Concerto for Cootie' from *The Blanton-Webster Band*

15. Duke Ellington and his Famous Orchestra: 'Harlem Air Shaft' from *The Blanton-Webster Band*

Ellington's musical journey began well before the Swing Era, an early original, 'Harlem Twist (East St. Louis Toodle-oo)' was his signature tune when he recorded this version in 1928. It shows how he was building his band sound around distinctive soloists with a unique sound signature, such as trumpeter Bubber Miley's muted trumpet featured here. Even when Miley had left Ellington, the legacy of growling brass was continued in early classics like 'Echoes of the Jungle'. 'Jack the Bear' comes from 1940, as do the remaining Ellington examples, and reveals the remarkable rhythmic spring bassist Jimmy Blanton brought to the Ellington band's step, his virtuoso pizzicato technique seamlessly integrated into the orchestration. Interestingly, this composition combines a 32-bar songform (the section that begins and ends with Barney Bigard on clarinet) followed by 5 choruses of 12-bar blues. 'Ko Ko' is one of the great moments of twentieth-century music and is based on a 12-bar blues! Its ominous character and powerful ensemble playing look backward to his jungle style and forward with moments of dissonance in a truly memorable performance. 'Concerto for Cootie' is a brilliantly conceived feature for trumpeter Cootie Williams, who joined Benny Goodman shortly after recording this tour de force for trumpet. 'Concerto for Cootie' has such depth and artful construction that the French musicologist André Hodeir wrote a twenty-three-page analysis of this performance in his book *Jazz: Its Evolution and Essence* – its haunting melody would re-emerge a few years later as a vocal hit for Ellington as 'Do Nothing Until You Hear From Me'. Finally, 'Harlem Air Shaft' may reflect the Swing Era in its conception, but there is much more going on in Ellington's orchestration than the standard fare served up by most Swing Era bands. Note how his writing moves inexorably towards a climax that, despite being achieved in a short space of time, does not sound as if it has arrived too early; rather, it sounds inevitable.

16. Count Basie and his Orchestra: 'Harvard Blues' from *Blues by Basie*

17. Count Basie and his Orchestra: 'Avenue C' from *Jazz the Essential Collection Vol. 3*

Count Basie's piano playing was the essence of the less-is-more ethic, while guitarist Freddie Green, bassist Walter Page and drummer Jo Jones locked into a swinging groove which gave Basie's band irresistible momentum. The early arrangements emphasized 'simplicity of format and simplicity of texture';[118] riff tunes utilizing the 12-bar blues and a few basic progressions such as 'I Got Rhythm' and 'Honeysuckle Rose' that relied on exemplary soloists such as trumpeter Buck Clayton and saxophonists Lester Young and Herschel Evans for their musical interest. As Gunther Schuller has pointed out, Basie's riff-based style highlighted the 'melodic/thematic paucity' of much of their material, something that has been largely glossed over by commentators. Among their better blues performances was 'Harvard Blues' with vocalist Jimmy Rushing singing the inscrutable lyrics written by jazz critic and Harvard graduate George Frazier. '"Rinehart" was apparently one James B. G. Rinehart, who was frequently paged by a friend shouting his name from the courtyard outside his dormitory window. On one occasion, it is claimed, dozens of fellow students spontaneously chimed in, and out of all this evolved the myth of a lonely undergraduate who shouted his own name on campus so others would think he was sought after.'[119] 'Avenue C' is a superior riff tune, with solos by Basie on piano, tenor saxophonist Buddy Tate, trumpeter Harry Edison, and climaxed by drummer Shadow Wilson.

18. Artie Shaw and his Orchestra: 'Stardust' from *The Essential Artie Shaw*

19. Artie Shaw and his Orchestra: 'Suite No. 8' from *To a Broadway Rose*

20. Artie Shaw and his Orchestra: 'Summertime' from *The Very Best of Artie Shaw*

Benny Goodman's great rival in the Swing Era was clarinettist and bandleader Artie Shaw, who, like Goodman, had exceptional command of the instrument. It's interesting to note that after the Swing Era, hardly anyone bothered to play the clarinet, the general consensus being that between Goodman and Shaw, everything that could be said on the instrument had just about been said. Yet there was no mistaking Artie Shaw for Benny Goodman, or vice versa. Shaw was a perfectionist, and this version of 'Stardust' was described by musicologist Gunther Schuller as 'near perfect'.[120] Arranged by Lennie Hayton, soloists are Billy Butterfield on trumpet, Shaw and nine bars by trombonist Jack Jenney that can only be described as magnificent. A lot happens in a short space of time. Strings are to the fore in the introduction of 'Suite No. 8' that's about as far removed from the concept of dance music as you can imagine. Clearly, the intro is informed by classical forms and techniques, but as the arrangement unfolds, the jazz dimension is unequivocal, featuring solos by Shaw, Georgie Auld on tenor and Hot Lips Page on trumpet. Listen out for Shaw's high-register intervention climaxing the performance – that note, an altissimo B flat, is so high and so difficult to achieve that you will never have heard before played on clarinet! Shaw's version of 'Summertime' is arranged by Eddie Sauter. The haunting introduction, using electric guitar, gives way to a muted-growl trumpet solo by Roy Eldridge (known as a plunger solo) who succeeds in avoiding sounding like an Ellington brass musician, such is the integrity of his playing. Listen for unique Sauter touches in sustaining the mood and then exploiting it via a stunning climax when the saxophone section swop their saxes for clarinets and join Shaw in a clarinet choir whose mild dissonance is powerful and edgy. It's a superb example of concert jazz meant for listening rather than dancing.

21. Tommy Dorsey and his Orchestra: 'On the Sunny Side of the Street' from *Smash Hits of the '40s*

One of the most memorable introductions of the Swing Era, this Sy Oliver arrangement is rightly considered a classic and provided a gold record for Dorsey. The attention-getting brass stabs answered by baritone saxophone was a rallying cry to get the dancers onto the dance floor. It's a performance that is of its time yet timeless, as much for the elegant execution of Sy Oliver's arrangement as the memorable four-part harmony of the Sentimentalists with lyrics that had been given a 'hip' makeover.

22. Claude Thornhill and his Orchestra: 'Arab Dance' from *Snowfall*

In his book *The Swing Era*, Gunther Schuller refers to the 'illustrious work' arranger Gil Evans contributed to the Claude Thornhill Orchestra that 'represent some of the more glorious moments in jazz history'.[121] The Thornhill Orchestra was something of an anomaly in the Swing Era, whose centre of gravity rested in exploring textures and timbres. Evans's rearrangement of Tchaikovsky's 'Arab Dance' was recorded in July 1946, and once again we have an example of a big band moving beyond the functionality of dance music in favour of jazz intended for serious contemplation in the concert hall. Evans's ability to rearrange an established orchestration found equally eloquent voice in his treatment of Joaquín Rodrigo's 'Concierto de Aranjuez' on the Miles Davis classic *Sketches of Spain*,[122] recorded in November 1959.

23. Woody Herman and his Orchestra: 'Apple Honey' from *Blowin' Up a Storm (The Columbia Years 1945–47)*

By 1945, bebop was beginning to make itself felt within jazz. Among the first of the established big bands to buy into its ethos was that led by Woody Herman. His transformation from dance band to modern jazz orchestra rested on an excellent rhythm section, a talented infusion of young jazz musicians versed in the technical skills of bebop style and a young pianist and arranger called Ralph Burns. 'Apple Honey' was based on the chord sequence of 'I Got Rhythm' and the opening roar of the ensemble – and here 'roar' is not misplaced – announces the sound of jazz was changing. It was a performance in keeping with the times: the sound of a confident America emerging triumphant after World War II.

8

Jazz Goes Modern

Bebop

By the 1940s, the standard of musicianship required to be a member of one of the leading big bands of the day was approaching that of a symphony musician. Let's consider for a moment what was required: mastery of their chosen instrument; playing fluently in any key and at any tempo; the ability to read at sight often complex arrangements; the ability to play expressively, in tune and with dynamic control (meaning the ability to play at all gradations of volume between soft and loud); and on top of all that, the best players would be expected to improvise convincingly. It is perhaps worth noting that not all big band musicians were improvisers. Many were section men, but the best were also first-rate jazzmen. Yet for an improvising musician, a big band could be a restricting place to be. Arrangements might call for just 8 or 16 bars of improvisation in a tune, while a full chorus was a relatively rare bird. It is perhaps a function of human nature that many musicians, having reached the level of excellence required to be a member of one of America's leading big bands, looked around and said, 'Is this all there is? There must be more.' And of course there was.

By the early 1940s, several young, musically curious musicians based mainly in Harlem, many of whom were employed in the big bands of the time, were attempting to incorporate chord extensions into their music, in other words making use of the ninth, eleventh and thirteenth of a chord, plus the good old flattened fifth that when added to a chord made it sound modern.[123] This was hardly new. As early as the 1920s, musicians had been similarly engaged in exploring what were then referred to as 'adventurous' harmonies. The difference between the musicians of the 1920s[124] and the young musicians experimenting in the jazz clubs and after-hours clubs of Harlem was that any recognition the 1920s experimenters might have enjoyed was usually as a single musician, whereas the collective impact of a community of similarly orientated and competing artists playing in a single coherent, unified style was not so easy to ignore. A feature of what became known as bebop was not so much in the use of the upper intervals of chords to get that elusive modern feeling, since that had been done before – in fact it's hard to find a bebop chord that didn't exist in earlier jazz – but how the flatted fifth, the ninth, eleventh and thirteenth were consistently emphasized in a way that formed a coherent style. As Charlie Parker, the leading figure in bebop, later said: 'I'd been getting bored with the stereotyped changes that were being used all the time and I kept thinking there must be something else … Well, that night I was working over "Cherokee" and as I did I found by using the higher [or upper] intervals of a chord … I could play the thing I was hearing. I came alive.'[125] Bop also introduced a degree of rhythmic intricacy that had not been present in earlier styles of jazz, while solos sounded faster because musicians often played in double time, sometimes beginning and ending musical phrases in unexpected places. Pianists and drummers were more inclined to interact with the soloist in bebop, a technique that at its best sounded like a rhythmic dialogue. Bebop drummers shifted to keeping time on a cymbal rather than pumping out four beats to the bar on the bass drum like the Swing Era drummers; now the bass drum was only used for accents. This gave bebop a lighter, shimmering, rhythmic feel, in tune with its fast tempos and dazzling instrumental athleticism.

As with so many of the great breakthroughs in the arts, no matter how radical they may have appeared at the time, most have flowed creatively from the developments that preceded them. Clearly bebop didn't happen overnight, although when it did emerge into public consciousness in 1945 its appearance was akin to a shock announcing the new since a recording ban had been in force between 1942 to 1944/5, organized by the American Federation of Musicians. It meant that the public at large, other than New York fans who frequented clubs in Harlem like Minton's (the scene where many bebop experimenters worked out their style by trial and error in live performance), had no idea of the winds of change that were blowing through jazz, since there were no recordings to alert them to the new developments. When new recordings did get released after the ban, it appeared as if this new style had arrived fully formed out of the blue, a 'palace revolution', so to speak, to displace the prevailing order (big bands), rather than the evolutionary development it really was. A lot of rationalization after the fact in bebop history overlooks the fact that its prime movers, alto saxophonist Charlie Parker and trumpeter Dizzy Gillespie, learned their trade in big bands and far from cutting ties with larger ensembles, continued to appear with them, albeit off and on, for rest of their careers. Dizzy Gillespie, for example, formed a big band as soon as he was able that became the talk of the New York jazz scene in 1947. In fact, his career can be traversed, rather like stepping stones, by the big bands he led during his career right up until his death in 1993, when he was leading his United Nation Orchestra. Parker did not form a big band, but for a while led a string ensemble and frequently guested with big bands. In fact, Parker's solos were very much shaped by his big band experiences[126] where space for improvisation was limited, so we seldom hear a long Parker solo among his many studio recordings where he makes maximum use of minimum solo space.[127]

The step from swing to bebop was not simply musical, it was also philosophical. It marked a change from communal celebration of the music in huge dance halls to its private contemplation in jazz clubs. With the rise of bebop, jazz quickly became a one-to-one experience; audiences were smaller, usually seated, and the performing situation more intimate. Initially, bebop enjoyed a flurry of interest in the music press as 'the latest and newest development in jazz' and enjoyed a small following of hip fans, in America's northern cities. For them the leading figure was the

JOHN BIRKS 'DIZZY' GILLESPIE (1917–93)

Gillespie was a musically gifted child, studying trumpet at the Laurinburg Institue in North Carolina. In 1935 he moved to Philadelphia, gaining experience in Frankie Fairfax's band before moving to New York and joining Teddy Hill's big band. In 1939 he joined Cab Calloway's Orchestra, then one of the most popular black bands in America. In 1940 he met Charlie Parker in Kansas City, an association that was renewed in 1943–4 in the Earl Hines Orchestra and the Billy Eckstine Orchestra. When he formed a bebop quintet with Parker in New York in 1945 it would revolutionize jazz; two master improvisers bringing to the fore the rhythmic and harmonic changes that were the essence of bebop. His late 1940s big band included conga drummer Chano Pozo, and compositions such as 'Manteca' and 'Cubana Be/Cubana Bop' helped bring Afro-Cuban jazz into the jazz mainstream. In 1956 he formed another big band that toured extensively for the American State Department. 'To live longer than 40 years is bad manners', said Dostoevsky's Underground Man, but Gillespie remained unromantically alive, unlike Parker who had enjoyed martyrdom since 1955, and as the *New Grove Dictionary of Jazz* noted, Gillespie became 'a regular performer on Caribbean cruise ships that featured jazz artists'.[128] By the 1970s and '80s he began to enjoy emeritus status as one of jazz's Elder Statesmen, which guaranteed him a walk-on part at any jazz festival in the world. It ensured his popularity, but since the 1950s he had failed to make any significant advance on his art.

extrovert Dizzy Gillespie, a gifted trumpet player and theorist of the music who touted a beret, horn-rim specs and a goatee beard. It was a trait that was quickly echoed by fans. By the late 1940s, *Downbeat* magazine was carrying adverts for 'Bop Berets' and 'Real Gone Bop Glasses' (horn-rim specs *à la* Dizzy Gillespie) and stick-on goatee beards.[129]

Gillespie was bebop's front man, a rare combination of clown and master musician, an ideal media person who could be relied upon for good copy; he was photogenic and witty and would always oblige with a zany quote or humorous pose. Alto saxophonist Charlie Parker, the key figure of the era, remained in the background as far as the public were concerned and shunned such extravagant behaviour. His extravagances were acted out in private through his addiction to alcohol, tobacco and hard drugs. He also displayed characteristics that we would today associate with a psychopathic personality disorder. But he was also a genius. His solos seemed perfectly constructed, masterpieces in their own right that students and musicians still study today. Parker's chaotic life came to a premature end on 12 March 1955. He was thirty-four. His original compositions, recorded variously on the Savoy, Dial and Verve record labels are now regarded as classics of jazz and include 12-bar blues such as 'Billie's Bounce', 'Cheryl', 'Barbados', 'Bloomdido', 'Now's the Time', 'Cool Blues', 'Au Privave'; variations on the blues (that became known as 'Bird changes') which included 'Si Si', 'Laid Baird' and 'Blues for Alice'; and contrafacts (songs based on the chord sequence of another song) which included 'Donna Lee', 'Ah-Leu-Cha', 'Anthropology', 'Constellation', 'Bird Gets the Worm' and 'Confirmation'. Yet Parker's contribution to jazz far exceeded the sum total of his compositions and recordings. His style, his sound, his mastery of the saxophone and his conception of jazz quickly became the standard for almost every post-1945 jazz musician. Interestingly, you can hear bebop popping up in a contemporary pop song on Billy Joel's 'Just the Way You Are', where the memorable alto solo is played by Phil Woods (1931–2015), the pre-eminent alto saxophonist in jazz after Parker's death. Woods became something of a jazz legend himself – check out his version of 'Cheek to Cheek' from the album *Live at the Showboat* for a jazz solo with the wow factor. No wonder it won a Grammy!

CHARLIE PARKER (1920–55)

Parker was born in Kansas City and worked in semi-professional groups before dropping out of school to become a jazz musician in 1935. In 1940 he joined Jay McShann's Orchestra, moving to Earl Hines's Big Band where he was in the company of several young modernists including Dizzy Gillespie. In 1943–4 Hines's band formed the nucleus of singer Billy Eckstine's Band, known as the hot house of bebop. During these years Parker participated in jam sessions at Minton's Playhouse and Monroe's Uptown House, the informal atmosphere at both lending itself to the sharing of ideas and the refinement of bebop which saw its apotheosis in a quintet he co-led with Dizzy Gillespie. Although the media have made much of his unsavoury lifestyle – he was addicted to tobacco, alcohol and hard drugs – he enjoyed brief celebrity as the leading figure in jazz. His addiction to heroin derailed his career, at one stage reducing him to busking in the streets for drug money. When he died at thirty-four, the doctor who attended his death estimated his age to be between forty and fifty, such were the ravages of his lifestyle. In 1988, the Hollywood motion picture *Bird*, directed by Clint Eastwood and starring Forest Whitaker, was a well-intentioned, if unsuccessful, attempt to portray Parker's life.

Two Key Pianists

Bud Powell is regarded today as one of jazz's great pianists, mentioned in the same breath as Parker or Gillespie and perhaps second only to Parker in terms of influence, setting the standard for how the piano should be played in the modern jazz idiom. Translating the ideas of Parker and Gillespie onto the piano keyboard, he was a master of up-tempo playing and a composer of several enduring jazz standards such as 'Un Poco Loco', 'Hallucinations', 'Parisian Thoroughfare' and 'Tempus Fugue-it'. Yet for all his remarkable ability, he was also the most inconsistent of the jazz immortals from this period, the lurid aspects of his life – his addictions, idiosyncrasies, mental struggles, breakdowns and periodic institutionalization – have at times threatened to shake his position as bebop's greatest pianist and the most talented composer after Thelonious Monk.

While the technical requirements for playing jazz increased significantly through the influence of Parker, Gillespie and Powell, even more compelling was their attitude to innovation, their embrace of the new and their willingness to experiment. This ethos might be said to encapsulate pianist Thelonious Monk's playing; using dissonance and angular melody to a degree that was unusual in the 1940s, his playing and compositions were strikingly different from anyone else's in jazz, then and now. In fact, his compositions–perhaps his best known are 'Round Midnight', 'Blue Monk', 'Straight No Chaser' and 'Epistrophy'–seem to be an extension of his solo piano style; certainly one seems to run parallel with the other. Even with the changes to jazz bop precipitated, Monk was a pianist who played in a style where he was the only practitioner. He was given welcome exposure on six sessions for the Blue Note label, between 1947 and 1952, who initially released his performances on two sides of a 78 rpm disc, later anthologizing them on an LP as *Genius of Modern Music Vol. 1* and *Vol. 2*. Subsequent opportunities to play and record were thin on the ground for such an idiosyncratic player, but Monk never made any musical concessions. In the 1950s he was recorded first by Prestige and then on the Riverside label, whose sympathetic producer Orrin Keepnews helped give his career momentum. Gradually his work found an audience, even though his style represented a type of anti-virtuosity[130] at a time when jazz musicians were heading in precisely the opposite direction.

When he was signed by Columbia Records he enjoyed a degree of worldwide acclaim as a bona fide jazz original in the 1960s and '70s that perhaps even he had never dreamt of. An eccentric whose odd behaviour began to increase, he withdrew from public performance after a Carnegie Hall concert in 1976.

The Birth of Cool

If bebop was 'hot', then with perfect timing, Newton's third law of motion − that every action has an equal and opposite reaction − kicked in with the emergence of cool jazz at the end of the 1940s. The antithesis of bebop, the style can be traced back to three recording sessions under the auspices of trumpeter Miles Davis for the Capitol label in January and April 1949 and March 1950. They were made with a nine-piece band that had gravitated into the orbit of arranger Gil Evans. These musicians had been enormously impressed by Evans's arrangements for the Claude Thornhill Orchestra,[131] and were looking, along with Evans, to reproduce them with the smallest possible ensemble that could do them justice. Using six instruments in three groups each an octave apart[132] − trumpet and trombone; alto and baritone sax; French horn and tuba − plus piano, bass and drums, they exploited the three-and-a-half-octave span this unusual combination of instruments permitted, featuring the solo talents of saxophonists Lee Konitz and Gerry Mulligan and the trumpet of Miles Davis. Davis became the band's leader, calling rehearsals and assuming responsibility for organizing the band. The recordings they made are now regarded as classics of modern jazz which combined a disciplined integration of the written (the arrangements) and the improvised (the solos). What is striking about these recordings is their non-frantic approach to jazz; even though they include a couple of bop pieces, the sharp edges of bebop had been smoothed down in a way that was less strident and angular, highlighted by a rhythm section that tended to be more subtle than the interactive approach of bebop. Initially, eight of these recordings were released by Capitol, each as two sides of a 78 rpm disc and in 1955 they were collected on a 10-inch LP as part of Capitol's 'Classics in Jazz' series. Three years later, with the addition of three further tracks, all eleven of the nonet's instrumental performances were released as a 12-inch LP under the title by which they have been known ever since: *Birth of the Cool*.

The Cool School

Baritone saxophonist Gerry Mulligan was the most prolific of the four arrangers who contributed to the *Birth of the Cool* sides, responsible for seven of the twelve numbers recorded. In 1952 he hitch-hiked, Kerouac-like, to the West Coast, where he met trumpeter Chet Baker, forming a quartet that took up residency at The Haig, an 85-seater club on Wilshire Boulevard, Los Angeles on Monday nights. What was unusual (for the time) was how the quartet dispensed with a piano, something that quickly became something of a cause célèbre in jazz circles. Recording for Pacific Jazz, the group had a minor hit with 'My Funny Valentine' that attracted national attention, prompting a write-up in *Time* magazine: 'The hot music topic in Los Angeles last week was the cool jazz of a gaunt, hungry young (25) fellow named Gerry Mulligan.'[133] Mulligan and Baker quickly came to terms with how their lines stood out in sharp relief with just bass and drums accompaniment and, under Mulligan's shrewd leadership, found ways of following the spirit of the *Birth of the Cool* sessions – indeed, the group actually recorded 'Rocker', which had been recorded by the larger group – albeit distilled to its essence with contrary voicings and elegant counterpoint. Later, Mulligan would say that much of what he wrote in the 1950s (and it was a lot) was based on what he wrote for Davis, which found voice in his Concert

Jazz Band, an important, if overlooked ensemble that shone brilliantly between 1960 and 1962 and whose recordings 'offer a stunning view of progressive big band music during the era'.[134]

After the break-up of Mulligan's quartet, Baker would go on to a solo career, he perhaps more than any other jazz musician at the time epitomizing 'cool', his best work coming in the period immediately following his association with Mulligan, with a quartet featuring pianist Russ Freeman – recommended is a live set from 1953–4: *Chet Baker Quartet Live Vols 1–3* plus two studio albums: *Quartet: Russ Freeman Chet Baker* and *Chet Baker Quartet featuring Russ Freeman* – before his career became hopelessly dogged by drug addiction. In the 1980s he enjoyed a certain celebrity as a jazz survivor, his heavily lined and much-photographed face a testament to a lifetime's addiction to hard drugs. 'They're laugh lines,' he once quipped to fellow trumpeter and arch humorist Jack Sheldon, who responded, '*Nothing* in life is that funny.'

Alto saxophonist Lee Konitz would enjoy less public celebrity post-*Birth of the Cool*, performing for a while as a featured soloist in the Stan Kenton Orchestra, but also coming under the influence of Lennie Tristano, a pianist, theorist and pedagogue who had a quite distinct approach to jazz improvisation which he taught from his studio in New York. Konitz would record some classic sides with Tristano, including 'Intuition' and 'Digression' in 1949 (that also included tenor saxophonist Warne Marsh) that which presaged free jazz. Konitz's recordings under his own name during the 1950s – such as *Inside Hi-Fi* and *Lee Konitz with Warne Marsh* – are generally regarded as classics of cool jazz.

From around 1954, pianist John Lewis – whose *curriculum vitae* included service in Dizzy Gillespie's 1947 big band and as an accompanist for Charlie Parker and vocalist Ella Fitzgerald – became the *ipso facto* musical director of the Modern Jazz Quartet with Milt Jackson on vibes, Percy Heath on bass and Kenny Clarke on drums, the latter soon replaced by Connie Kay. Lewis set the tone of the group with his compositions, not least 'Django' from the album of the same name. Lewis realized early on that bop, for all its instrumental virtuosity, relied on traditional forms and structures, and that by using alternative compositional forms he might enrich the music's basic design. One way he did this was by drawing on classical music models such as the conventions of Bach and of *commedia dell'arte*. This marked a break with conventional jazz probity of the time and was not without controversy among critics, but the public loved it. Lewis demanded the precision and correctness of a classical group which he contrasted with vibrant, swinging solo interludes from Jackson and himself that are especially effective on the live set *Blues on Bach*. The group shared a collective ambition to move their music out of the jazz club and onto the concert stage and, attired in immaculate evening dress, they had largely achieved their ambition by the end of the 1950s – quite an achievement in the racial climate of the United States at the time. The group created a strong body of recorded work but their Parthian shot before going into temporary retirement in 1974 was also one of their finest albums: *The Modern Jazz Quartet – The Complete Last Concert*.

The Influence of Rhythm and Blues

Since bebop was primarily aimed at a listening audience it soon lost touch with the dancing public, the primary source of revenue for jazz musicians during the Swing Era. But people had not stopped dancing; they had simply migrated to another style of music, and that for the majority of black audiences was rhythm and blues, the respected jazz commentator Bob Blumenthal referring to the 'depressed nature of the jazz business'[135] in the late 1940s and early 1950s. In March 1951, Jackie Brenston and his Delta Cats (actually Ike Turner's Kings of Rhythm) recorded a song called 'Rocket 88' for the Chicago-based Chess label. The record went to No. 1 on the *Billboard* R&B chart (in America, the

R&B chart was the black music chart; before World War II it was known as the 'race' chart), and is a strong contender for the first rock n' roll record. It's a 12-bar boogie blues with a strong back-beat and a 'back to basics' feel, with Brenton's vocal followed by his tenor saxophone solo. What is interesting about 'Rocket 88' and Fats Domino's 'The Fat Man', another back-to-basics 12-bar blues from around the same time and also a contender for the first rock n' roll recording, is that they retained the saxophone (Domino used a small sax section on 'The Fat Man'), the trumpet and sometimes the trombone, and for a while the upright bass (before it was later replaced by a Fender bass guitar). On 'The Fat Man' Domino even sings two falsetto choruses in what could be mistaken for a whah-whah trumpet.

The *instrumentation* of the early rhythm and blues bands – with the exception of an amplified guitar and the use of vocals – was surprisingly similar to the instrumentation of the bebop combos of the day. Rhythmically, however, the key element that differentiated them was the back-beat; Earl Palmer, Domino's drummer on 'The Fat Man', claimed the recording was the first time a drummer had played 'nothing but a backbeat for the whole recording'. R&B was down-to-earth music that was ideal for socializing and dancing. The clubs and social spaces where the R&B bands played in places like Harlem, Philadelphia, Pittsburgh, Baltimore and Chicago were very often the same clubs and social spaces where the bebop bands found work. Audiences were predominantly blue collar and wanted music they could dance to in a 'Hell, it's Friday night and I don't give a damn' way.

The problem was that bebop bands were not delivering that kind of music, and you can imagine club owners taking bandleaders aside: 'C'mon guys, play something with a bit of a beat, get these people up dancing, the bar is quiet, takings are down.' Jazz musicians were forced to take stock of the socio-economic reality around them – if they wanted work then their music had to reflect something of what their audiences wanted. As David H. Rosenthal noted: 'The early fifties saw an extremely dynamic rhythm-and-blues scene take shape ... Young jazz musicians, of course, enjoyed and listened to these R&B sounds ... and it is in this vigorously creative black pop music, at a time when bebop seemed to have lost both its direction and its audience, that ... hard bop's roots may be found.'[136]

The Emergence of Hard Bop

Pianist Horace Silver and drummer Art Blakey initially remained true to the bebop style in the late 1940s and early 1950s, but they could see the way the wind was blowing. In 1954–5, they were both playing together fairly regularly and on the album *A Night in Birdland Vol. 1* recorded under Blakey's name in February 1954, something different is in the air. Writer Jack Cooke points to 'the astonishing violence of the rhythm section ... a style in which the drummer no longer functions as accompanist pure and simple but often, and for long periods, becomes a contributor on the same level as the soloist'.[137] Violent and explicit the drummer may have been, but Blakey's playing resonated with R&B audiences: the other part of the R&B equation was provided by Silver going back to the blues basics, or roots, albeit with a jazz twist. Musicians started talking about getting a bit of 'funk'[138] into their music, providing the kind of commercial stimulus jazz needed at this point.

In 1958, a feature in *Downbeat* magazine by Barry Ulanov headlined 'How Funky Can You Get' observed that 'Everybody's doing it now. The most unlikely of jazz musicians have discovered "roots".'[139] The Horace Silver Quintet, Art Blakey and his Jazz Messengers and later saxophonist Cannonball Adderley's Quintet emerged as excellent working definitions of what funky hard bop was all about. Silver delivered its impact with his 1959–63 quintet with Blue Mitchell on trumpet and Junior Cook on tenor saxophone on albums such as *Blowin' the Blues Away*, *Finger Poppin'* and *Doin' the Thing at the Village Gate*. Playing memorable 'bluesy' themes that the ensemble performed with audible joy plus an implicit beat, the band enjoyed a run of popularity in the late 1950s and early 1960s.

In 1958 Art Blakey's pianist Bobby Timmons gave the drummer a 'soul' jazz hit with 'Moanin', from the album of the same name, with Blakey's saxophonist Benny Golson providing 'Blues March' and 'Along Came Betty', making this one of the classic soul jazz albums of the period. By 1959–61, Blakey had one of his finest versions of the Jazz Messengers with trumpeter Lee Morgan and saxophonist Wayne Shorter, who can be heard on albums such as *The Freedom Rider*, *Like Someone in Love* and *The Big Beat* – the latter title an allusion to the powerful beat Blakey was famous for on the one hand while on the other signifying on the name of DJ Alan Freed's popular television show in the 1950s. The show was infamously cancelled in 1957 when a black man was seen dancing with a white woman on screen. In 1958 a rock n' roll film of the same name was released to considerable box-office success.

Alto saxophonist Cannonball Adderley would have been a soulful player even without funky hard bop and, after his sojourn with Miles Davis, came into his own and rode the funky tide with distinction; 'Walk Tall' and 'Hummin'[140] from *Country Preacher* catching his band, with Joe Zawinul from Vienna on piano, in fine form.

Blue Note Records

Blue Note Records, whose label carried the proud boast 'The best in jazz since 1939', came to define a whole world of hard bop sophistication in the 1950s and '60s. Run by Francis Wolff and Alfred Lion, two German émigrés who had fled from Hitler's clutches in the late 1930s, they produced some 1,000 albums, of which some 900 are now sought-after classics,[141] before they eventually sold the label to Liberty Records in 1966. Their first success was with the classic jazz of Sidney Bechet's 'Summertime', recorded on 8 June 1939, which effectively created the cash flow that enabled the label to continue and grow.[142] Even though today the Blue Note label under Wolff and Lion's stewardship is primarily associated with hard bop, they actually began by recording classic New Orleans styles of jazz and boogie-woogie. Bop and hard bop came later, when Wolff returned from military service after World War II. Blue Note recordings not only came to define the sound of hard bop, but they influenced the evolution of jazz in terms of recorded sound, style and technical standards and a large chunk of their catalogue provides a model for young jazz artists today. Blue Note reissue programmes have occurred on a fairly regular basis over the years, enabling subsequent generations of fans to discover the enduring appeal of the artists who recorded for the label. While in a book of this nature space precludes an examination of the Blue Note legacy of Wolff and Lion, readers are encouraged to seek out albums from the 1950s and 1960s on vinyl or CD since Blue Note albums form the basis of many modern jazz record collections.

TEN 'MUST HAVE' BLUE NOTE RECORDINGS

1. John Coltrane *Blue Train*
2. Eric Dolphy *Out To Lunch*
3. Kenny Burrell *Midnight Blue*
4. Art Blakey *A Night at Birdland 1 & 2*
5. Tina Brooks *True Blue*
6. Donald Byrd *Fancy Free*
7. Herbie Hancock *Maiden Voyage*
8. Horace Silver *Blowin' the Blues Away*
9. Jackie McLean *Bluesnik*
10. Andrew Hill *Smokestack*

Charles Mingus – a Major Figure

It's fair to say the bassist, composer and bandleader Charles
Mingus was a volatile character. A troubled soul, he even checked
himself into a mental institution in 1958. His sprawling discography includes both notable successes and noble failures,[143] but
albums such as *Mingus, Mingus, Mingus, Mingus, Mingus* and
Black Saint and the Sinner Lady (both on the Impulse! label) and
a series of albums on the Atlantic label such as *The Clown*, *Pithe-
canthropus Erectus*, *Blues and Roots* and *Mingus Oh Yeah* attest to
his greatness as an artist. Certainly his best work is suffused with
a funkiness, or an earthiness, that's imbued with the blues – not
least the latter two titles on the Atlantic label – and his use of
collective improvisation that dates back to New Orleans jazz
sounds fresh, dynamic and modern. For many, the two albums
Mingus recorded for the Columbia label in 1959, *Mingus Ah Um*
and *Mingus Dynasty* take some beating. They are an excellent
realization of Mingus the bassist, bandleader and composer – the
swirling, dense ensembles with both written and improvised
counterpoint – that provided a different take on the soul jazz
of the period. Among the highlights from the two Columbia
albums are 'Better Get It In Your Soul' with a catchy 6/4 beat,
the energetic 'Boogie Stop Shuffle' and the affecting ballad
'Goodbye Pork Pie Hat', a in tribute to Lester Young based on a
12-bar blues (albeit with altered harmonies).

Miles Davis Kicks the Habit

After recording the *Birth of the Cool* sides and leaving Charlie
Parker's Quintet, Miles Davis succumbed to the temptation of
drugs in the early 1950s and suffered the chaotic lifestyle that
accompanied addiction. However, in mid-1953, he returned to
his parents' farm in Millstadt, Illinois, some fourteen miles south

of East St Louis, to shed his addiction 'cold turkey'. He returned to the jazz scene in early 1954 determined to make up for lost time, signing a three-year record deal with the Prestige record label. With a pick-up band that included pianist Horace Silver, he recorded the album *Walkin'*, in April 1954, which is now regarded as a hard bop classic and was an important step towards rehabilitating his career.

MILES DAVIS (1926–91)

Born in East St Louis, Davis was playing the trumpet professionally at fifteen. In 1944 he moved to New York, ostensibly to study at the Juilliard School of Music but his plan was to further his musical education with Charlie Parker. In 1945 he was a member of Parker's quintet and in 1949–50 he was at the helm of the *Birth of the Cool* sessions. During the early 1950's, addiction was interfering with his career and although he recorded with several name musicians, he was in danger of spinning off the rails until he returned to the family home in St Louis to rid himself of his addiction. When he returned to New York in 1954, he recorded for Prestige, a small independent label, but was determined to achieve the career boost that signing with Columbia Records, then *the* major record label in the USA, would bring.

Almost as an afterthought (his name didn't appear in the main programme, for example), Davis was invited to participate in a jam session on the night of 17 July 1955 at the Newport Jazz Festival, Rhode Island. Aware that Columbia executive George Avakian was in the audience, Davis pulled out all the stops with a moving performance of the Thelonious Monk ballad 'Round Midnight'. Avakian was impressed, and by the time Davis came off stage, he was in the trumpeter's dressing room ready to discuss a recording contract. It was no coincidence that 'Round Midnight' was selected as the title track of Davis' Columbia debut, and when it was released in 1956, his career was given a much-needed boost. His subsequent work for Columbia with his quintet was more nuanced and less rigidly bound to the dogma of the hard bop style than earlier Prestige recordings such as *Workin'*, *Relaxin'*, *Steamin'* and *Cookin'*. Key to his band's fortunes during this time was saxophonist John Coltrane, a player given to arbitrary over-statement, and the contrast of his prolix style with the economical Davis, who seemed to pare melody down to its very essence, proved to be a compelling combination. The albums he left in his wake on the Columbia label during this period neatly divide themselves into two specific areas of musical activity: his regular quintet/sextet that produced *Round About Midnight*, *Milestones* and his magnum opus *Kind of Blue*; and his collaborations with arranger Gil Evans for a large orchestra that produced *Miles Ahead*, *Porgy and Bess* and *Sketches of Spain*, all jazz classics.

Bill Evans – Musical Poet

Pianist Bill Evans was the pianist on Miles Davis's *Kind of Blue*, and if the jazz world had not woken up to his talent before, then his period as Davis's pianist from April to November 1958 certainly gave his career a lift. His first album had been *New Jazz Conceptions* in 1956, followed by *Everybody Digs Bill Evans* two years later, but it was two 1961 albums recorded live at the Village Vanguard – *Sunday at the Village Vanguard* and *Waltz for Debby* – where Evans encouraged a more interactive 'conversational' approach between piano, bass and drums that ensured he claimed the ear of the jazz world. By now Evans was emerging as a major artist in his own right, and although he succumbed to drug addiction he continued to develop as an artist and kept his career largely on track. Evans' playing was always elegant and probing and was matched by a mastery of harmony that set his playing apart from every other pianist in jazz. There are very few contemporary jazz pianists who have not come under his spell, noted jazz writer Gene Lees calling him 'The most influential pianist of his generation, altering the approach to tone and harmony. He ... built a style on subtle rhythmic displacement, fresh and sometimes ambiguous chord voicings, thoughtful voice leadings and an exquisite golden tone.'[144] One album among the many that Evans recorded which captures these elements of his style in perfect recorded fidelity is *You Must Believe In Spring*.

John Coltrane Goes it Alone

Thanks to his association with Miles Davis, saxophonist John Coltrane's profile in jazz rose from that of a complete unknown to rising star by 1960. In 1958, a leave of absence from Davis saw Coltrane performing with Thelonious Monk and recording *Blue Train* under his own name, his best recording to date by his own admission.

JOHN COLTRANE (1926–67)

Born in North Carolina where he learned woodwind instruments in school, Coltrane furthered his education in music in Philadelphia (1946–7) before working with bandleaders such as King Kolax and Eddie 'Cleanhead' Vinson. His early career was that of picking up work where he could with people like Jimmy Heath, Dizzy Gillespie, Earl Bostic and lesser-known musicians. A period with Johnny Hodges (1953–4) preceded a period of infrequent work for about a year before receiving the call to join Miles Davis.

After a spring tour of Europe in 1960 with Miles Davis, Coltrane left to pursue his own musical agenda, helped by the release of *Giant Steps* in January 1960 that immediately grabbed the jazz world's attention. The album's centrepiece was 'Giant Steps', a 16-bar theme where every note of the melody, regardless of its duration, is harmonized (that is, has a fresh chord to go with it). This has the effect of de-emphasizing the melody and places harmony at the forefront of the improviser's mind. The harmonic rhythm on 'Giant Steps' is fast – which in turn was accentuated by the brisk tempo in which Coltrane chose to play it. 'Giant Steps' was a challenge to the improviser back then, just as it is today. To unlock the complexities of improvising on such fast-moving 'changes', Coltrane utilized a procedure known as 'pattern running'.

On 'Giant Steps' Coltrane uses melodic pattern running, which is when the relationship of a group of notes one to another in one chord is preserved in the next chord. For example, a pattern Coltrane used frequently was the first, second, third and fifth notes of the scale (in other words, the doh-ray-me-so of the chord). The same pattern is then applied to the next chord where it becomes the 1-2-3-5 or doh-ray-me-so of *that* chord, and so on.

If this sounds a bit complicated, check out the opening move-ment of Beethoven's *Symphony No. 5 in C minor*. It begins with a distinctive four-note pattern that goes short-short-short-long which has been called the 'fate motif'. Breaking this down, this is a 3-3-3-1 pattern (in other words the me-me-me-doh of the chord). Listen to how Beethoven preserves this pattern in different pitches – both higher and lower – as the first move-ment develops. Since it's a simple phrase we have no difficulty in picking it out, try singing along with the opening few bars of Beethoven's symphony as the 'pattern' goes up and down in pitch. Once you hear how Beethoven moves this 3-3-3-1 pattern around in different pitches, you will get a clear idea of what Coltrane is doing with his 1-2-3-5 patterns as he moves them through the different pitches, or chords, of 'Giant Steps'.

Coltrane also mixes his 1-2-3-5 pattern with other patterns, such as 5-3-2-1, but these other patterns do not occur as frequently. Although jazz soloists had used melodic patterns before in jazz, Coltrane brought their use suddenly and sharply into focus as a means of negotiating a route through tricky chord progressions. In his book *Elements of the Jazz Language for the Developing Improviser*, leading jazz educator Jerry Coker points out that Coltrane's 'Giant Steps' solo comprises almost forty percent of patterns,[145] which had been learned by rote through assiduous practice and applied individually to each chord change of the composition. Subsequently, pattern running became a skill that is widely taught in jazz education and is a technique that can be heard in the playing of many young musicians today, albeit resulting in a similarity of concept and execution among some young players.

Giant Steps was Coltrane's finest recording up to that point in his career. For most musicians this would be a crowning achievement, but for Coltrane it was a waystation along a path that would be dotted with further triumphs. Within a year he turned his attention to the kind modal concepts that Miles Davis introduced on *Kind of Blue*. With a quartet comprising McCoy Tyner on piano, Jimmy Garrison on bass and Elvin Jones on drums – referred to as his 'Classic Quartet'[146] – Coltrane blazed a trail through the jazz of the period, leaving a legacy of remarkable albums including *Coltrane* (1962), *Live at the Village Vanguard* (1962),[147] *Impressions* (1963), *Crescent* (1964) and his magnum opus *A Love Supreme* (1965).

The Enigmatic Mr Rollins

While Coltrane owed much to his five year on-off association with Miles Davis, it's interesting to speculate how his career might have developed had Davis secured his first choice saxophonist, Sonny Rollins. When Davis returned to New York after withdrawing from heroin addiction, he turned his attention to forming his own group. On 29 June 1954 he recorded four numbers for Prestige with a group that he hoped to take on the road. Sonny Rollins was his first choice of saxophonist, but Davis was unable to find work for the band. When he signed with Columbia in 1955, he formed another group with Rollins on tenor saxophone, Red Garland on piano, Paul Chambers on bass and Philly Joe Jones on drums. Davis had lined up a string of bookings starting in September, but in-between jobs Rollins, who was addicted to drugs, left for Chicago to rehabilitate himself.

Once he had withdrawn from drugs, Rollins received an offer to join the Clifford Brown/Max Roach Quintet. For me, Clifford Brown is among the finest trumpeters in all of jazz. The Brown/Roach recordings are well worth checking out simply to marvel at the joy, warmth, fluency and invention of Brown's playing. Rollins was both rejuvenated and inspired by Brown and during the next two years, he entered what could only be described as a creative high. He was involved in fifteen recording sessions under his own name that started with *Worktime* and ended in *Freedom Suite*, taking in *Saxophone Colossus* and *Way Out West*, plus a couple of classic Blue Note sessions for good measure. *Saxophone Colossus* made Rollins' reputation with aficionados and public alike. However, four days after the first five tracks were recorded, Clifford Brown was killed in a car crash. Rollins' brief period of collaboration with Brown marked one of the great trumpet/tenor saxophone combinations in jazz, a meeting of two giant talents. Subsequently Rollins took two lengthy career breaks to rejuvenate his health at crucial points in his career – one from 1959 to 1962 and another from 1966 to 1972 – so that he effectively had to rebuild his career twice. On his return to jazz in 1972 he led an electric ensemble, but by the end of the 1970s he was back with an acoustic ensemble in which he played a dominant role; many of his solos were stream-of-consciousness miracles of invention that gradually enveloped his audiences like a one-sided argument. If you were in the right place at the right time, then Sonny Rollins seemed to be jazz's greatest living improviser. However, there were occasions when his fans felt he was working comfortably within himself, genius on hold, his audiences waiting for him to scale the summit yet again.

West Coast Jazz

From the late 1940s, the West Coast jazz scene was almost entirely centred around the clubs and after-hours spots of Central Avenue where a small but talented group of black bebop players held court, such as Dexter Gordon, Wardell Gray, Sonny Criss, Teddy Edwards, Hampton Hawes, Frank Morgan and Harold Land. It is fair to say that drug problems interfered with the career of many of these musicians, with Dexter Gordon moving to Europe in 1962, finally returning to the USA in 1976 to much acclaim while Frank Morgan and Teddy Edwards were 'rediscovered' in the 1980s, the latter through his association with singer Tom Waits.

Today, however, West Coast jazz is primarily associated with a number of white musicians, many formerly associated with the bandleader Stan Kenton, who settled in Southern California and whose day jobs were as studio musicians for the big Hollywood sound stages. Many of these musicians gravitated to The Lighthouse jazz club on Hermosa Beach to indulge their love of jazz. Despite their relatively young ages, they had come through the ranks of the big bands while some had seen war service and were able to apply through the GI Bill to further their musical education at university. All were au fait with bebop, but their musical curiosity resulted in looking farther afield to music that explored a wider diversity of approaches including serialism, modalism, counterpoint and ad hoc compositional structures, often organized within carefully arranged originals, and some even anticipated free jazz.

In West Coast jazz relaxed tempos and unhurried improvisations were the norm, well and truly breaking ranks with the bop and funky hard bop paradigm. Clearly, there was something agreeable in the West Coast air, and Lester Koenig's Contemporary label, Richard Bock's Pacific Jazz label and the Weiss brothers' Fantasy label documented developments there as assiduously as the Blue Note label documented developments on the East Coast. While Gerry Mulligan on the West Coast initially attracted attention with his piano-less quartet, other musicians such as Shorty Rogers and his Giants, alto saxophonist Art Pepper, saxophonist Jimmy Giuffre, drummer Shelly Manne and, for a while André Previn (in his guise as jazz pianist[148]) began to attract international attention. Pepper was especially enigmatic, with a string of excellent albums on the Contemporary label such as *Art Pepper Meets the Rhythm Section*, *Art Pepper + 11*, *Smack Up* and *Intensity*, but his here-again-gone-again career as he served time for drugs offences kept his profile low with the public. It was a reckless squandering of talent, although he finally got things back on track to enjoy a brief career renaissance in the late 1970s before his death in 1982.

Tenor saxophonist Stan Getz did not really consider himself a West Coast musician – he was born in Philadelphia and his family moved to the Bronx a few years later – but he did record the album *West Coast Jazz* while living in California in 1955 which is a classic, principally for his superb 9-chorus solo at 76 beats per minute on 'S-h-i-n-e' that's preceded by a remarkable unaccompanied 8-bar introduction. He recorded a further two albums during this time – *The Steamer* and *Award Winner* – his sound on the saxophone marking him out as the quintessential cool jazzman. Getz's subsequent career was one of continually refining his style: his early 1950s quintet with guitarist Jimmy Raney; his successful collaboration with guitarist Johnny Smith on the 1952 album *Moonlight in Vermont*, the year's top jazz album; the improvised counterpoint with trombonist Bob Brookmeyer on *Stan Getz at the Shrine*; his work with a quartet and quintet with Lou Levy on piano that produced *West Coast Jazz* and the classic *The Steamer*; his 1961 collaboration with arranger Eddie Sauter on *Focus*, an album with strings that stands as the finest of a distinguished career, and the bossa nova years between 1962 and 1964 when his hit singles 'Desifanado' and 'The Girl from Ipanema' reached fifteen and five on the *Billboard Hot 100* pop chart and the album *Jazz Samba* topped the *Billboard Top LPs* chart for seventy weeks. In the 1980s, he still remained on top of his game and along with pianist Kenny Barron produced two latter-day career highlights in *Serenity* and *Anniversary*.

Cool and Hot – Dave Brubeck

In 1954 pianist Dave Brubeck made the cover of *Time* magazine. 'In a matter of five years, Brubeck fans have grown from a small, West Coast clique to a coast-to-coast crowd ... what people hear and cheer is ... a new type of jazz,'[149] said the magazine. Stylistically, Brubeck was a difficult musician to pin a label on. After military service in Europe, he was one of many musicians who furthered their musical education under the GI Bill, in his case studying under the famous European composer Darius Milhaud at Mills College in California. Brubeck's style incorporated the sum total of his learning with Milhaud leavened by the whole history of jazz from boogie-woogie and stride piano through to modern jazz.

Although Brubeck played modern jazz, it did not share characteristics in common with the modern jazz mainstream, which was something East Coast critics in the 1950s and 1960s found hard to forgive. Nevertheless, they were outvoted in huge numbers by

WHAT MADE DAVE BRUBECK SO POPULAR?

In 2012, *Scientific American* asked, *Uncommon Time: What Makes Dave Brubeck's Unorthodox Jazz Stylings So Appealing?* The answer was 'Brubeck's music doesn't swing the way jazz "should", but it combines novelty and familiarity in a way that stimulates the brain.' Professor Justin London of Carelton College in Minnesota, whose speciality is music perception and cognition, argued Brubeck's asymmetrical rhythms, such as 9/8 and 5/4, test people's native entrainment ability so keeping the brain more active when listening. 'The asymmetrical meters do make you work a little harder to make you stay along with them,' he said. 'That's part of their appeal, attraction and charm.'[150]

the general public and in 1954, after releasing several successful albums on the Fantasy label, Brubeck was signed by record giant Columbia. In all, Brubeck recorded some fifty albums for Colum-bia and all are of uniformly high standard, with *Time Out* from 1959 a runaway bestseller; it peaked at No. 2 on the *Billboard Pop Album* chart and was the first jazz album to be certified platinum.

Two years after *Time Out* was released, the tune 'Take 5' was put out as a single to became the biggest-selling jazz single of all time, all the more remarkable since it used time signatures not then normally used in jazz – 'Take Five' was in 5/4 while the flip side of the single, 'Blue Rondo à la Turk', was in 9/8 alternating with 4/4. 'Creating a "hit" out of the odd-meter experiments of *Time Out* was the farthest from any of our minds when Paul Desmond [alto saxophone], Joe Morello [drums], Eugene Wright [bass] and I went into the studio to record,' said Brubeck in 1996.[151]

A Golden Period?

Jazz education, concerned with educating and preparing students to become jazz musicians, requires a core curriculum designed to achieve a satisfactory level of professional competence on gradu-ation. By the new millennial years, the globalization of not just jazz, but of jazz education, meant that aspiring young musicians had the option of studying jazz to degree and doctoral level. Universities, colleges and music conservatoires around the world broadly opted to follow the American model of jazz educa-tion. Charles Beale, one of the UK's foremost jazz educators, has pointed out that the development of jazz education has tended to 'codify jazz education and slant players it produces towards the mainstream styles and tunes of the United States and towards tunes that are deemed educationally useful as well as those that remain musically significant', and that the majority of educators today argue that, 'The U.S. "tradition" should be the basis of the jazz learner's experience early on.'[152] The core of the jazz curriculum in jazz education worldwide is based on the bop styles, mastery of which enables jazz students to gain 'an insight into jazz processes at the highest level'.[153] This is generally referred to as 'the jazz tradition', and playing 'in the tradition' means playing in American bebop-derived styles; the degree to which this has been mastered by many young musicians can be breathtaking.

This has tended to valorize post-1945 developments in jazz at the expense of pre-1945 developments, since these earlier styles are broadly considered irrelevant for the contemporary jazz musician and thus receive significantly less emphasis in the curriculum. But for a broad appreciation of jazz, which is quite different to acquiring the necessary instrumental and theoretical skills to function as a jazz musician, I would argue that knowledge of the pre-bop styles of jazz is essential to understanding the music, since there were certainly Golden Periods in pre-bop jazz. Nevertheless, Fred Kaplan, in his book *1959: The Year That Changed Everything,* argues that 1959 was a year of stylistic culmination and revolutionary breakthrough, which was certainly true in jazz, a year when four major jazz albums were released, each suggestive of new directions the music might follow and whose implications continue to be felt: Miles Davis' *Kind of Blue*; Dave Brubeck's *Time Out*; Charles Mingus' *Mingus Ah Um*; and Ornette Coleman's *The Shape of Jazz to Come* (which we will look at in the next chapter). These albums can be seen as a declaration of jazz's self-awareness as a serious, socially relevant art form, a summation of jazz in the 1950s which many people now consider to be jazz's Golden Period.

Jazz Goes Modern Playlist

It may be that you have noticed two of the jazz musicians encountered in this chapter in earlier playlists. For example, we heard Dave

Brubeck's 'Blue Rondo à la Turk' in the Blues Playlist for Chapter 2, and his version of Cole Porter's 'What Is This Thing Called Love' from the Instrumental Solo Playlist in Chapter 5. John Coltrane's 'My Favourite Things' was also encountered in The Instrumental Solo Playlist. To keep the length of this playlist manageable, Brubeck is not included here, but the reader is most certainly directed to his album *Time Out* as well as *Jazz at the College of the Pacific* that Brubeck himself believes has some of his quartet's finest playing.[154]

1. Jay McShann and his Orchestra: 'Hootie Blues' from *Jazz Collection 1941.*
2. Supersax: 'Parker's Mood' from *Supersax Plays Bird.*
3. Charlie Parker: 'Parker's Mood' from *Bird/The Savoy Recordings (Master Takes).*
4. Supersax: 'KoKo' from *Supersax Plays Bird.*
5. Charlie Parker: 'KoKo' from *Bird/The Savoy Recordings (Master Takes).*
6. Thelonious Monk: 'Blue Monk' from *Jazz on Summer's Day.*
7. Miles Davis: 'Godchild' from *Birth of the Cool.*
8. Gerry Mulligan: 'Walkin' Shoes' from *Complete Recordings 1951–56.*
9. Lee Konitz: 'All of Me' from *Motion.*
10. Modern Jazz Quartet: 'Django' from *Django.*
11. Jackie Brenston and his Delta Cats: 'Rocket 88' from *Chess Pieces: The Very Best of Chess Records.*
12. Horace Silver: 'Filthy McNasty' from *Doin' the Thing at the Village Gate.*
13. Charles Mingus: 'Hora Decubitus' from *Mingus Mingus Mingus Mingus Mingus.*
14. Miles Davis: 'Walkin'' from *Walkin'.*
15. John Coltrane: 'Giant Steps' from *Giant Steps.*
16. Sonny Rollins: 'Blue Seven' from *Saxophone Colossus.*
17. Stan Getz: 'Shine' from *West Coast Jazz.*

Listening Notes to the Jazz Goes Modern Playlist

1. Jay McShann and his Orchestra: 'Hootie Blues' featuring Charlie Parker

Any band that was not from New York, Chicago or Los Angeles was known as a 'territory' band. Jay McShann's orchestra came from Kansas City, which had previously launched the careers of Count Basie, Andy Kirk and Harlan Leonard, and was the last territory band to make anything near the big time in the Swing Era. Kansas City bands were big on riffs and blues, and McShann remained true to type on this studio version of 'Hootie Blues', recorded 30 April 1941 when Parker was twenty-one. His solo, just twelve bars of it, is a perfectly balanced statement that has poise, originality and assurance that is startling for one so young. A later version of this tune by McShann and Parker, recorded live at the Savoy Ballroom on 13 February 1942, available on the album *Early Bird*, is at a faster tempo, and this time Parker takes two choruses of the blues. The first chorus is largely based on the studio recording; the second, although interrupted, shows him on the cusp of his great recordings for the Savoy label in a matter of three years' time.

2. Supersax: 'Parker's Mood' from *Supersax Plays Bird*

3. Charlie Parker: 'Parker's Mood' from *Bird/The Savoy Recordings (Master Takes)*

Hearing Parker's solos performed by Supersax, a sax section plus rhythm and trumpet, is for many an ideal introduction to a Parker solo where the clarity of his ideas assume greater definition when presented as 'a work of art worthy of being extracted from its original context and expanded through the medium of orchestration'.[155] Parker's own version of 'Parker's Mood' is developed from the basic blues changes and then progressively finessed with additional harmonies; after the piano solo his rhythmic fluency allows him to imply double time (playing at twice the tempo) with some remarkable flourishes that are impeccably articulated. Part of Parker's genius was his ability to manipulate his rhythmic delivery in subtle yet vibrant ways.

4. Supersax: 'KoKo' from *Supersax Plays Bird*

5. Charlie Parker: 'KoKo' from *Bird/The Savoy Recordings (Master Takes)*

'KoKo' is based on a pre-existing set of chord changes, in this case the chords of a tune written by British bandleader Ray Noble called 'Cherokee'. It's an AABA song, but instead of being 32 bars long (each section 8 bars) it is 64 bars long (each section is now 16 bars long). Parker's two solo choruses continue to be widely admired in jazz, presenting 'the ultimate in flowing ideas, flawless execution and cohesion of thoughts ... This is the one Parker record that must be present in any jazz collection.'[156] Once again, the Supersax version is easier to follow in modern fidelity, and once you are familiar with it you should be better able to engage with Parker's original version.

6. Thelonious Monk: 'Blue Monk' from *Jazz on Summer's Day*

By now you should be able to recognize a 12-bar blues, so the underlying form of 'Blue Monk' means you're on familiar ground. Monk's piano playing, however, is anything but. At first hearing he can sound like someone trying to teach himself the piano. But keep with it; he is one of the most original composers and soloists in jazz. On his 1958 album *Underground*, Monk included an original called 'Ugly Beauty' (the only waltz, or composition in 3/4, among his recorded work, incidentally), a title that provides an apt description of his playing. With the passage of time, Monk's playing and composing has become so influential there's been a veritable deluge of Monk tribute albums to the point that his style, once derided by critics, has become so parodied in contemporary times it's become something of a cliché. But when you hear the real thing, it's clear Monk was a one-off; he still sounds fresh, innovative and *modern* even though his best work, in the late 1940s and 1950s, was recorded well over fifty years ago.

7. Miles Davis: 'Godchild' from *Birth of the Cool*

Miles Davis left the Parker Quintet on 23 December 1948, and on 21 January 1949 was recording 'Godchild' with a nonet under his own name on the first of three sessions whose combined output would later be dubbed *Birth of the Cool*. Arranged by Gerry Mulligan, 'Godchild' became a favourite of many jazz musicians during this period. Mixing individual part writing with blocks of sound made possible by the unusual instrumentation, the piece is surprisingly light on its feet. The solos are by Davis, Mulligan and trombonist Kai Winding.

8. Gerry Mulligan: 'Walkin' Shoes' from *Complete Recordings 1951–56*

Mulligan's 'piano-less quartet' recordings have proved remarkably enduring. Note how the absence of a chordal instrument (piano, guitar or vibes) makes Mulligan and Baker's lines stand out in sharp relief and assume a greater clarity of expression, both in leading and secondary roles. 'Walkin' Shoes' is a 32-bar AABA composition.

9. Lee Konitz: 'All of Me' from *Motion*

The first thing you notice about Konitz's 'All of Me' is that there is
no statement of the theme – it's held back until the end. Listen to
how his improvisation flows in unexpected ways – phrases begin
and end in ways you do not expect. This is known as 'playing over
the bar lines', where the improvisation does not neatly fit into the
demarcation of bar lines, lending a curiously off-centre, or asymmetrical, feeling to the improvised line. What is interesting about
this piece, and the accompanying four tunes from the same LP, is
that there was no rehearsal beforehand. Konitz preferred the fresh,
newly minted feel of spontaneous improvisation, and throughout
his life scrupulously avoided rehearsal. *Motion*, from which this
track is taken, is for my money Konitz's finest.

10. Modern Jazz Quartet: 'Django' from *Django*

There is no shortage of original compositions in jazz (meaning compositions written by the jazz musicians themselves) but
among the very best is 'Django'. Written by John Lewis, the
Modern Jazz Quartet's pianist and musical director, it features a
sublime solo by vibraphonist Milt Jackson – the bassist is Percy
Heath bass and the drummer Kenny Clarke. First, a word about
the composition. The 'Django' theme is a composed 20-bar
theme we'll call A, a solemn lament for the guitarist Django
Reinhardt. What is interesting is that unlike most jazz originals where the solos are taken over the chords of the theme, on
'Django' the soloist plays off a completely different set of chords.
After the exposition of the initial 'Django' theme 'A', the soloist then moves to a BBCD structure. When the soloist reaches
the end of 'D' it is followed by a pre-written 8-bar transition,
'E', in double time (twice the tempo of the overall piece) to
hand over to the next soloist, who returns *a tempo* to the BBCD
structure. It doesn't stop there – the bass player has some pretty

specific instructions too. The bass line at 'C' is a simple repeated note on each beat of the bar for each of the 8 bars (known as a Pedal Note) and on 'D', the bassist plays a pre-written figure for the final 8 bars of the section. When the last solo is finished, the 8-bar transition 'E' is dropped and the ensemble move back to the statement of the 20-bar 'Django' theme 'A'. If all this makes the Schleswig-Holstein question seem simple, take heart; once you've heard it a couple of times you'll discover it's a remarkably organic performance, and knowing what they get up to behind the scenes with the clever BBCD scheme between the two A sections and the transition 'E' simply deepens your respect and understanding of a remarkable performance.

11. Jackie Brenston and his Delta Cats: 'Rocket 88' from *Chess Pieces: The Very Best of Chess Records*

Here's a bit of light relief, but with a serious purpose. Recorded in March 1951 by Jackie Brenston and his Delta Cats, its inclusion here is to illustrate the style of music that was sweeping through the urban black communities in the United States in the early 1950s. Earthy and primal, it was the kind of music that was popular in clubs and bars for dancing and socializing. 'Rocket 88' was often called a 'dirty blues' because of the distortion created by guitarist Willie Kizart's broken amp. R&B bands playing in a raw, earthy style like 'Rocket 88' were hugely popular among urban black audiences at the time, persuading many jazz combos to adopt a similar funky, down-to-earth approach that became known as hard bop.

12. Horace Silver: 'Filthy McNasty' from *Doin' the Thing at the Village Gate*

Along with Art Blakey, Horace Silver became the most popular of the hard bop bands of the mid-1950s, early 1960s. This live recording, with what is generally regarded as Silver's finest line-up – Blue Mitchell on trumpet, Junior Cook on tenor saxophone, Silver on piano, Gene Taylor on bass and Roy Brooks on drums – captures the infectious spirit of the band in live performance. The Mitchell/Cook frontline stayed together from 1959 to 1964, making five albums for Blue Note, any one of which are now regarded as classics.

13. Charles Mingus: 'Hora Decubitus' from *Mingus Mingus Mingus Mingus Mingus*

Like all great cooks, Charles Mingus was able to take simple ingredients, in this case a 12-bar blues, and make them into something special. Mingus himself opens the performance with a 12-bar introduction on bass before the baritone sax instrumentally outlines the classic blues form. The genesis for this composition came from Mingus' memory of a band called the Savoy Sultans, the resident eight-piece band led by Al Cooper at the now legendary Savoy Ballroom in Harlem during the 1930s to '40s, saying they, 'used to outswing most big bands, just by building on riff patterns. Here I wanted to do the same thing – to swing hard!' Solos are by tenor saxophonist Booker Ervin, alto saxophonist Eric Dolphy, whose solo suggests a trail left by a spider who has escaped from an ink bottle, and trumpeter Richard Williams.

14. Miles Davis: 'Walkin'' from *Walkin'*

Miles Davis's solo on 'Walkin' really catches the ear. A 12-bar blues, Davis plays seven choruses with exceptional clarity and lucidity; he never sounds rushed, leaving spaces between his notes that lend a pleasing sense of balance and symmetry to his line; as Gil Evans once observed, Davis has 'the courage to wait'. Interestingly, Horace Silver is the pianist here, and along with Percy

Heath on bass and Kenny Clarke on drums, creates an insist-ent swing feeling that offers a compelling contrast to the studied nonchalance of Davis.

15. John Coltrane: 'Giant Steps' from *Giant Steps*

Coltrane's solo on 'Giant Steps', as was explained in the text, comprises some forty percent 'patterns'.[157] As an 'exhibition' piece to showcase his virtuosity it's impressive, and remains a landmark in jazz. Coltrane never played this piece live (as far as we know), and after recording it, headed towards the next phase of his career, the modal phase, where the sheer passion of his play-ing would pin audiences to the backs of their seats for upwards of two hours at a time.

16. Sonny Rollins: 'Blue Seven' from *Saxophone Colossus*

Saxophone Colossus was recorded when Sonny Rollins was twenty-five. It would establish him as a jazz great. The album's status was enhanced by an analysis of 'Blue Seven' by Gunther Schuller in the then influential magazine *Jazz Review* that's worth sourcing on the Internet.[158] Key to understanding its significance is the way in which melodic motifs were moved through thematic variation (and repetition and motivic elision) to produce a work of great structural cohesiveness and aesthetic unity.

17. Stan Getz: 'S-h-i-n-e' from *West Coast Jazz*

The difference between Stan Getz and, say, John Coltrane, is that listening to the latter makes you *feel* saxophone-playing is a stern discipline that only a few successfully master, while Getz makes you feel that anyone can pick up a saxophone and play it. One of the few times he permitted a glimpse of his virtuoso technique was on the opening 8 bars of 'S-h-i-n-e'. When one great musician said he wished he could hear that opening 8 bars for the first time every time he heard the recording, you know what he meant. It immediately catches the ear and sets up a buzz of anticipation for what is to follow. A tune from an earlier era of jazz, the 1920s, it is a 32-bar AABA form, but is taken at a very brisk tempo. After a statement of the theme, Getz takes nine choruses, which can lead to repetition if inspiration flags, but Getz was a constantly inventive musician. His solo sounds truly inspired throughout and, as Max Harrison has pointed out, '["S-h-i-n-e"] remains one of the great *tours de force* of tenor playing ... marked by unflaggingly intelligent melodic invention and no little wit.'[159] It was an observation underlined by the pianist on the date, Lou Levy, who said simply, 'I think that "S-h-i-n-e" is a masterpiece. When it came out all the tenor players shook their heads and said, "It's flawless".'[160]

9

Change – and More Change

The 1960s – a Decade of Protest and Change

The 1960s was a period of immense political and social change in the United States, enacted against a backdrop of an increasingly acrimonious Civil Rights campaign and the social and political fall-out of America's war in Vietnam. By the end of the decade the President of the United States, his Attorney General and the charismatic leader of the Civil Rights movement, Dr Martin Luther King, had all been assassinated and the incoming president, Lyndon Johnson, was facing the prospect of defeat in America's war in Vietnam. Yet the 1960s was also a period of startling originality in pop music. It heralded the age of the artist as singer/songwriter, so breaking the dominance of professional songwriting teams who had hitherto provided pop artists with their hits (and misses). Now the songs were by America's youth for America's youth, sending reverberations through a music business that was about to be turned on its head. The sudden and unexpected rise of pop and rock music in the mid-1960s caused the collegiate audience for jazz to haemorrhage to rock almost overnight. Something new and exciting was in the air and it wasn't jazz. 'The times are a changing', warned Bob Dylan, yet the writing had been on the wall for some time. When Elvis Presley encountered jazz lovers in the 1957 movie *Jailhouse Rock*, they were depicted as pretentious and elitist. It was rock 'n' roll that young audiences now saw as the music of adolescent rebelliousness.

Free Jazz

Just as the final frontier for the *Star Trek* series was outer space, the final frontier for jazz was freedom from the laws that governed music. The concept had tentatively been tried out by pianist Lennie Tristano in 1949 and in the early and mid-1950s, musicians such as Shorty Rogers, André Previn and Shelly Manne also flirted with the concept, but nobody had made it central to their style. That was about to change when alto saxophonist Ornette Coleman, who had been wrestling with the concept for some years, gathered a circle of like-minded musicians around him to attempt to improvise without any preset chord changes. As Coleman put it, 'What do you do after you play the melody if you don't have nothing to go with?'[161]

FREE JAZZ

According to the *Encyclopedia Brittanica*, the main characteristic of free jazz is that there are no rules. Musicians do not adhere to a fixed harmonic structure (predetermined chord progressions) as they improvise; instead, they modulate (i.e. change keys) at will. Free jazz performers often improvise without observing fixed metres or tempos. Solo and accompaniment roles tend to be fluid, as does the balance of composition and improvisation in a performance. The ultimate development of free jazz is free improvisation, which combines all these qualities – using no fixed instrumental roles or harmonic, rhythmic, or melodic structures and abandoning composition altogether.[162]

Even though at the time Coleman was working intermittently, in 1958 he nevertheless came to the attention of one of the more established musicians on the West Coast, bassist Red Mitchell, who introduced him to Lester Koenig, the owner and producer of Contemporary Records. Koenig was sufficiently intrigued with Coleman to offer him a chance to record, but on his first album he wanted Coleman to play his original compositions with chord changes rather than abandoning them, which was not what Coleman was about.

ORNETTE COLEMAN (1930–2015)

Born in Fort Worth, Coleman began playing saxophone at the age of fourteen, working on a style based on Charlie Parker. This important formative influence (even in the 1970s and '80s Coleman would astonish friends in informal gatherings by playing Parker solos from memory) would play an important role in helping shape his subsequent style. His early professional work included rhythm and blues bands, playing in Pee-Wee Crayton's band in 1950. However, his ideas about free jazz were met with hostility, and while working as an elevator operator in Los Angeles he evolved a style that, while drawing on the blues, also incorporated highly personal readings of music theory. Thereafter, the blues feeling would appear as an important ingredient in his music.

However, Coleman agreed to Koenig's terms and the results, *Something Else! The Music of Ornette Coleman*, contains nine original compositions: 'Alpha', 'The Disguise' and 'When Will the Blues Leave' based on blues chord changes; 'Angel Voice', 'The Sphinx' and 'Chippie' loosely based on 'I Got Rhythm'; 'Jayne' largely based on the chords of 'Out of Nowhere', while 'Invisible' and 'The Blessing' had Coleman's own chord progressions. What is striking about this album is how Coleman's playing sounds fully formed, even at this stage of his career.

In the spring of 1958, advertisements in *Downbeat* magazine's 'Where to Go' spot for the Los Angeles area included a regular entry for the Hillcrest Club, featuring pianist Paul Bley's quartet.[163] Bley and his musicians were also interested in 'breaking the bondage of chord structures', as the pianist later put it.[164] When Coleman began working with Bley at the club, the sessions from October 1958 were recorded and released in 1976 as *Live at the Hillcrest Club*. Here we get a sense of Coleman's ideas in the raw, since his next album for Contemporary Records, *Tomorrow Is The Question!*, while not exactly giving full rein to Coleman's ideas was enough to get him noticed by East Coast promoters, resulting in a two-week engagement with his group at the Five Spot Café in New York City, beginning on 17 November 1959. It was an event that would send shockwaves through jazz. Was this the future of the music? The abandonment of predetermined harmony and form?

For a while Coleman and his group – with Don Cherry on pocket trumpet, Charlie Haden on bass and Billy Higgins on drums – were the centre of attention in the jazz world. A-list celebrities of the day, such as Leonard Bernstein and Dorothy Kilgallen said yes, while Kenneth Tynan said no. The press, jazz musicians and curious fans all turned out to see what the fuss was about, and it quickly became clear that as many went to bury Caesar as to praise him. Coleman's next album, *The Shape of Jazz to Come*, came out on the more sympathetic Atlantic label. Recorded with his Five Spot ensemble, it was followed by the more emphatic *Change of the Century*.

Despite the controversy the mild-mannered Coleman was causing, no one seemed to notice that many of his themes were reassuringly diatonic.[165] His improvisations, using a plastic alto saxophone, were for some exhilarating, to others unnerving. The role of bassist Charlie Haden was key; he shadowed the soloist, making sure his bass line correlated with whatever the improviser was playing, as chord changes had been abandoned. It took well-trained ears to do this, and Haden proved to be a masterful accompanist. This form of soloing and accompaniment became known as 'time – no changes', meaning the musicians played in time, but there were no chord changes. This artistic licence was taken a stage further by Haden during his solo on Coleman's composition 'Ramblin'' from *Change of the Century*. As he later pointed out: 'We recorded two records, one of them was called *The Shape of Jazz to Come*, the other one was called *The Change of the Century* and on one of my bass solos I played a series of folk songs that I learned with my family ... "Old Joe Clark" and "Fort Worth Jail House" and "John Henry", a lot of different songs.'[166] It's interesting to note that no one else at the time, or indeed subsequently, realized Haden was drawing on country and western melodies during his solos, marking a true meeting of two indigenous American forms in jazz and country.

After another four albums from Atlantic – *This Is Our Music* (1960), *Free Jazz* (1960), *Ornette!* (1961) and *Ornette On Tenor* (1961) – Coleman became suspicious that he was being ripped off by unscrupulous management, and by 1962 had temporarily retired from public performance. He rarely worked in New York clubs thereafter; he appeared about ten times until the 1980s, and gave about as many concerts there. He made no records between 1962 and 1965, at the height of free jazz, and only three between 1969 and 1975.

John Coltrane and the New Thing

When Ornette Coleman withdrew from public performance in 1962, he could have had little idea of what he had set in motion, as free jazz became increasingly woven into the socio-cultural fabric of the 1960s. The growing influence of the Civil Rights movement gave expression to both political awareness and the rejection of racial injustice, and many young black jazz musicians became swept along by fast-accelerating events. They felt that by freeing themselves from bar lines, harmony and rhythm they were participating, both literally and metaphorically, in the black crusade for freedom and social justice. For many, free jazz or, as it became known during these years, the 'New Thing', became the anthem that screamed rejection of racial inequality. Certainly, much free jazz of the period was inextricably linked to the social climate from which it emerged and, like American society at this time, saxophonist John Coltrane's music was also in flux.

In December 1964 he recorded his solemn dedication to God, called *A Love Supreme*, with his 'classic quartet' of McCoy Tyner on piano, Jimmy Garrison on bass and Elvin Jones on drums. It would come to represent the culmination of his modal period, but he also recorded further versions of Part I of the suite called 'Acknowledgement', adding 'New Thing' saxophonist Archie Shepp and bassist Art Davis, suggesting his music was already in transition. During 1965, the classic quartet found themselves witness to their leader's deepening engagement with the New Thing, something that became clear with the appropriately named album *Transition*, recorded on 10 and 16 June 1965 that, while including 'Suite', in an obvious continuum of his religious preoccupations, in its totality – 'Transition', 'Welcome', 'Suite' and 'Vigil' – suggested a gathering of forces that presaged his major work *Ascension*, recorded on 28 June 1965, barely two weeks later. In an August 1966 interview, Coltrane was asked whether the kind of social and political issues Malcolm X talked about were expressed in his music, and whether he thought they were important. 'Well, they're *definitely* important,' Coltrane responded. 'And as I said, they are, the issues are part of what *is*, you know, at this time. So naturally as musicians, we express whatever, whatever it is.'[167]

However, labelling the music 'New Thing', like the label 'film noir' in the movie world, would, over time, have the effect of glossing over each genre's inherent social criticism. *Ascension* marked the beginning of what has become known as 'Late Period Coltrane', portrayed as a rupture with the past and the beginning of the saxophonist's musical roller-coaster ride into eternity – he died on 17 July 1967. It was a period that is as controversial now as it was then, with Jim Merod observing, 'A great deal of John Coltrane's late-period, avant-garde experimentation is without charm, utterly devoid of beauty in any sense that I can corroborate, yet nonetheless profoundly, disturbingly musical in every sense of the term's innate meaning.'[168] Others have taken a different view, such as academic Tony Whyton: 'I argue that the late works of Coltrane can play a central role in understanding jazz as a discursive cultural practice and in developing an understanding of the ideologies that lie beneath the celebration of jazz as a linear tradition.'[169]

Although it seldom forms part of the Coltrane discourse, Coltrane's biographer Lewis Porter has pointed out that Coltrane had dabbled with LSD, while the writer Stanley Crouch has written of 'rumours about hallucinogenic drugs, which intensify narcissism and spiritual fantasies'.[170] Certainly, in the worlds of rock and jazz on both sides of the Atlantic at this time the ready availability of LSD to both musicians and fans was a fact of life. But whether Coltrane did, or did not, take mind-bending drugs, there is no shortage of reports that his music was moving into a highly experimental phase where noise and volume were key components of his conception. Perhaps this was reflecting what was going on in the streets, with the chaos, noise and violence of the race riots being reflected on the bandstand. A *Downbeat* review of a Coltrane performance in November 1965 noted the band had 'more power than Con Ed', a reference to Consolidated Edison, who supply the electricity for the whole of New York City. Describing the concert as: 'Trane + 7 = A Wild Night at the Gate', *Downbeat* reported that 'One simply couldn't hear anything but drums on "Out of This World." I had no idea what the soloists were saying and I doubt the players could hear each other [either] … at one point I saw Coltrane break out a bagpipe and blow into it, but damned if I heard a note of what he played.'[171] Performances such as this did not go down well with audiences, as Stanley Crouch notes: 'By 1966 Coltrane was not only having troubles in clubs, sometimes being fired on opening night, he could also empty an entire park, which, as [his drummer] Rashied Ali recalls, he did in Chicago.'[172] Indeed, Ali also recalls performing with Coltrane when 'He'd put the horn down, beat on his chest and screamed into the microphone. People really thought he had lost his mind then.'[173] John Coltrane died on 17 July 1967, but the debate about the music of his 'final period'— especially among academics – has continued unabated and, rather like the debate about the number of angels that can dance on the head of a pin, has served to detract from the very real achievements of his earlier years.

Whither Freedom?

You might have thought the New Thing would have been in tune with the *zeitgeist* of the 1960s, a music of protest and rebellion that reflected the social unrest in American society, but paying customers were hardly beating down the doors to get in, as saxophonist Eddie 'Lockjaw' Davis discovered when he worked for a booking office between stints as a featured soloist with Count Basie's Orchestra: 'If a person comes into a club and does not understand or enjoy what the musicians are playing, he's not coming back. Therefore there's no business ... [This] is why there are no clubs to speak of today [1970] ... Freedom has done more harm to the industry than any other form of music. It's a fact.'[174]

Certainly, free musicians were encountering difficulty in finding an audience for their music. Avant-garde saxophonist Albert Ayler (1936–70), for example, was considered 'The *ne plus ultra* of free jazz', who 'performed the musical equivalent of speaking in tongues: he left chord changes and swinging rhythms far behind and emitted great spiritual wails and shrieks from his horn.'[175] Yes, you read that correctly, it's taken from *The New Yorker*. Ayler relocated to Sweden in 1962, where he gained a degree of recognition, returning to New York in 1963 to record for ESP-Disc, and later the Impulse! label. His music, though, 'evoked incredibly strong and disparate reactions from critics and fans alike',[176] said *The Biographical Dictionary of Jazz*, albeit his final three albums returned to a basic R&B formula with a backbeat and vocals. On 5 November 1970, he was found dead in New York City's East River, the circumstances of his death still unknown. Listening to his recordings today – despite his influence extending over a wide range of jazz musicians and even today's thrash metal bands – it's impossible not to think Ayler took jazz further than it had ever gone, and probably as far as it could go before casting off into meaningless noise.[177]

The pianist Cecil Taylor once symbiotically recorded with Ayler but forged his own path into the twenty-first century when his eighty-fifth birthday was honoured in 2014 at the Painted Bride Art Centre in Philadelphia with a tribute concert. Taylor's modest early explorations into free jazz were captured on the album *Looking Ahead! The Cecil Taylor Quartet* in 1958, and he subsequently developed a very vigorous, physical style at the piano; his 1976 solo album *Air Above the Mountains* is a good example of this. There was a fascination in his explosive approach, as well as in the fluency of his swirling, dissonant flurries; in the 1980s he would often begin a concert with a period of somewhat disconcerting chanting. *In Florescence* captures in broad brushstrokes the diversity of his free jazz vision in sympathetic surroundings.

Spiritual Jazz

For many black jazz musicians, the New Thing was too extreme – literally too far out. They felt closer to Coltrane's spiritual offering, *A Love Supreme*, than albums like *OM*, *Meditations*, *Interstellar Space*, *Live in Seattle* and *Ascension*. These musicians were more in tune with a religious revolution in urban black America that had sprung up in opposition to America's dominant Christian faith, such as Elijah Muhammad's Nation of Islam or ideas rooted in Eastern mysticism, Zen philosophy and Egyptology. Many sought to reflect the transcendent in their music, some embracing the sound of the Southern Baptist holy-roller meetings, while others sought enlightenment from Southeastern Asian practices like transcendental meditation and yoga. After Coltrane's death, the leading figures in this movement were his wife Alice Coltrane and his former co-saxophonist Pharaoh Sanders. Their work, and that of others inspired by them, was devoted to meditative and spiritual concerns. Often infused with the timbres of Indian music and sometimes called astral jazz, others drew on contemporary sounds such as funk and soul music, as well as African and Middle Eastern influences and rock music. Inspired by the Civil Rights and Black Power movements, this was music of its time, often with funky bass lines, a strong backbeat, strings, electronic instruments such as the electric piano and early synthesizers and spiced with vocals by the likes of Jean Carn and Kellee Paterson. Recorded by small independent labels like Black Jazz, Strata East, Tribe, Nessa, Muse and Prestige, the music was largely ignored by critics at the time, but began to resurface as collectors discovered it, along with US hiphop producers looking for breaks and samples. In more recent times, saxophonist Kamasi Washington's three-CD set, *The Epic*, inspired by, and almost an extension of spiritual jazz, catapulted him to worldwide recognition. In Britain he appeared in the 2016 Henry Wood Promenade Concert season, winning over many converts to the music.

Was that It? The Dust Settles on Free Jazz

In the social context of its time, the role of free jazz as a vehicle for social protest was seen by some as worthier than musical or aesthetic merit. Free jazz appeared to weigh more heavily on some critics' consciences on than their pleasure centres, and whatever the 'shock of the new', a certain critical discretion preceded valour, lest history mark the denigrator of the new Picasso or Joyce. 'For every one Coleman,' wrote musicologist Gunther Schuller, an Ornette Coleman advocate, 'there were ten lesser or no-talents who sought refuge in the anarchy and permissiveness of the avant-garde',[178] and certainly there were many free jazz recordings from this period that sounded like a dysfunctional family squabbling over control of the TV remote. In the face of what George Russell called the 'war on chords', where audiences were confronted with seemingly random notes against an abstract background and a disorder alien to their previous listening experiences, the audience for free jazz waned. One possible reason for this was that the language of free jazz had raced ahead of public taste – the oblique nature of the music meant that a popular audience for it, even within the black community, was never a possibility. It was songs like Sam Cooke's 'A Change Is Gonna Come', widely adopted as a black anthem, Curtis Mayfield's 'People Get Ready'and, in 1968, James Brown's 'Say It Out Loud–I'm Black and Proud' that captured the spirit of the times. Looking increasingly beleaguered at the barricades of socio-political issues, free jazz turned inwards, into enclaves of its true believers, forming artists' collectives such as the Jazz Composers Guild, formed in New York in 1964, the Association of Advancement of Creative Musicians in Chicago and the Underground Musicians Artists Association on the West Coast – both formed in 1965 – and the Black Artists Group in St Louis formed in 1968, that emphasized pride in the whole black music tradition and maintaining cultural identity through jazz and improvised music.

As the 1960s gave way to the 1970s, several leading musicians from these collectives gravitated to the New York loft scene playing for small but enthusiastic audiences, while in 1976 Ornette Coleman recorded *Dancing In Your Head* with his band Prime Time that employed electric instruments and funk rhythms. This ensemble, with his son Denardo on drums, preached harmolodics, a 'philosophical concept'[179] Coleman used to explain his music, which is a contraction of harmony, movement and melodics that in its reasoning, to use one of Coleman's album titles, was *Something Else!*

With the passage of time, free jazz musicians were forced to confront the dual reality that their music had lost touch with the public, other than its true believers, and that in the end, total freedom could in itself be limiting. 'It all started sounding the same,' said saxophonist Steve Lacy. 'It wasn't free anymore.'[180] In summing up this period of jazz history, *The New Grove Dictionary of Jazz* said free jazz was 'Highly regarded by the critics', but Mark Gridley, in *Jazz Styles: History and Analysis* noted it was 'one of the least popular styles in jazz history'.

Shock Waves: the Rise of Rock in the 1960s

Although free jazz has been blamed for the downswing in the popularity of jazz in the 1960s among promoters, artists and fans, it was undoubtedly exacerbated by the unexpected rise in popularity of rock music among young audiences, which while not exactly casting jazz into outer darkness, did at least relegate it to the commercial twilight. 'One treacherous night John Coltrane played in Chicago's "Birdhouse"', wrote *Downbeat* reporter Gordon Kopulos. 'He played to an audience that numbered ten at its height. I counted. As if to underscore the whole thing in living theatre, another group appeared that night on the South West Side: Kenny Klope Fantastics – a rock group. And Jimmy Loundsberry, then a popular emcee. They packed in 600 kids paying two dollars apiece and turned away 300.'[181] As the *Daily Telegraph* has noted, 'The 1960s proved a thin time for jazz'[182] as the collegiate audience for jazz migrated almost en masse to rock music, which was considered to be more in tune with the times. By 1967, the British music weekly *Melody Maker* contained a requiem for 'a jazz we loved and knew so well', while the American *Downbeat* magazine, a solid and reliable chronicler of the jazz scene since 1934, declared 'Jazz is Dead'. Jazz clubs were closing down and reopening their doors as discotheques, while record companies had lost interest in the relatively small returns produced by jazz albums and were rubbing their hands at the prospect of the huge returns produced by rock recordings. 'All of a sudden jazz became passé', wrote Miles Davis in his autobiography. 'Something dead you put under a glass in the museum and study. All of a sudden rock n' roll was in the forefront in the media.'[183]

Miles Davis Reacts to the Changing Times

Since the departure of John Coltrane from his group, Davis had gradually rebuilt his band, and by the mid-1960s his group – usually referred to as his 'second great quintet', comprising Wayne Shorter on tenor sax, Herbie Hancock on piano, Ron Carter on bass and Tony Williams on drums – was reaching an unparalleled level of creativity. In 1965 the group recorded *Live at the Plugged Nickel* that was followed by *Miles Smiles* (1966), *Nefertiti* (1967), *Miles in the Sky* (1968) and *Filles de Kilimanjaro* (1968), all bona fide jazz classics. Shorter emerged as a leading catalyst within this group through compositions that reversed the burden of complexity between the front line and rhythm section with slow-moving melodies on top for sax and trumpet that did not have bridges or complex turnarounds, so giving the rhythm section latitude to create rhythmic interest and complexity down below. In bebop and most other forms of jazz it was the other way around: the complex stuff was the province of the trumpeters and saxophonists, while the rhythm section kept time and generally steered clear of too much fancy stuff. Many of the compositions Davis's quintet played at this time were specifically fashioned around the 'time, no changes' principle we heard Charlie Haden and Ornette Coleman employ earlier in the chapter. Here, a theme served to set key and tempo and, once played, conventional chord changes were abandoned – such as 'Prince of Darkness', that used a mixture of prearranged harmonies and 'time, no changes'. While Davis' band was in the vanguard of jazz at this time, the only problem was that his albums were popular with everyone except the record buying public.

Davis was aware that with the huge popularity of rock music, his record company was concerned that he was not selling albums in the kind of quantities that were attractive to them. '[They] started talking to me about trying to reach this younger market,'[184] he said. Gradually he began feeling his way towards incorporating elements from the rock world into his music, albeit in his own very personal way. On 'Stuff' from *Miles in the Sky* and 'Vonetta' from *Sorcerer*, we hear Tony Williams using the square rhythm patterns we associate with rock. On *Miles in the Sky* he uses electronic sounds associated with rock – an electric guitar (on the track 'Paraphernalia') and pianist Herbie Hancock playing an electric Fender Rhodes piano. On *Filles de Kilimanjaro*, a classic although neglected Davis album, bassist Ron Carter plays a bass line closer to rock than jazz on the title track, while 'Mademoiselle Mabry' is almost an abstraction of 'soft soul'. Reining in the free-flowing creativity of *Live at the Plugged Nickel*, Davis and his musicians distantly reflect and comment on what was happening in popular culture without surrendering to commercial impulse. Davis seems to suggest change is not only inevitable in his music, it was necessary. However, the question he must have been asking himself was how far could he reach into pop culture without surrendering the essential ingredients that made jazz jazz?

That was largely answered on his next album *In a Silent Way* in February 1969. By now, pianist Herbie Hancock, bassist Ron Carter and drummer Tony Williams had left, replaced by Chick Corea on electric piano, Dave Holland on acoustic and electric bass and Jack DeJohnette on drums. With this new album, Davis embraced rock more unequivocally. Using three keyboards (Corea, Hancock and Joe Zawinul) for the sessions, plus guitarist John McLaughlin, he succeeded in proving the artistic feasibility, if not commercial viability, of a jazz-rock union (it only reached 134 on the *Billboard* album chart). Although *In a Silent Way* was characterized by subdued musical events, in live performance the music of his quintet was quite another story: 'He put a cap on a certain style of acoustic jazz music with Herbie [Hancock] and Ron [Carter] and Wayne [Shorter] and Tony [Williams],' said Corea. 'Every tune we played [live] was in this incredible abstract form; the meat of the rendition was free improvisation.'[185] This new direction went largely unrecorded: 'I wish this band had been recorded live,' Davis would reflect later. 'Columbia missed out on the whole...thing.'[186] The group was even dubbed 'The Lost Quintet' since it was so scantily recorded by Columbia, and it was not until 2013 when Columbia/Legacy put out *Miles Davis Quintet: Live in Europe 1969*, using material that had been recorded on tour by European radio and TV broadcasters, that the extent of their invigorating brand of free jazz electric experimentation over rock-style rhythms became clear.

Something's in the Air – A Marriage between Jazz and Rock?

Davis was not alone in trying to find some sort of accommodation with rock. For a young generation of jazz musicians, rock was the music of their generation, the music they socialized to, the music they partied to, the music they made love to. The talented young jazz guitarist Larry Coryell spoke for many young jazz musicians of his age when he said, 'We love Wes Montgomery, but we also love Bob Dylan, we love Coltrane, but we also love the Beatles, we love Miles Davis, but we also love the Stones. We wanted people to know we were very much part of the contemporary scene, but at the same time we had worked our butts off to learn jazz too.'[187] Popular culture was being swept with unusual connections and new ideas and for many, the idea of integrating jazz and rock seemed the most logical thing in the world. On the West Coast, the San Francisco rock bands such as the Grateful Dead, Jefferson Airplane and Country Joe and the Fish were already playing long sets of three and four hours for stoned-out, hallucinating hippies that opened up songs with long periods of improvisation, often based on modes. There was genuine curiosity among rock musicians about jazz techniques – indeed, many players in these bands were jazz fans, such as Grateful Dead's lead guitarist Jerry Garcia and Jefferson Airplane's Jorma Kaukonen.

In 1967, *Time* magazine did a feature that was full of optimism that a jazz-rock hybrid as a specific genre of music in its own right might emerge, and even went as far as wishing the newlyweds bon voyage. The climate was such that jazz-rock was now beginning to be seen, not as a possibility, but more of a probability. Jazz musicians such as tenor saxophonist Charles Lloyd's quartet, alto saxophonist John Handy's quintet and pianist Mike Nock's Fourth Way began playing the big West Coast rock emporium Fillmore West, incorporating rock rhythms into their jazz improvisations. In New York, Larry Coryell formed a group called the Free Spirits that combined jazz with rock, as did flautist Jeremy Steig with his group Jeremy and the Satyrs. Vibraphonist Gary Burton's quartet fluidly slipped in and out of rock rhythms, while in 1968 the commercial potential of jazz-rock was illustrated by the groups Blood Sweat and Tears and Chicago, using a simple formula of big band riffs played by a horn section and rock rhythms played by electric piano, electric guitar, electric bass and drums.

Jazz Meets Rock in Britain

In the United Kingdom during the 1960s, some musicians were further along the road to a jazz-rock fusion than their American counterparts. Guitarist and vocalist Alexis Korner used jazz musicians in his ensembles in a mix of blues and rock that many consider was a harbinger of jazz-rock, especially his band Blues Incorporated that included bassist Jack Bruce and drummer Ginger Baker. Forgive the broad brushstrokes at this point, which are bound to irk those seeking finer detail, but there were many musicians who would emerge from Korner's circle, plus others quite separately experimenting with the idea of jazz and rock, the key development at the time being when Jack Bruce and Ginger Baker hooked up with guitarist Eric Clapton to form Cream in 1966. 'Eric was a straight blues player and Jack and I were both jazz players ... There weren't three musicians around like us; that's how the name came about, we considered we *were* the cream,' said Baker.[188] What's significant is that Baker and Bruce both considered themselves jazz musicians in what is now considered one of the major rock bands of the 1960s. Later Clapton would reflect: '[Ginger Baker] was really a leader. I always felt ... I [had] to fit into whatever concept he wanted to lay down ... because he's much more of a jazz-based musician; the Cream were really a jazz group, a jazz-rock group.'[189] When they toured the USA in 1967,

Rolling Stone magazine pointed out that 'they have been called a jazz group',[190] and today it seems clear they were pretty close to a working model of what a fusion between jazz and rock might actually sound like before a jazz-rock genre became defined and a community of similarly orientated musicians emerged that could collectively be called a trend.

Equally, bands like Colosseum and Soft Machine had a strong jazz underpin, while Robert Fripp's King Crimson made an impression on young American jazz musicians with their jazz-rock experimentation – not least Gary Burton and Chick Corea. But perhaps aesthetically the most successful British jazz-rock pioneer was trumpeter Ian Carr with his band Nucleus. In January 1970 they recorded the album *Elastic Rock*, and later that year they appeared at the Newport Jazz Festival at Rhode Island. '*Bitches Brew* was out when we went to New York in 1970,' recalled Carr. 'But what surprised me was that musicians were coming up to us and saying, "What do you call this music, what is it?"'[191] Nucleus subsequently recorded a series of albums that were never released in the States. Taken together, *Elastic Rock*, *We'll Talk About It Later*, *Solar Plexus*, *Belladonna* and *Labyrinth*, represent an important, if overlooked, area of jazz-rock that genuinely suggests the artistic potential of a jazz-rock fusion – indeed, original-issue vinyl albums today fetch between three and four figures in the collector's market.

Miles Makes His Move

It took from February 1969's *In a Silent Way* and a tour that lasted until August with the experimental 'Lost Quintet', before Miles Davis felt ready to make his first major jazz-rock statement. With his next album *Bitches Brew*, Davis came to personify jazz-rock, and as a result was often credited with 'inventing' the genre; he didn't. Perhaps more importantly, though, his stature in the jazz world meant he was bestowing a kind of blessing on the new hybrid, so triggering the dawn of a new era. *Bitches Brew* was as enigmatic as Davis himself, purposely avoiding pop music's smooth contours with a gritty dissonance and angular, open-ended improvisation that flew in the face of commercialism. There were no cadences, nothing resolved as solos rose out of the mix and sank back into a matrix of sound that seemed to define its own process. This mysterious brew extended across a two-LP set that had stunning cover artwork by Mati Klarwein that served as a gateway into the music. By the end of its first year of release it had sold 400,000 copies and won the 1970 Grammy Award for Best Jazz Record, going on to become Davis's first RIAA Gold album. Neither prophet nor martyr, Davis had succeeded in making sense of the fast-changing world around him and had shown the jazz world that the boundaries musicians and fans had created for themselves were in flux.

For all the success and media attention *Bitches Brew* attracted – and still attracts – Davis was yet to confront the electronic *power* of rock. Here Jimi Hendrix emerges as a key figure, since he had grasped something that Davis, and jazz musicians in general, had not. Quite simply he treated the electric guitar as an *electronic* instrument, rather than an amplified acoustic one. Harnessing volume, feedback and distortion as aspects of authenticity, he took the electric guitar to places it had never been. Davis would grasp the nettle in April 1970 on the track 'Right Off' from the album *Jack Johnson*. It was a piece that began innocuously enough, as John McLaughlin recalls. 'We were in the studio, Herbie Hancock, Michael Henderson, Billy Cobham and me. Miles was talking with [producer] Teo Macero in the control room for a long time. I got a little bored and I started to play this shuffle, a kind of boogie in E with some funny chords. The others picked it up and locked in. The next thing, the door opened and Miles runs in with his trumpet and we played for about 20 minutes. It was a large part of the record yet it came out of nowhere.'[192] McLaughlin's Hendrix-like power chords were forward in the sound mix, and at around bar 50 he begins to set the stage for Davis, dropping in volume, and from around bar 60 begins a climactic build-up to frame Davis's commanding entry at bar 75. It's one of the great moments in recorded jazz, as memorable in its own way as the entry of Scarpia in Act 1 of *Tosca*. Like all his finest solos, it has great structure and poise. But it's quite unlike his work with his acoustic ensembles; instead of introspection and control, his playing is extrovert and full of drama, often contrasting staccato passages with fast, sweeping runs that leap into the high register of his instrument. In live performance, however, Davis's music increasingly became characterized as what might be called an electronic free-for-all, and subsequent albums such as *Live-Evil, On the Corner, Pangaea* and *Dark Magus* came to be overshadowed by the work of musicians who had emerged from his ensembles. To paraphrase Gertrude Stein on Hemingway, Davis did it first and others came along and did it better.

Sons of Miles

The first of Davis's late-1960s band members to leave and strike out on his own was pianist Herbie Hancock, who took a leave of absence from the Miles Davis Quintet to get married in August 1968, only to learn that his place in the group had been taken by pianist Chick Corea. In November that year Hancock debuted his new sextet at the Village Vanguard. It gradually evolved, through albums such as *Mwandishi, Crossings* and *Sextant* into a somewhat esoteric space jazz group, whose main claim to fame was being one of the first bands to go out on the road with a synthesizer. Concerned with free forms and textures, their music is highly regarded now, but in the context of its time the band struggled to get work. When they were booked to support The

Pointer Sisters, an extrovert vocal threesome, at the Troubadour Club in Los Angeles, Hancock was forced to acknowledge that in comparison to the sort of crowd reaction the Pointers received, his band was nowhere. Then followed an abrupt change of musical direction; within a month he had dissolved his band and re-formed a new one. After listening to James Brown, Stevie Wonder and Sly and the Family Stone, he sought out musicians who could play in a similar idiom as well as jazz. The resulting album, *Headhunters*, was an instant hit, with the single 'Chameleon' appearing at No. 42 on *Billboard's Hot 100*, while the album went to No. 13 on the *Billboard* pop album chart and by the end of the year had sold 750,000 units, making it one of the biggest-selling jazz albums up to that point in jazz history. Overnight, Hancock became a major attraction on both the rock and jazz circuits. Other than a few excursions into acoustic jazz,[193] by his own admission some of the records he made during this time were never intended to be considered 'jazz' albums, such as 1983's *Future Shock* and its Grammy-winning single 'Rockit' one of the biggest instrumental dance singles and video hits of the 1980s.

Davis's drummer Tony Williams was next to leave, his departure not quite as abrupt as Hancock's, but by the end of 1968 he had formed a trio with guitarist John McLaughlin and organist Larry Young called Lifetime. If *Bitches Brew* was characterized by an absence of significant musical events, then Tony Williams' Lifetime gave apodictic testimony to a new way of reconciling jazz and rock. The music was manic and desperate, and for a moment it seemed as if it were to Lifetime and not Davis that destiny was beckoning. But the band had burnt itself out by 1973, a victim of personal tensions and bad management. Williams was largely inactive until 1975, and by degrees gradually returned to acoustic jazz, touring in a group called VSOP – essentially the Miles Davis Quintet of 1968 but with trumpeter Freddie Hubbard in Davis' stead – and with his own acoustic jazz quintet in the 1980s.

At the end of 1969, tenor saxophonist Wayne Shorter ended his five-and-a-half-year association with Davis to form a band called Weather Report with the formidably talented Austrian keyboard player Joe Zawinul. Initially, the band began as an electric free jazz ensemble, but after two albums on the Columbia label, a change of musical direction was heralded by *Sweetnighter* in 1973, with a more structured, compositional approach using rock-orientated rhythms. Two tracks from the album, 'Boogie Woogie Waltz' and '125th Street Congress' have been extensively sampled by DJs in today's pop culture. Subsequent albums including *Mysterious Traveller* (1975), *Tale Spinnin'* (1976) and *Black Market* followed, the latter mark-ing the point when virtuoso bassist Jaco Pastorius joined the band. 'Before Jaco came along we were perceived as a kind of esoteric jazz group,' said Zawinul. 'After Jaco joined the band we started selling out concert halls everywhere.'[194] Their next album, 1977's *Heavy Weather,* earned them a Grammy Award and with initial sales of over 500,000 the album went gold, representing the high point, both artistically and commercially, of the evolution of Weather Report. The band continued to record successfully into the 1980s, and by the time of their final release – *Sportin' Life* (1985) – Zawinul and Shorter had produced fifteen albums in an association that had lasted almost fifteen years. Often described as a 'jazz-rock' or even a 'fusion' band, with the passage of time it is now clear they were *sui generis*, since their stylistic outlook was extremely broad and any success they enjoyed was achieved on their own terms. 'We play *our* brand of music,' Zawinul once asserted. 'Nobody plays tunes like we play';[195] and he was right. Both Zawinul and Shorter would re-emerge with their own successful ensembles as the late 1990s gave way to the early millennium years – the Zawinul Syndicate and the Wayne Shorter Quartet laying seri-ous claim to being among the finest electric and acoustic jazz bands respectively of the period.

Pianist Chick Corea ended his stint with Davis after a summer tour of festivals in 1970, taking with him bassist Dave Holland. They wanted to pursue a non-electric approach to free jazz playing, but Corea soon felt the need for a more lyrical context for his music. From 1971 he led a band called Return to Forever that began life as an acoustic band before combining somewhat grandiose electronic orchestral effects with stunningly fast passages of meticulous precision combining guitar, keyboards, bass and drums on albums such as *Hymn of the Seventh Galaxy* (1973), *Where Have I Known You Before* (1974) and *Romantic Warrior* (1976). The group was among the most commercially successful of the jazz-rock fusion bands, spawning countless imitators, reaching beyond jazz to appeal to progressive rock fans. However, as prog rock became discredited by rock critics for its empty virtuosity, then so too was the high-powered jazz-rock of Return to Forever, condemned by jazz critics who claimed their music was beginning to sail perilously close to prog.[196]

Guitarist John McLaughlin, who made his first recorded appearance with Miles Davis in 1969 with *In A Silent Way*, actually turned down several requests from Davis to join his band. Nevertheless, he did guest on other Davis albums from the period, including *Bitches Brew* and a series of live recordings made at Washington, D.C.'s Cellar Door jazz club in 1970[197] before going on to form his own band, the Mahavishnu Orchestra in July 1971. Nothing quite like this band had been heard in jazz before. Inspired by McLaughlin, they were illuminated by the rhythmic complexity of drummer Billy Cobham, and together with Jerry Goodman on violin, Jan Hammer on keyboards and bassist Rick Laird, everyone played as if their lives depended on it. Abrupt gear shifts of metre, astonishing ensemble cohesion and an ability to launch into passages of improvisation so powerful they threatened to overwhelm their audiences, Mahavishnu created an impact that could be overwhelming. 'Its coherence and control come as a shaft of light on the muddied and confused', reported

Melody Maker in 1972.[198] The band's first two albums, *Inner Mounting Flame* from 1971 and *Birds of Fire* from 1972, were their most successful both artistically and commercially (they reached Nos 89 and 15 on the *Billboard* album chart respectively). Then suddenly, after just one more album, they were gone.[199] Subsequent versions of the band came and went, but you can only make a first impression once and none was able to capture the energy of the band's startling debut, as pianist Chick Corea later acknowledged: 'I feel the formation of the Mahavishnu Orchestra was equally important [as Miles Davis's bands],' he said. 'What John McLaughlin did with the electric guitar set the world on its ear, no one ever heard an electric guitar played like that before and it certainly inspired me. John's band, more than my experience with Miles, made me want to turn up the volume and write music that was more dramatic and made your hair move.'[200]

Miles Retires (for a While)

When Miles Davis played a midnight concert on 1 July 1975 at Avery Fisher Hall in New York – billed as 'The Midnight Miles' – he was distracted by painkillers and an arthritic hip. His music, a sprawling free jazz electronic miasma without resolution or direction – captured on live albums such as *Dark Magus* (1974) or *Pangaea* (1975) – was now only attracting lukewarm reviews. When he played the Schaefer Festival in Central Park on 5 September, for example, *The New York Times* noted that 'Miles Davis' ability to leave his listeners languid was given pointed display.'[201] Two days later, Davis's band members and equipment were in Miami for a concert at the Gussman Hall, but Davis failed to make it, cancelling at the last minute with the promoters impounding his equipment to set against their losses. One more concert, on 12 October at the Auditorium Theatre, had been planned, but Davis again pulled out, finally recognizing treatment for his hip was his only option. His withdrawal from jazz at this point led to a six-year furlough, a point at which it seems appropriate to lower the curtain on the jazz-rock era.

Like all new movements in the arts, it's usually the first flush of creativity that produces its greatest works. In the case of jazz-rock, its musical potential was gradually undone by recording company executives keen to cash in on bestselling albums by Miles Davis, Herbie Hancock, Chick Corea, Weather Report and the Mahavishnu Orchestra. They began casting around for artists deemed to have 'crossover appeal' and thus commercial potential at the expense of artistic integrity. In general, by 1975 the promise of jazz-rock had pretty much been undone by commercial ambition because the dominant non-jazz elements of the jazz-rock equation no longer came from the creative side of rock music, but from pop music with simple melodic hooks, a repetitious back-beat and easy-listening solos variously marketed as smooth jazz, quiet storm, lite jazz, hot tub jazz or yuppie jazz. Record companies, catering to a perceived demand for this slick, flawlessly executed instrumental candyfloss continued to crank out countless albums well into the 1990s. Sadly, this is what jazz-rock is usually remembered for and it has become fashionable to write off the whole genre as some ghastly aberration that should never have happened – trumpet player Wynton Marsalis and the writer Stanley Crouch were among the most vocal in expressing such sentiments during the 1980s and beyond – a classic case of throwing the baby out with the bathwater. Nevertheless, there is no denying that as a musical concept it eventually ended up obeying the laws of the marketplace – perhaps the inevitable price of jazz's dance with popular culture. Taking a music from the margins and marketing and mainstreaming it for wide popular acceptance is a continuous cycle enacted in the music business. Once jazz-rock entered this cycle it was inevitable that it would be diluted to serve the needs of populism, a dumbing-down process that has had countless parallels in pop music.

The 1980s Beckon

Jazz covered a lot of ground in a relatively short period of time during the 1960s and into the 1970s; for example, the classicism of John Coltrane's *A Love Supreme* from December 1964 was replaced by the energy and abstraction of his 'New Thing' experimentation within just twelve months, while Miles Davis, having taken jazz improvisation to the mountaintop on *Live at the Plugged Nickel* from December 1965, had changed direction by the end of 1968 and was experimenting with the electronic sounds and rhythms associated with rock music. Like American society itself, with the Civil Rights protests and anti-Vietnam war protests at their height, no one was quite sure where it would all end up. Just as the hope for a better society was dashed in the aftermath of the Watergate scandal that forced President Nixon to become the only serving US President to resign from office, so too jazz's hopes for a better future were dashed; *The Atlantic Monthly* magazine reflecting that, 'Jazz seemed dominated and diminished by rock-oriented fusion, marginalised by outré experimentation ... and disconnected from the youth audience that has driven American popular culture since the postwar era.'[202] Even more troubling was the absence of any major, coherent jazz movement waiting in the wings of the sort that had periodically re-energized jazz in the past when, for example, bebop swept aside the big bands, free jazz had challenged the certainties of everything that had preceded it, or the way jazz-rock took over jazz's centre ground in the late 1960s and early '70s. Perhaps unsurprisingly, many people began wondering whether jazz had run its course and all that was left was echoing and re-echoing the past.

Playlist for Change – and More Change

This playlist reflects major musical changes in jazz. These tracks have been selected to provide both an interesting listen and a broad overview of the events under discussion. Miles Davis features quite a bit here, since I am using him as a metaphor for the kind of changes that were occurring elsewhere in Jazz, as musicians attempted to find an accommodation with rock music.

1. Ornette Coleman: 'Ramblin'' from *Change of the Century*.
2. John Coltrane: 'Pursuance' from *A Love Supreme*.
3. John Coltrane: 'Ogunde' from *Expression*.
4. Miles Davis: 'If I Were a Bell' from *Cookin' at the Plugged Nickel*.
5. Miles Davis: 'Shhh/Peaceful' from *In a Silent Way*.
6. Miles Davis: 'Bitches Brew' from *Bitches Brew*.
7. Nucleus: 'Crude Blues Parts 1 & 2' from *Elastic Rock*.
8. Miles Davis: 'Right Off' from *Jack Johnson*.
9. Mahavishnu Orchestra: 'Birds of Fire' from *Birds of Fire*.
10. Weather Report: 'Birdland' from *Heavy Weather*.
11. Herbie Hancock: 'Chameleon' from *Headhunters*.

Listening Notes for the Change – And More Change Playlist

1. Ornette Coleman: 'Ramblin'' from *Change of the Century*

Recorded in October 1959, 'Ramblin'' opens *Change of the Century*, Coleman's fourth album (his second for the Atlantic label). Coleman was from Texas and no stranger to the blues, and 'Ramblin'' is infused with a blues feeling (to some ears this piece is not a stone's throw from early rock n' roll), but is not a traditional 12-bar blues. It works well: Coleman is the most effective soloist, and listening to this music today it is hard to imagine the controversy he caused in 1959.

2. John Coltrane: 'Pursuance' from *A Love Supreme*

'Pursuance' is part three of Coltrane's *A Love Supreme* suite dedicated to God and is a minor 12-bar blues, introduced by a drum solo by Elvin Jones before the exposition of the melody by Coltrane for two choruses. Then follows a dramatic, uplifting piano solo from McCoy Tyner; notice how he creates tension by moving away from the home key with phrases that sound angular and edgy. It's called 'sideslipping', or playing outside the chord change by subtly creating dissonance and thus tension. In his final chorus he ups the intensity to set the scene for Coltrane's entry; the saxophonist makes the most of it, ploughing into eighteen choruses of the blues at such force you can't help thinking this level of energy usually *climaxes* a solo. But Coltrane commands our attention by the sheer technical command of his instrument, using devices such as increasing the rhythmic intensity by implying double tempo, dubbed 'sheets of sound' by the American critic Ira Gitler. Elsewhere we hear Coltrane developing musical motifs, sideslipping and utilizing the rising line.

3. John Coltrane: 'Ogunde' from *Expression*

Here is a brief glance of Coltrane as he heads into New Thing territory. It dovetails nicely with the previous track where we heard both McCoy Tyner on piano and Coltrane sideslipping. Here he takes things a bit further out; it's only 3 minutes 36 seconds long, but you get an uneasy feeling that the notes they're playing are somehow wrong because of musical tension they create by their relationship to the underlying harmony. As discussed in the text, this marked the beginning of the final period when Coltrane went deeper into the free jazz New Thing and, as Coltrane's biographer Lewis Porter has noted, 'was into sheer sound – harsh shrieks and wails of wavering pitch that put him into the same camp as Albert Ayler (1936–70)'[203] – indeed, all the things guaranteed to give you iPod whiplash if one of his later period tracks comes up on your playback device's random shuffle. As Porter points out, Coltrane was interested in Ayler because he thought his approach 'was the next frontier, "beyond notes",[204] and into noise as a thing in itself.

4. Miles Davis: 'If I Were a Bell' from *Cookin' at the Plugged Nickel*

In 1965, the Miles Davis Quintet was still playing a collection of Standards that had not changed much since John Coltrane was in the band in the 1950s, but was approaching them from a very different perspective. 'If I Were a Bell' is a Standard the band had recorded in 1956 on the album *Relaxin' With the Miles Davis Quintet* and had become associated with Davis in live performance. The band's familiarity with it meant they began taking huge liberties in live performance. Listen to how Davis merely alludes to the melody after the 'bell-like' chimes in the piano intro and is quickly into his solo. Note too how rhythm is also messed about with, Williams constantly challenging the improviser (the beginning of Shorter's solo, for example). It was high-risk/high-gain stuff and required enormous ability to carry it off.

5. Miles Davis: 'Shhh/Peaceful' from *In a Silent Way*

As Davis historian Bob Belden points out,[205] 'Shhh/Peaceful' was a result of a studio jazz session that was edited to give shape to the performance. Davis' solo at 1:35 minutes into the performance is repeated at 13:31, which in effect bookends the middle section, giving the piece a rough and ready form – a beginning, a middle and an end! The subdued opening was recorded at the beginning of the session when the guitar (John McLaughlin) was tuning to the organ (Joe Zawinul) and was used again near the end to suspend the momentum of the piece and provide a sense of resolution. The result, after the tape surgery, is a surprisingly convincing foray into a new musical hybrid that mixed elements from popular culture (one can hardly say 'rock' in the instance of *In a Silent Way*) and jazz in a subdued yet aesthetically pleasing way. It promised much for the future.

6. Miles Davis: 'Bitches Brew' from *Bitches Brew*

No doubt about it, Davis plunged headlong into the electric jazz milieu with *Bitches Brew*, but strangely the album seems in no hurry to get anywhere and as it searches for a new jazz Jerusalem it defines its own mysterious process. Once again the result has been culled from studio jam sessions. The form is roughly AB, the A section strongly haunting and ominous with trumpet blasts as searing as a flashing neon sign that's answered by the ensemble. On the 'groove' B section, both Davis and Shorter show how they can sculpt solos of lasting beauty out of nothing – well, okay, a drone. As Davis would say in his autobiography, nothing was written down; it all had to come out of a process in the studio.

7. Nucleus: 'Crude Blues Parts 1 & 2' from *Elastic Rock*

In mid-1969 trumpeter Ian Carr formed Nucleus with the express aim of exploring a union between jazz and rock. When he recorded *Elastic Rock* in 1970 it was quite different to the loose, unstructured electric music of Miles Davis; although Nucleus stretched out in live performance, their repertoire was firmly compositionally based, acknowledging the blues but also metrically subdividing pieces into different sections and time signatures. 'Crude Blues' is a good example of their work, so too is '1916' from the same album, which is also worth checking out.

8. Miles Davis: 'Right Off' from *Jack Johnson*

The guitarist Jimi Hendrix exerted a profound influence on Miles Davis's music – 'Filles de Kilimanjaro,' for example, was based on the chords of Hendrix's 'The Wind Cries Mary' – but it was not until 'Right Off' that Davis confronted Hendrix's power and visceral impact. This is reflected in John McLaughlin's power chords, which created the context for Davis' solo. Here he eschews the brooding intensity that characterized the majority of his acoustic work with a solo that's as exuberant as it's expansive. Three days later, Davis recorded his first live album since the Plugged Nickel engagement in 1965, and *Black Beauty: Miles Davis at Fillmore West* saw his ensemble building on the textural density of *Bitches Brew* in extended electronic free jazz improvisations.

9. Mahavishnu Orchestra: 'Birds of Fire' from *Birds of Fire*

'Birds of Fire' is one of the great moments of early jazz-rock: the ominous gong that announces the piece followed by the entrance of John McLaughlin's overdriven guitar in a time signature of 18/8, then the statement of the theme in unison with Jerry Goodman's violin against the obsessive arpeggiated figures from Jan Hammer's keyboards all given greater impact by Billy Cobham's dramatic drum accompaniment. Note the power and drama of McLaughlin's guitar solo was inspired by the intensity of John Coltrane's playing. A year later their performance inspired arranger Don Sebesky to combine 'Birds of Fire' with extracts from Stravinsky's *The Firebird*, a juxtaposition that should have worked better, on his three-album set *Giant Box*. Mahavishnu communicated an intense virtuosity that even today conveys something of the shock of the new that so impressed audiences at the time. The form, despite the arching, loping time signature is AAB, with the A sections suggesting, albeit like a shimmering image glimpsed in a desert heat haze, elements of the blues.

10. Weather Report: 'Birdland' from *Heavy Weather*

Grammy-nominated for 'Best Instrumental Composition', it's easy to see why. 'Birdland's' sophisticated ad hoc form always seems to be leading somewhere new; full of catchy, hummable themes, it's hard not to join in, especially in the coda's repeated 8-bar sections when Jaco Pastorius's falsetto voice adds to the synth riffs. Composed by Joe Zawinul and orchestrated in a way that echoes the big bands (in this case the Maynard Ferguson Big Band of the 1950s of which a young Zawinul was a member when it played the Birdland jazz club), 'Birdland' put Weather Report well and truly on the map, reaching No. 30 on *Billboard*'s singles chart.

11. Herbie Hancock: 'Chameleon' from *Headhunters*

Composed by Herbie Hancock in conjunction with the members of his Headhunters band, the album track clocks in at 15:44, and is basically based on a two-chord vamp. The funky, hypnotic bass line, played by Hancock on an ARP Odyssey synthesizer, immediately catches the ear and has subsequently been widely sampled in DJ Culture, while 'Chameleon's' influence has extended beyond jazz into funk, soul and hiphop. The album, *Headhunters*, peaked at No.13 on the *Billboard 200*, becoming the bestselling album in jazz history up to that point (1973–4), and the first jazz album to receive an RIAA Platinum Award.

10

The Postmodern Paradox

We're All Leaders Now

The 1980s would turn out to be the first decade in jazz that wasn't associated with a major *new* style or movement. While it was a period of regrouping, reassessment and retrenchment, it was also a period of restless experimentation by a diversity of musicians pursuing new ideas and new ways of doing things. As we have seen in the past, jazz has been inexorably linked to the social fabric from which it emerged. In Reagan's America of the 1980s, just as in Thatcher's Britain, the dominant theme was 'small government', decentralization and extolling individual enterprise. 'There is no such thing as society,' said Thatcher, 'there are individual men and women.' In jazz, individual pianists, drummers, bass players, saxophonists, brass musicians, guitarists and vocalists were no longer content to play in other people's bands but now wanted to do their own thing. Jazz was unravelling in unexpected ways, not into new genres – like bop, hard bop, cool, free jazz, New Thing or jazz-rock – but in all the directions *individual musicians* wished to pursue. This was unsettling for those advocating the values centred around the 'jazz tradition'. Just as in politics, where many lamented the absence of a great visionary leader like a Roosevelt or a Churchill to give direction in the pluralistic times they lived in, so too in jazz, where many yearned for a Louis Armstrong or Charlie Parker to bring unity and direction to the music. But, as the writer Laurens van der Post reflected: 'I hear people everywhere saying that the trouble with our times is that we have no great leaders any more. If we look back we always had them. But to me it seems there is a very profound reason why there are no great leaders any more. It is because they are no longer needed. The message is clear ... Every man must be his own leader. He now knows enough not to follow other people.'[206]

Postmodernism Rears its Head

With the rationalization hindsight affords us, we can now see that the 1980s was a decade when certain key elements of post-modernism coalesced in jazz, suggesting it had entered a post-modernist phase. First was the fragmentation of jazz's master narrative, blurring distinctions between genres. Postmodernism is effectively a critique of grand narratives, arguing that there is no 'universal truth', or metanarratives as they are called, so the sheer diversity and plurality of jazz during the decade (and the decades that followed) placed the certainties of a jazz tradition under threat. Other characteristics of postmodernism that became apparent were, in no particular order: intertextuality, or the merging of genres and styles; that anything – no matter how wild – was considered jazz (adopting aspects of pop music such as turntable scratching or hiphop rhythms); that the traditional distinction between high and low cultures was eroded (the gods in the jazz pantheon and lesser names were considered by some equally worthy); style, no matter how ephemeral or fleeting, was preferred by some critics over substance and 'bricolage', or jazz constructed from a diverse range of styles, all contributed to a feeling that the centre was not holding and there was less need to look to it for a model of correctness.

Free Jazz reinvents Itself

It remains a truism in the arts that no artist can work outside the tradition because the tradition will eventually stretch to accommodate whatever artists do. In the case of free jazz this seemed broadly true in two ways as the 1970s gave way to the 1980s. First, many free jazz musicians began looking for areas of common ground with the jazz mainstream, seeking restraint after the perceived excesses of the New Thing and the extended solos and collective mayhem that had made the New York loft scene famous or notorious, depending on your point of view. Musicians adept at playing 'outside' preconceived harmonies began creeping 'inside' the chord changes, anticipating the 1980s stylistic regroupings. Having spent twenty years levelling the site, the time had come for rebuilding, and playing 'in the tradition', and 'intertextuality', however creatively interpreted or distorted, became a leitmotif of the 1980s and '90s.

Second, from the mid-1970s on, free jazz devices had begun cropping up in performances that would not otherwise be considered free jazz at all. This had a lot to do with the influence of Miles Davis's 'Second Great Quintet' in the mid-1960s and their use of 'time, no changes' (the principle Ornette Coleman introduced with Charlie Haden) which effectively sanctioned and inspired its use in non-free jazz contexts. Other elements of free jazz that were adopted by the mainstream were an occasional use of dissonance by sideslipping (something we heard on John Coltrane's 'Pursuance') and brief episodes of spontaneous interaction.

Saxophonist Arthur Blythe was one of the most passionate and lucid players to emerge from the avant-garde and was signed by Columbia records in 1979, making his debut with *Lennox Avenue Breakdown*. His subsequent work was split between two bands: In the Tradition, with piano, bass and drums accompaniment, and his guitar band with cello, guitar, tuba and drums. For a record-buying public who like their heroes plainly labelled, this was probably a mistake and by the time he realized his best shot with a major label was to concentrate on one band, Columbia had signed trumpeter Wynton Marsalis, who in 1981 achieved the kind of breakthrough widely predicted for Blythe.

Saxophonist Chico Freeman's reconciliation with the jazz mainstream came with *Spirit Sensitive* in 1979, but despite a run of fine albums, it was saxophonist David Murray, earning *Village Voice*'s 'Musician of the Decade' award in 1980, who captured the jazz media's attention. Working with an array of ensembles – duets, quartets, an octet and a big band – it was the albums he made between 1980–7 with his octet, *Ming*, *Home*, *Murray's Steps*, *New Life* and *Hope Scope*, that brought him most acclaim. But as work began drying up he moved to Europe in 1996 – initially to Paris, then Portugal – where his work continued to be as diverse as ever, ranging from projects with Macy Gray, the Gwo Ka Masters and his own Fo Deuk Revue.

A Prophet Looking Backwards – Wynton Marsalis

In 1981 George Butler of Columbia Records signed the twenty-year-old trumpet sensation Wynton Marsalis, explaining to *Newsweek*, 'I thought if I went after young artists at least that would pique the interest of kids.'[207] As a strategy to connect with college-age consumers, proven record buyers, it was largely successful, while older consumers were equally persuaded to buy his latest CDs to see what all the fuss was about. Marsalis's arrival in jazz, championing a return to an acoustic post-bop mainstream, was seen by many to be as timely as the arrival of the 7th Cavalry in the film *Destry Rides Again*. A young man equally at home in the European tradition of classical music – at the age of fourteen, for example, he had performed Haydn's Trumpet Concerto with a

Symphony Orchestra under the baton of Gunther Schuller – and jazz – at eighteen he took leave of absence from his studies at the prestigious Juilliard School of Music in New York to feature with Art Blakey's Jazz Messengers. With Columbia Records he became the first person to win simultaneous Grammies for a classical recording (*Trumpet Concertos*, a collection of trumpet concertos by Haydn, Hummel and Leopold Mozart) and a jazz recording (*Think of One*). Assigned the high-powered publicist Marilyn Laverty, whose clients included Bruce Springsteen, he became 'one of the most promoted jazz artists in the history of the idiom'.[208]

Columbia's success with Marsalis created a bandwagon effect among the major recording companies to sign similarly talented *wunderkinder*. 'There is no doubt there is copy-catting in the record business,' said Nathan Graves, former Head of Jazz at Universal UK. 'Companies see something working and say, "Let's take this direction."'[209] Soon young, photogenic jazz musicians in suits who played in the hard bop style of the 1950s and early 1960s began featuring in newspapers, style magazines and Sunday supplements, their initial success promoting *Newsweek* to observe it had 'Given the jazz-record industry a huge shot in the arm.'[210] A cynosure for a reborn jazz, Marsalis's artistry, youthful image, a penchant for sharp opinions and Cassius Clay I-am-the-greatest-isms – 'Everyone was saying jazz was dead but when they heard me they knew I was takin' care of business'[211] – seemed for some both a diagnosis and remedy for the problems they considered ailed jazz – it was a reaction against jazz for growing old (these musicians were, after all, youthful); it was a reaction against free jazz for having lost touch with an audience, and it was a reaction against fusion for having lost touch with the jazz tradition.

In the past, jazz's potential had often been expressed as a flight *from* the status quo. Marsalis and his followers who championed a return to a tradition-centred synthesis of earlier styles was, of course, the reverse of that, a flight *back* to the status quo, which the trumpeter was careful to present in the broader context of America's cultural heritage. However, if history teaches us anything it's that any return to a past tradition, whether it be music, art, literature or life, usually limits horizons rather than extending them. Movements define themselves by that which they exclude, thus to Marsalis and others who followed his example, the outsiders were the free jazzers, the jazz rockers and the non-tradition-based experimenters who became branded as exponents of non-jazz. As his fame grew, Marsalis consolidated a vision of jazz in conjunction with the writers Albert Murray and Stanley Crouch. Their interpretation of jazz was as much musical as it was ideological – dubbed neoconservatism in the jazz press – and when in 1987 Marsalis accepted the role as artistic adviser for a series of jazz concerts promoted by the Lincoln Centre of Performing Arts in New York City, he had a prestigious pulpit from which to preach what he believed jazz should be. He advanced this vision by separating the jazz sheep from the jazz goats to both controversy and success in what became known as the 'Jazz Wars' of the 1990s, when the pro and anti factions fought out their differences in the music press. Marsalis, Murray and Crouch argued that for jazz to be jazz, it must possess certain elements – most notably a blues sensibility and swing – that were present when jazz was a shared expression of black engagement with modern life. This was a new ball game altogether: a musician, in conjunction with two writers, was seeking to influence the future course of jazz through an idealized representation of the past.

This trend towards conformity coincided with jazz courses in academe to graduate level reaching an all-time high. The style of jazz that was taught in universities and conservatoires was in matchless synchronicity with the style of jazz that had become identified with the so-called 'Young Lions' that followed in Marsalis's wake. Educators such as David Baker, Jamey Aebersold and Jerry Coker had, by the 1980s, written exhaustive textbooks based on the methodology and techniques of jazz improvisation based on the quantifiable and analysable aspects of bop that were widely studied by students on jazz courses in colleges, universities and conservatories throughout the United States. They served to reinforce an underlying set of standards and a community of belief with shared ideas for training young musicians in achieving professional competence. The tenets of bop became the core of American jazz pedagogy, the means by which music theory was taught, rather than classical music. Bop was now institutionalized as the basic requirement for a musician to participate in jazz and tangible evidence of his or her instrumental and theoretical proficiency. The dichotomy of the 1980s and '90s was that many young American musicians, fresh from college and university, saw no need to attempt to extend the boundaries of jazz or even question them, as had happened in the past, because the prevailing jazz climate favoured the certainties and mechanical perfection of bop-based styles.

Miles Smiles, Again

Miles Davis was kept on a retainer by his record company (an honour only previously bestowed by Columbia on concert pianist Vladimir Horowitz),[212] during his six years' withdrawal from music between 1975 and 1981. During this period Columbia sought to offset their outlay by regularly releasing previously unreleased recordings from their vaults. These releases kept his name in front of the jazz public so that when news of his 'comeback' concert on 5 July 1981 at Lincoln Center leaked out, tickets sold out within two hours. Newswires around the world were soon buzzing, and the event became the most publicized jazz concert in history. Subsequently, Davis sought to capitalize on his celebrity with high-grossing tours across Europe, America and Asia, establishing himself as *the* must-see draw in jazz during the 1980s. Fans turned out in huge numbers wanting to celebrate a jazz legend who, if not quite returning from the dead, had at least returned from self-imposed exile. Paradoxically, the music was less important than the event. This became apparent with his first post-comeback album *The Man With the Horn* (1981). Davis had now returned to simple theme-solos-theme songs against a strong funk-rock backdrop, leavened with a bawdy dose of Hendrix-inspired guitar from Mike Stern. More cogent was the Grammy-winning *We Want Miles* (1982) and in November 1982 Davis began work on the album *Star People*, adding guitarist John Scofield to his band, whose disciplined, blues-based approach provided welcome contrast to Stern's flights. Critical reaction to these albums was mixed, with 1983's *Decoy* continuing this ambivalence. At the end of 1984, Davis recorded *You're Under Arrest* appropriating three tunes from popular culture: D Train's 'Something's On Your Mind', Cyndi Lauper's 'Time After Time' and Michael Jackson's 'Human Nature' that gave the crowds something to cheer in live performance, Lauper's 'Time After Time' becoming a personal lament by Davis on harmon-muted trumpet and a guaranteed crowd pleaser.

Davis's final album for Columbia records was *Aura*, his first recording with a large orchestra since his collaborations with Gil Evans in the 1950s. Davis considered it his latter-day masterpiece; Columbia didn't, the trumpeter having to secure funding from the National Endowment of the Arts to finish it. Although recorded in 1985, it was not released until 1989, when it won a Grammy. The episode brought to a head something he had been brooding over for a while. Given his long and distinguished career with Columbia, Davis had begun to feel miffed by the attention the label was lavishing on Wynton Marsalis. He resolved matters by moving to Warner Bros in what became the music media event of 1986. The dramatic Irving Penn photograph of Davis on the cover of *Tutu* announced his new affiliation, and from the opening bars of the title track he had the attention of the jazz world. Produced by bassist and multi-instrumentalist Marcus Miller and dedicated to the South African bishop, *Tutu* ended Wynton Marsalis's three-year reign as Grammy-winning Top Instrumental Jazz Soloist. It was a pity that Davis was not able to sustain the momentum of this album in subsequent releases.

In June 1991 he appeared as part of a double bill with B. B. King in the New York JVC Jazz Festival, the *New York Times* noting it was 'a particularly bad night' for Davis 'the problem seemed simple, Mr. Davis was incapable of sustaining more than a few notes at a time'.[213] In July, Quincy Jones persuaded Davis to confront his honourable musical past and recreate a selection of triumphs from the *Birth of the Cool*, *Miles Ahead* and *Porgy and Bess* albums on the occasion of the Montreux Jazz Festival's 25th Anniversary. *Miles Davis and Quincy Jones* suggests the music again came second to the event (billed simply as *L'Evenement*) with trumpeter Wallace Roney sharing the spotlight when Davis ran out of puff. Two days later, Davis appeared in Paris with musicians who represented certain phases of his career and on 25 August he played the Hollywood Bowl, one eyewitness account saying he looked and sounded frail.[214] One month later, on 29 September 1991, Davis died at St Johns Health Centre in Santa Monica, California. According to his doctor, Jeff Harris, in a statement released by the hospital, the causes were pneumonia, respiratory failure and a stroke. He was laid to rest with one of his trumpets in the Woodlawn Cemetery in the Bronx.

Davis's whole career had been one of musical reinvention; as one phase of jazz passed he looked around him and took stock of what was going on, but rather than substantially altering his playing style, he changed the musical backdrop by bringing in younger musicians in tune with the times – each time putting his own creativity on the line. Some of these transitions were difficult; after John Coltrane left it took him three years to find the right replacement, but when he did he entered a new period of creativity with the 'Second Great Quintet'. The distinction in his music was that as he transitioned from one phase to the next, the changes in his music often influenced change within jazz itself.

After his death, new Davis album releases continued unabated, just as they had done during his gap years between 1975 and 1981. Columbia embarked on an extensive reissue programme, often repackaging previous releases in expensively produced 'complete' box sets with all known takes. The reissue programme continued well into the new millennium, and almost twenty-five years after his death, in August 2015, a compilation of every known recording Davis made at the Newport Jazz Festival between 1955 and 1975 appeared as *At Newport: 1955–75*, entering the *Billboard* Jazz Chart at No. 2 and was prominently featured in newspapers and jazz magazines around the world. Miles may have died, but his music has not.

M-Base adds its voice

One musician who successfully rode the postmodernist tide in the 1980s was alto saxophonist Steve Coleman and his band Five Elements, whose music put into practice his somewhat arcane M-Base theories. 'I call my music M-Base because I figure I should have the right to name it,' he said in 1988.[215] The group debuted with *Motherland Pulse* that included a fine Cassandra Wilson vocal, followed by *On the Edge of Tomorrow* and *World Expansion*, but the impression was of an austere, rococo funk music. Nevertheless, M-Base became the critics' flavour of the month for, well, months. A thoughtful and articulate man, underneath the metaphysical theories (such as 'Melodic Material Generated by Symmetrically Derived Laws of Motion' or 'Harmonic Material Generated by Symmetrical Space')[216] was a shrewd musical mind, whose experimentation with metre, rhythm and form was quietly influential. Perhaps Coleman's best playing of this period could be heard during his time in bassist Dave Holland's ensemble – *Razor's Edge*, *Seeds of Time* and *Jumpin' In* – where he sheds the somewhat arty self-consciousness displayed with his own band to produce expansive and edgily exciting performances. By the early 1990s Coleman's music, deeply linked to his musical theories, ironically fell victim to one of the tenets of postmodernism – that the consumer creates the meaning of the text, not the creator, and that regardless of the deep meanings creators want their text to carry, if the audience does not 'read' them they become meaningless. As his audience drifted away, most of his musicians went back to more conventional styles of jazz, most notably the vocalist Cassandra Wilson, who developed her own highly individual approach (*Blue Light Till Dawn*, *New Moon Daughter*), but even though Coleman's audience had decreased, his M–Base collective evolved into an informal Coleman 'school' that espoused his theories in clinics and residencies for young musicians.[217]

The Downtown Scene

From the mid–1980s onwards, some of the most interesting, radical and exciting developments were centred around Downtown Manhattan, most notably in a venue called the Knitting Factory at 47 East Houston Street, just below Greenwich Village. Here two, three and even four groups nightly, who might never have had performance opportunities, began to get recognition. These groups were often highly experimental and non-genre specific, becoming known as 'Downtown Jazz' after the experimental Downtown classical music scene of the 1960s that produced Steve Reich and Philip Glass. Downtown jazz quickly assumed the cachet of a breaking underground scene and the best-known Downtown experimenters had, by the end of the 1980s, begun to acquire an international profile, such as alto saxophonists John Zorn and Tim Berne, drummer Bobby Previte, keyboard player

Wayne Horvitz and guitarist Bill Frisell. They all made some interesting albums; perhaps the most enduring today are John Zorn's *The Big Gundown* and *Naked City*; Bobby Previte's *Pushing the Envelope* and *Claude's Late Morning*; Wayne Horvitz's *Bring Yr Camera* and *Miracle Mile* and Bill Frisell's *Lookout for Hope*.

Jazz-Rock Becomes Electric

Following the Second Coming of Miles Davis, jazz-rock, now commonly dubbed 'electric jazz' to escape the connotations of jazz-rock excesses in the 1970s, began to be taken seriously. Ex-Miles Davis guitarist John Scofield formed a band in 1987 that was probably the finest of his career. Certainly his album *Blue Matter* was one of the better albums of the decade – all his band members–Robert Aires on keyboards, Gary Grainger on bass and the impressive Dennis Chambers on drums–collectively jumped into a groove and stayed there; this was neither commercial cop-out, 'fusion' or smooth jazz but solid, creative and intense music.

Guitarist Pat Metheny arrived during the tail end of the 1970s as a leader with The Pat Metheny Group which became, in jazz terms at least, hugely popular, built on assiduous touring and regular releases. A child prodigy, teaching guitar at the University of Miami at the tender age of seventeen and a faculty member of Berklee College of Music in Boston at nineteen, he came to prominence under the aegis of vibist Gary Burton. Debuting on the ECM label, a series of albums he recorded for the Geffen label were all Grammy winners, including *Still Life (Talking)*, *Letter from Home*, *The Road to You*, *We Live Here*, the excellent *Imaginary Day*, *Speaking of Now* and *The Way Up*. However, the significance of his music seemed to escape many critics, deeply suspicious of anything that even vaguely smacked of commercial success, an oversight that Mervyn Cooke's in-depth study *Pat Metheny: The ECM Years* (2016) sought to correct.

A New Acoustic Fusion?

Steps, a collaboration between tenor saxophonist Michael Brecker, vibist Mike Mainieri, pianist Don Grolnick, bassist Eddie Gomez and drummer Steve Gadd, was originally formed in 1979 and was quickly dubbed 'the new acoustic fusion'. Formed to play Seventh Avenue South, a club in Greenwich Village, New York owned by Michael and Randy Brecker, some one-off dates in Japan resulted in two albums – *Step by Step* and *Paradox* – for the Japanese Better Days label. After a further tour of Japan, they decided to commit to a regular group, changing their name to Steps Ahead. A one-of-a-kind ensemble that promised much for the future, *Steps Ahead*, their first album for an American label recorded in 1983, had Eliane Elias on piano and Peter Erskine on drums in for Grolnick and Gadd respectively. The album stood out for the sophisticated musicianship of all concerned and exemplary soloing by Elias, Mainieri and especially Brecker. *Modern Times* (1984) saw the group adopting the tone colours of electronic instrumentation with Brecker continuing to impress, both on saxophone and EWI (Electronic Wind Instrument). By then he was regarded as the most influential saxophonist since John Coltrane, but although he was well into his thirties, he still hadn't recorded under his own name, something quite unusual for a major soloist in jazz. He remedied this in 1987 with *Michael Brecker* and throughout demonstrates a mastery of the saxophone that set him apart from his peers. Although influenced by John Coltrane, he developed a style that built on Coltrane's achievements, both harmonically and technically, that continues to be widely admired (and imitated) by saxophonists. Today his work on *Michael Brecker* marks him out as the most important soloist to emerge in the 1980s and '90s. Brecker sadly died after a long illness in 2007.

Encoding Multiple Significances – the Emergence of ECM

In 1969, just as Blue Note was being swallowed up by the huge United Artists conglomerate, a tiny operation in Munich run by Manfred Eicher released its first jazz album by the American jazz pianist Mal Waldron. Eicher called his new company Editions of Contemporary Music, or ECM. From the outset, he paid scant regard to conventional notions of what was, or was not, considered 'commercial' or indeed, jazz. Thus the range of music he recorded is astonishingly broad, embracing not just American jazz but musicians with something to say from Europe, Scandinavia, South America, North Africa, India, Eastern Europe and, well, just about anywhere. From the very beginning, the ECM label had a vibe about it, be it the highly distinctive yet moody album art, the expensively packaged high-quality vinyl recording contained inside (or later, high-quality, high-resolution Compact Disc) or the enigmatic label motto, 'The most beautiful sound next to silence'. As the *Observer Music Monthly* put it, an ECM recording 'comes with an element of seductive difficulty – a sense that the effort of the listener will be both required and rewarded [is something] that can be peculiarly compelling, even addictive'.[218]

Emerging at a period in jazz history when the major recording companies were devoting most of their attention to rock and jazz-rock and neglecting jazz, ECM sought musicians with original ideas and approaches, emphasizing improvisation from the outset, with standard-setting recordings by Keith Jarrett, Paul Bley, Jan Garbarek, Chick Corea, Gary Burton, the Art Ensemble of Chicago and many more. Eicher responded to jazz with a European sensibility and one of the key albums of ECM's early period was *Afric Pepperbird*, the seventh ECM release, recorded in Oslo in 1970. Here Eicher introduced a saxophonist who would become one of the label's most enduring stars,

Norwegian Jan Garbarek. Together with fellow countrymen Terje Rypdal on guitar, Arlid Andersen on bass and Jon Christensen on drums, *Afric Pepperbird* had its roots in American free jazz, but nevertheless projected a specific European identity. 'After we recorded it we knew we had something special,' reflected Eicher. 'It was not in the way of American jazz, but was Scandinavian.'[219]

Eicher also encouraged musicians to record in a variety of performing situations, sometimes conceiving collaborations between American and European musicians who had never encountered each other, encouraging them to respond to the challenges of hearing different ideas in new musical surroundings by giving themselves to the music. 'There are many instances of this in our catalogue,' says Eicher. 'I think of *Solstice*, the recording with Ralph Towner – which to me is a classic recording in the early ECM days–with Ralph Towner, Eberhard Weber, Jon Christensen, Jan Garbarek. Then the recording with Egberto Gismonti and Charlie Haden, *Folk Songs* – these recordings were also based on a high risk, whether it would work or not.'[220]

An ECM Star – Keith Jarrett

Ever since its release in 1975, pianist Keith Jarrett's solo *Köln Concert* began selling in numbers not usually associated with a jazz recording. 'We had no idea it would be so big,' Eicher recalls. 'It just kept selling and selling.'[221] While the label had several albums that had sold well up to that point, the four-million-plus-selling *Köln Concert* helped broaden ECM's profile with the record-buying public. It also created a demand for more solo concerts of total improvisation from Jarrett, ECM documenting many of them including *Solo Concerts: Bremen/Lausanne*; *Sun Bear Concerts*; *Paris Concert*; *Vienna Concert*; *Radiance*; *The Carnegie Hall*

Concert; *London/Paris: Testament* and *Rio*. Each album is totally different, each one revealing yet another facet of this remarkable improviser's invention. In 1977 he revisited an earlier collaboration with Jan Garbarek, which produced the critically acclaimed *Belonging* with Palle Danielson on bass and Jon Christensen on drums, by recording *My Song* that proved equally influential and the group toured together for the first time that year. Their final tour took place in 1979 and produced a further three albums. Taken together with *Belonging* and *My Song*, the live albums *Nude Ants*, *Personal Mountains* plus the 2012 release *Sleeper*, prompted Jarrett's biographer Ian Carr to claim they 'take the art of the classic jazz quartet to its highest pinnacle'.[222] As Eicher himself has pointed out: 'In the case of Keith Jarrett and Jan Garbarek, their recordings were incredibly influential as far as a lot of musicians in America were concerned, and I do not regret that I did take the risk to make the attempt to bring these musicians together.'[223]

In 1983 Jarrett embarked on a new venture, the formation of a piano trio with bassist Gary Peacock and drummer Jack DeJohnette. After the success of his solo concerts, Jarrett, it seemed, was missing interaction with other musicians – in fact he abandoned solo concerts for the next three years. The trio's first endeavours were recorded in January 1983 at New York's Power Station studio. As the Swiss writer Peter Rüedi has noted: 'From the very beginning Jarrett emphasised two imperatives: they must take the standards seriously, as great if unrecognised art on a small scale, and they had to do so from an up-to-date and radically improvisational vantage point.'[224] With *Standards Vol. 1* and *Standards Vol. 2*, 'The Standards Trio' emerged onto the world stage, building a substantial discography on the ECM label including *Standards Live*, *Standards in Norway*, *Tokyo '96*, *Whisper Not*, *Still Live*, *Inside Out* and *Always Let Me Go*. Widely regarded as one of the finest contemporary piano trios in jazz, the group was finally wound up by mutual consent in 2015.[225]

ECM Becomes a Major Voice

By the end of the 1970s, ECM's roster of talent had begun to draw major critical acclaim. In 1979 the label earned the first of many Grammy Awards with *In Concert – Zurich, October 28, 1979* by Chick Corea and Gary Burton with the duo earning another Grammy in 1981 for *Duet*. Countless awards would accumulate over the years,[226] and in 1994 the label scored a major commercial success with Jan Garbarek's *Officium* with the Hilliard Ensemble, an early-music vocal group. Sales exceeded two million, and the album was described by novelist Marius Gabriel as 'What Coltrane hears in heaven.'[227] Although Jarrett and Garbarek were undoubtedly major artists for ECM, Eicher also played a significant role in developing the careers of many of his artists, not least guitarist Pat Metheny: 'I think he was a really quite remarkable artist when he was starting with ECM,' says Eicher. 'We did a recording with him, Jaco Pastorius and Bob Moses called *Bright Size Life*.'[228] In 1977, Metheny formed The Pat Metheny Group, and the albums that followed on ECM helped establish Metheny as a major jazz artist: *The Pat Metheny Group* (1978), *American Garage* (1978), *Offramp* (1982) that produced the label's third Grammy Award, *Travels* (1983) and *First Circle* (1984). 'I'm still proud of the records we made in the early time of Pat Metheny,' reflected Eicher.[229]

At the end of the 1970s, former Miles Davis drummer Jack DeJohnette emerged with a group called Special Edition that was both a reflection and commentary on the late 1970s and early 1980s alignment of freedom with the tradition – *Special Edition* (1980), *Tin Can Alley* (1981), *Inflation Blues* (1983) and *Album Album* (1984). The latter is especially worthy of note, with DeJohnette's deft compositional and arranging skills rejecting 'open-ended' soloing, focusing instead on creating a balance between solo ingenuity and compositional wisdom. 'In the late '70s and early '80s when we made these records, it felt like an open time,' reflected DeJohnette in 2012. 'There was a lot more room to reach for new things than there would be later in the 1980s, when the scene got more predictable.'[230]

TEN MUST-HAVE ECM RECORDINGS

1. Keith Jarrett: *Personal Mountains*
2. Charlie Haden: *Ballad of the Fallen*
3. Kenny Wheeler: *Angel Song*
4. Jack DeJohnette: *Album Album*
5. Tomasz Stanko: *Soul of Things*
6. Jan Garbarek: *Dis*
7. Bobo Stenson: *War Orphans*
8. Keith Jarrett: *Köln Concert*
9. Charles Lloyd: *Fish Out of Water*
10. Pat Metheny: *First Circle*

ACT RECORDS — A MAJOR INDEPENDENT JAZZ RECORD LABEL

Described by *The Guardian* newspaper as being a 'strong contender for the same podium' occupied by other legendary jazz independents such as 'Blue Note, Riverside, Impulse! or ECM', ACT is a 'Munich based based independent with a striking house style'. Founded by Siegfried 'Siggi' Loch, its first success came in 1992 with the double Grammy nominated *Jazzpaña* featuring saxophonist Michael Brecker with arrangements by Vince Mendoza. Since then the label has won countless awards and has helped further the careers of many important young European jazz musicians, most notably the late Esbjorn Svensson, pianist Michael Wollny, Nils Landgren, bassist Lars Danielsson and Leo Tolstoy's great, great granddaughter, vocalist Viktoria Tolstoy. It has also focussed the attention of the jazz world on some of the striking young jazz talent to be found in Germany with its Young German Jazz series. Born in 1940, Loch, who formerly enjoyed a glittering career in the record business culminating in a top executive role in Warner Bros. once said, 'My only regret is why I waited so long to be the oldest new independent owner in the business.'

Today, with a catalogue of well over a thousand releases, ECM continues to command the collective ear of the jazz world. In 2015, ECM released *Break Stuff* by the pianist Vijay Iyer, born in Albany, New York and the son of Indian Tamil immigrants. In many ways the album could stand as a metaphor for the musical diversity the label stands for, touching base with the American jazz tradition with compositions by Thelonious Monk, John Coltrane and Billy Strayhorn but also incorporating influences from West African drumming, South Indian mridangam-playing, Brooklyn hiphop and Detroit techno.

The Postmodern Paradox

With the onset of the 1990s, jazz was in a classic postmodern paradox. Wynton Marsalis was clinging to modernist values that, as he saw it, were being violated by the crass pluralism of the present. With the 'master narrative' of jazz fracturing into a series of decentred forms, he turned to the continuity of values embedded within the jazz tradition. His was a modernist position based on eighteenth-century Enlightenment values rooted in the truth and in Marsalis's case, the truth lay in the primacy of the jazz tradition. Postmodernism, however, is generally regarded as a rejection of, or dissatisfaction with, modernity, arguing that there's not one truth but many, a multitude of cognitive and cultural perspectives each of equal validity. However, although modernism is contested by postmodernism, it is nevertheless deeply dependent on it in the way all oppositions are to what they oppose. Thus Marsalis's rationality of a 'purist' vision of jazz coexists alongside the postmodern condition in jazz where a decentred multiplicity of strands are becoming harder to contain in safe categories.

The postmodern paradox was that one could not do without the other; on the one hand the modernist jazz mainstream had tradition, history and an air of permanence that matched conventional notions of musical culture. It was here the roots of jazz resided, the source from which the diverse branches of jazz grew. On the other hand, postmodernism's multiplicity of different 'versions' of jazz supported the notion that jazz is as much about the present as it is the past; that it was not a historical endeavour – such as Renaissance or Baroque music in the classical music field – but a music in flux whose continued evolution had relevance to the here and now. Nowhere was this more apparent than in the world outside the United States, where, in the early millennium years, it was becoming apparent that the interaction between globalized American jazz and local cultures was fracturing into even more hybridized forms whose approaches were differentiated by location. It was here, in the Global Village – to borrow Marshall McLuhan's term[231] – where some of the most interesting developments in jazz were now occurring.

The 1980s and into the New Millennium Playlist

This playlist stretches from the beginning of the 1980s to the new millennium years, a period that saw the fragmentation of jazz into countless multicoloured shards that produced countless albums documenting a trend so broad that it is impossible to properly represent it in a playlist such as this. However, what it is possible to do is highlight some of the more interesting developments that might inspire the reader to embark on their own voyage of musical discovery into jazz of this period.

1. Arthur Blythe: 'Miss Nancy' from *Illusions*.
2. David Murray Octet: 'Train Whistle' from *New Life*.
3. Wynton Marsalis Quartet: 'Knozz-Moe-King' from *Live at Blues Alley*.
4. Miles Davis: 'Human Nature' from *You're Under Arrest*.

5. John Zorn: 'Latin Quarter' from *Naked City*.

6. John Scofield: 'Blue Matter' from *Blue Matter*.

7. The Pat Metheny Group: 'Minuano (Six Eight)' from *Still Life (Talking)*.

8. Steps Ahead: 'Pools' from *Steps Ahead*.

9. Michael Brecker: 'Sea Glass' from *Michael Brecker*.

10. Wayne Shorter Quartet: 'Footprints' from *Footprints Live!*.

11. The Zawinul Syndicate : 'N'awlins' from *World Tour*.

12. Keith Jarrett: 'New Dance' from *Nude Ants*.

13. Jack DeJohnette Special Edition: 'Ahmad the Terrible' from *Album Album*.

14. Tomasz Stanko: 'Soul of Things I' from *Soul of Things*.

Listening Notes to The Postmodern Paradox Playlist

1. Arthur Blythe: 'Miss Nancy' from *Illusions*

This example of Blythe's 'In the Tradition' band succeeds in conveying something of the edginess of his playing normally reserved for his more avant-garde performances. In many ways it's a classic example of building tension and deferring release; during Blythe's exposition of the composition we are waiting for the metre to open out into a hard swinging 4/4 time. It never quite comes, cleverly deferring our expectations until pianist John Hicks emerges swinging hard, a musician well capable of raising the temperature in any surroundings.

2. David Murray Octet: 'Train Whistle' from *New Life*

Here Murray's ensemble indulges in what postmodernists call 'intertextuality', the merging of genre styles – in this case the avant-garde with the spirit of the Duke Ellington Orchestra.

Ellington's band hired their own Pullman car for their tours that criss-crossed apartheid America of the 1930s. There is something innately romantic about a train journey, evoking thoughts of the lonesome whistle as it crosses the prairie and the rhythmic sound of the wheels on the track. It inspired Ellington to write pieces such as 'Lightnin'', 'Daybreak Express', 'Track 360', 'Happy Go Lucky Local' while his theme song, 'Take the A Train', was written by his protégé Billy Strayhorn. Murray evokes the spirit of these Ellington compositions in this programmatic performance, which is both tribute and personal statement.

3. Wynton Marsalis Quartet: 'Knozz-Moe-King' from *Live at Blues Alley*

Here his playing surges with energy, spontaneity and sophisticated rhythmic interaction between band members Marcus Roberts on piano, Robert Hurst on bass and Jeff Watts on drums. 'Knozz-Moe-King' appears in four versions on the album *Live at Blues Alley*; I prefer the first. It's a theme plus 'time, no changes' piece with Marsalis revealing a rhythmic and tonal intensity with a gusto that's quite compelling.

4. Miles Davis: 'Human Nature' from *You're Under Arrest*

Michael Jackson's 'Human Nature' came as a relief from the fairly thin material Davis had used on his previous four albums. Yes, 'Human Nature' largely followed Jackson's presentation of the song, but its anthem-like opening on keyboards and Davis's harmon-muted meditation that followed proved hugely popular in live performances. For a new, younger generation of fans, 'Human Nature', together with 'Something's On Your Mind' and 'Time After Time', became as important to them as 'Round Midnight' or 'My Funny Valentine' were to previous generations of fans.

5. John Zorn: 'Latin Quarter' from *Naked City*

With John Zorn, alto saxophonist and arch New York 'Down-town' musician John Zorn, jazz goes postmodern with a venge-ance. This abrupt collision of ideas – blues, surf guitars, film noir moods, country music and short, sharp shocks of rebarba-tive noise – is what postmodernists call 'bricolage', a mixture of seemingly incongruous elements creating a matrix of internal relationships where there is no fixed configuration, thus destroy-ing the traditional organic unity of a work of art. It was these Information Age sound bites from alien cultures decontextu-alized by juxtaposition that created the 'new' in Zorn's music. In 'Latin Quarter' bricolage is used to programmatic ends – it's as if Zorn is walking through the Latin Quarter, capturing the competing sounds as he walks past a restaurant, a deli, a liquor store, a bar and a raucous club.

6. John Scofield: 'Blue Matter' from *Blue Matter*

'Blue Matter' opens with a loping bass line that had become asso-ciated with Miles Davis during Scofield's time as a sideman in his band. It's contrasted by an 8-bar B section featuring the startling semi-quaver bass drum figures of Dennis Chambers before return-ing to the mysterioso opening section. Throughout, Scofield's horn-like guitar figures seem to wrench meaning from his instrument suggesting the emergence of an important soloist in his own right.

7. The Pat Metheny Group: 'Minuano (Six Eight)' from *Still Life (Talking)*

Metheny compositions have an orchestral quality with his use of voices and thickly voiced fret and keyboard ensemble colours. His compositions unfold with steadily evolving logic – Metheny calls this 'the trip factor' – and *Still Life (Talking)*, while draw-ing on electronic and acoustic instruments as in previous PMG albums, adds wordless vocals as an additional tone colour within the ensemble. By now, Metheny had begun to take account of the minimalist composer Steve Reich, especially in terms of rhythmic complexity and the use of a marimba – for example, the marimba obstinato that emerges to dramatic effect on this piece brings to mind impact the instrument had when it entered towards the end of Reich's *Drumming*. For all Metheny's increasing compositional sophistication (and it has to be said that in jazz, compositional theme and development broadly remains a relatively under-exploited resource), he is not afraid to make melody and rhythmic complexity work for him, as he does here.

8. Steps Ahead: 'Pools' from *Steps Ahead*

'Pools', written by Don Grolnick, captures the elegant poise of Steps Ahead. The form employs a simple AAB structure (the A sections 20 bars and B section 14 bars). Note that during Mainieri's solo Erskine moves from accompanist to play a prominent role alongside the vibes. Although the piece is in straightforward 4/4 rhythm, the rhythm section doesn't adhere to the traditional swing feel, and towards the end of Brecker's final solo a back-beat emerges which prompted critics to dub their music 'the new acoustic fusion'.

9. Michael Brecker: 'Sea Glass' from *Michael Brecker*

'Sea Glass' opens with haunting electronic tone colours of Kenny Kirkland's keyboards suggesting a 3/4 pulse, with Brecker's anthem-like exposition of the melody implying a rubato feel (it is not) above drummer Jack DeJohnette's cymbal and drum cascades. As DeJohnette and bassist Charlie Haden move into a flowing 3/4, Brecker's long legato lines give way to an increasing density of notes while reaching further and further up into the higher registers of his saxophone (a device we examined on

George Coleman's solo on 'They Say It's Wonderful') before a recapitulation of the theme.

10. Wayne Shorter Quartet: 'Footprints' from *Footprints Live!*

To understand where Shorter's coming from on the recordings he made with his quartet between 2002 and 2013, it's necessary to return to Miles Davis's *Cookin' at the Plugged Nickel* (see Chapter 9's playlist) as this is a continuation of the 'time, no changes' principles they explored. 'Footprints' was first recorded by Shorter on his 1966 album *Adam's Apple*[232] and more famously by Miles Davis on the 1966 album *Miles Smiles* (when Shorter was a member of his quintet) when it became a jazz standard. A modified minor 12-bar blues played against a 6/4 rhythm, there is an elusive, angular quality about the theme which Shorter exploits during his solo, while his accompanists – Danilo Perez on piano, John Patitucci on bass and Brian Blade on drums – each play musical epigrams in response, so taking the music in directions that – as you'll hear from the vocal responses to the music by the band members during the performance – surprise even themselves.

11. The Zawinul Syndicate: 'N'awlins' from *World Tour*

It took a while for Joe Zawinul to define the sound of the Syndicate, his earlier attempts on the Columbia record label lacking a cohesive group sound. Zawinul persisted, off and on, and by the mid-1990s he defined a sound with a group of musicians at one with his ideas – groove-based compositions within which he would spontaneously reorder form and cue solos. When this recording was made in 1997, the Zawinul Syndicate was the hottest band on the jazz circuit and in this tribute to birthplace of jazz, New Orleans, he uses a rhythmic figure made famous by New Orleans R&B bands like The Meters, Professor Longhair, The Neville Brothers and more. It's funky, and Zawinul and the band dig in with some infectious yet powerful playing.

12. Keith Jarrett: 'New Dance' from *Nude Ants*

Like the sinuous violin that links the movements of Rimsky-Korsakov's *Scheherazade Op. 35*, representing the voice of Scheherazade telling the stories of the *One Thousand and One Nights* to the Sultan, Jarrett is a musical storyteller, his playing unique and immediately identifiable. If you listen carefully you'll notice there are no clichés or gratuitous flourishes in his playing, rather he is concerned with melodic development and although this can sometimes be angular and gritty, it's also probing and questing. He's in great form on this joyous romp with his European Quartet – Jan Garbarek on tenor sax, Palle Danielson on bass and Jon Christensen on drums. Garbarek's playing here during the statement of the theme and in his solo (notice how Jarrett drops out, leaving it up to the saxophonist, bassist and drummer to carry the energy forward) is elegant, balanced and authoritative, with his powerful tone making each note memorable.

13. Jack DeJohnette Special Edition: 'Ahmad the Terrible' from *Album Album*

With *Album Album* from 1984, Jack DeJohnette created a classic. With David Murray on tenor sax, John Purcell on alto sax, Rufus Reid on bass and Howard Johnson on baritone sax and tuba, DeJohnette brought the full weight of his talent as a drummer, pianist, composer, arranger and bandleader to bear. Thanks to multi-tracking, DeJohnette shows what an accomplished pianist he was, and reining in the freer impulses of Murray and Purcell to fit the compositional structure of 'Ahmad the Terrible' – a tribute to the pianist Ahmad Jamal – the result is both powerful and majestic and grows and grows on you with each listening.

14. Tomasz Stanko: 'Soul of Things I' from *Soul of Things*

In many ways *Soul of Things* provides an answer to a question jazz fans have been debating since 1959. The question is simple: What album do you play after Miles Davis's *Kind of Blue*? The answer is less simple. Davis's album consumes the space around it, blotting out the memory of albums played before it and diminishing the effect of those played after. Yet when *Soul of Things* follows *Kind of Blue* there's no sense of disjunction, since it sustains *Kind of Blue*'s mood of quiet introspection without seeking to imitate it. Stanko, who lives in Warsaw, began his career five years after Stalin's ban on jazz in Poland was lifted in 1961, saying, 'Jazz was like freedom for us, the opposite of communism.'[233] Different though *Kind of Blue* and *Soul of Things* are, there is perhaps a commonality that lies deep beneath the surface of the music. The intensely felt emotions of the Afro-American musicians in apartheid America of 1959 that helped shape the former perhaps share something with the intensely felt emotions of Stanko which helped shape the latter. Davis experienced things in apartheid America and Stanko things in communist Poland that both preferred not to talk about. But to both Davis and Stanko jazz represented freedom, and this rings clear in the music.

11

Jazz in the Global Village

Jazz Goes Global

Jazz went global as soon as the first jazz recording – the Original Dixieland Jazz Band's 'Livery Stable Blues' – was released in April 1917, thanks to a sophisticated distribution network across the Western world established in the years before World War I. It meant that audiences in America and around the world could hear this startling new music without having to go to the nightclubs and dance halls of New Orleans, Chicago or New York to experience it; they could listen to it in their own living rooms. In fact, in the early years of jazz's development most people's first encounter with the music was via the gramophone. As jazz history evolved inside America, the globalization of the music through recordings meant it was acquiring other histories in other countries. What's interesting today is the remarkably similar way the music has been absorbed into the cultural and artistic life of quite different countries and cultures. At first the appeal was confined to the social function of the music – dancing, partying – but then serious fans began engaging more deeply with the music, often forming discussion groups, known as Rhythm Clubs or Hot Clubs. At the same time local musicians took their first tentative steps towards playing jazz by listening to recordings over and over and imitating what they heard. Local bands soon developed that attracted local crowds, creating a demand for the 'real thing': American jazz musicians. Finally, hybridity occurred when local musicians adapted the music to suit their social and cultural concerns by introducing local elements such as folk music, their classical music or local pop music, which in turn produced new meanings in local contexts, so giving the music greater relevance to its own community.

How the Global Becomes the Glocal

In the world of business, the interaction of the global with the local is a well-known outcome which is regarded as an inevitable bi-product of globalization. Local outcomes can occur in social, political, economic, cultural, artistic and commercial activities and in all forms of globalized media. In business circles this is called 'glocalization', meaning the interaction of a global product with the local consumer. You only have to think of how the modest Italian pizza has been localized, or glocalized, internationally: Japan has a sushi pizza, Bankok has a Thai pizza, Lebanon has a mezze pizza, and so on. Or the McDonald's hamburger chain adapting its products to local culinary traditions by serving a Big Mac with brie cheese in France or sauerkraut in Germany. I coined the use of the word 'glocalization' in jazz to describe the interaction between globally transmitted American jazz and local culture[234] simply because the word neatly describes a process that has steadily been gaining influence for decades as globalization became an increasingly powerful agent of social, cultural, economic and industrial change. In his book *The World Is Flat*, the three times Pulitzer Prize-winning journalist Thomas L. Friedman speaks of how, thanks to globalization, the world is taking on a distinctly American hue with a proliferation of 'American brands and American moviemakers, American singers and entertainers, American clothing designers and American fast-food chains'[235] which are contributing to a flattening, or a 'homogenizing of culture'. Clearly, cultural convergence is readily apparent to us all with shopping malls, skyscrapers, American fast-food retailers, American business practices, American cars, American beauty products and nail bars so common in cities around the world they barely warrant a mention. Thus glocalization can also be a *reaction* to globalization, a way of contesting the false universalism it implies as national and cultural values come under threat by the removal of trade barriers to encourage closer economic, industrial, technological and cultural convergence between countries. This effectively diminishes the importance of national borders, yet it's surprising how deeply our self-conception and self-perception is related to nationality. For example, at international sporting occasions such as the Olympic Games you only have to see the reaction of athletes standing on the winner's podium as their national anthem is played for evidence of this. We are more proud of our national and cultural heritage than we like to think. Here, glocalization can – and does – emerge as an expression of this, an assertion of local identity within the global and a way of preserving a degree of cultural autonomy in an increasingly homogenized – some may argue Americanized – world.

How does Glocalization Occur in Jazz?

For glocalization in jazz to take place, 'local' jazz musicians need to have become fluent in playing American jazz – in other words have a thorough understanding of the rules of the game. The glocalization process itself is then most commonly achieved by integrating local folkloric, pop or classical influences that reflect local identity. When we look a bit closer at this process we see that glocalization actually breaks down into a series of unique encounters, each culturally specific, explained in terms of local, social and cultural context where local musicians seek to create original music that is both part of a universal language of jazz and an individual expression of their own unique local, social and cultural identity. For example, in Sweden, the early 1960s album *Jazz pår Svenska* by pianist Jan Johansson took twelve traditional Swedish folk songs from the national collection of folk songs *Svenska låtar* and with just a bass accompaniment, gave precedence to the strong melodic content of each song and supported it with discreet, yet sophisticated jazz improvisation. Today it's the bestselling jazz album in Sweden, surpassing American jazz classics such as Miles Davis' *Kind of Blue*, John Coltrane's *A Love Supreme* or Dave Brubeck's *Time Out*, because local audiences and consumers generally find it easier to identify with *local* values, attitudes and customs. Thus *Jazz pår Svenska* emerges as a perfect example of glocalization – a *local* musician playing melodies taken from his *local* culture that have meaning to his *local* community – demonstrating how local values usually transcend those that come from a global source.

DJANGO REINHARDT – AN EARLY EXAMPLE OF JAZZ 'GLOCALIZATION'

The earliest example of the emergence of glocalization in jazz was the formation of Quintet of the Hot Club in Paris on 2 December 1934. Star of the quintet was guitarist Django Reinhardt, who integrated guitar techniques from his Manouche gypsy heritage into jazz improvisation. Together with violinist Stéphane Grappelli, they suggested that American jazz was not devalued or did not somehow become 'inauthentic' just because it reflected a 'local' cultural component (in this case elements taken from the Manouche gypsy folkloric tradition). Reinhardt is now credited with creating a viable subgenre of the music called *jazz manouche*, or gypsy jazz, a significant glocalized dialect of the music that can still be heard today in France and Belgium and by its adherents around the world. For example, since 2000, New York's Birdland jazz club has been host to the annual Django Reinhardt NY Festival where musicians from all over the world gather and demonstrate their prowess in playing in the Jazz Manouche style.

However, the glocalization of jazz is not an exclusionary process; glocal jazz musicians can perform American jazz in 'the American way' in some contexts and a glocalized, or localized version of American jazz in other contexts. Once again we turn to Sweden for examples of this – pianists Jan Johansson and Bobo Stenson once both played in bands led by leading American saxophonists: Johansson with Stan Getz in the 1960s, and Stenson with Charles Lloyd in the 1990s. In each case, they played in a forthright, swinging style we associate with much American jazz, but when they came to define their own music, they played in a glocalized, or local style, incorporating Swedish folkloric and classical influences (as we saw earlier with Johansson's *Jazz pår Svenska*). In the case of Stenson's association with Lloyd in the 1990s, we have a series of ECM albums with which to contrast and compare his globalized American style with his glocalized local style. Stenson's participation in the Charles Lloyd Quartet is documented on *Fish Out of Water*, *Notes From Big Sur*, *The Call*, *All My Relations* and *Canto* recorded between 1990 and 1997. 'You can say with Charles [Lloyd], this is "traditional American music,"' explained Stenson. 'It's a way of playing he likes, and I guess I understood what he wanted, quite literally, and I guess that's why he liked to play with me, and I liked to play with him. We had great concerts, I think.' However, referring to a series of exemplary piano trio recordings under his own name – *Reflections*, *Serenity* and *War Orphans* recorded between 1993 and 2000 – he says, 'With my trio it is different, we don't have to speak to the [American jazz] tradition, we are not bound to it like the Americans because that's their music and the way they are supposed to play their music, I think. We play in the language of American jazz but I guess we put other things into music. We have other traditions here [in Scandinavia], more from classical music and folk music and stuff, and I guess we put that into the thing more than "Traditional American Jazz". More important, we don't need to play the "American way"; we can leave that and come back to it. It allows you to take the music in new directions. That's the difference, we are more free.'[236]

The spread of glocalized jazz is analogous to language: English might be an international lingua franca, but English speakers around the world do not necessarily follow the rules of grammar and syntax used by English speakers in the United Kingdom. For example, Spanglish in the United States, which is predicted to become the majority spoken language there within fifty years; Singlish in Singapore; Franglais, a kind of Euro-speak that derives more from EU bureaucracy than real life; and countless 'local' versions of English, such as Swedish-English, Netherlands-English, Brazilian-English, and so on, where people speak English in a local way because of the influence of their mother tongue, which shapes the English language in different ways. Similarly, if we say jazz is an international musical lingua franca, it does not necessarily follow that jazz musicians around the world play jazz the same way Americans play it, because localizing elements have been introduced, such as folk music. In each case, in language and in music, the lingua franca breaks down into hybridized – or glocalized – forms on a country-by-country basis.

The Nordic Tone

The Nordic Tone is for some an elusive concept because of an absence of a precise definition, but broadly speaking it's a less-is-more approach to jazz adopted by many (but by no means all) Scandinavian musicians; a kind of understated Nordic blues. Norwegian pianist Tord Gustavsen reflects on the concept: 'It's fair to say many of the projects making up what perhaps is natural to label "typical", or more profiled, Nordic jazz, have a taste for minimalism, a taste for space and a taste for speaking with what lies between the notes [spaces] – that's something that many of us share to a larger extent than jazz that comes from other parts of the world.'[237]

In the 1950s, the Swedish baritone saxophone player Lars Gullin was one of the first to awaken the notion of a Scandinavian approach to jazz by turning to his folkloric heritage and Swedish classical composers such as Wilhelm Peterson-Berger and Hugo Alfrén. Trumpeter Bengt-Arne Wallin's *Old Folklore in Swedish Modern* and Jan Johansson's *Jazz på Svenska* gave further momentum to this notion. Johansson's approach was enormously influential among Scandinavian musicians – in contemporary times pianists such as Tord Gustavsen, Esbjorn Svensson, Jan Lundgren, Martin Tingvall and Helge Lien are among many Scandinavians who have taken account of Johansson in their approach to jazz piano.

From the 1970s, the Norwegian saxophonist Jan Garbarek came to personify what might be called a contemporary version of the Nordic Tone in jazz. In his early years Garbarek evolved a formidable saxophone technique derived from listening to Dexter Gordon and later John Coltrane (and to an extent Albert Ayler); in other words he was thoroughly versed in the rules of the game, but he subsequently became more interested in the saxophone *tone* as the main expressive force of the instrument rather than the exploitation of technique. While he was open to a wide range of influences, it was the incorporation of local elements specific to his own culture into his music – from ambient sounds (his 1976 album *Dis* was recorded with a wind harp), to folkloric themes (herding songs, lullabies, mountain calls and rowing chants, many of which are still extant in Norway) and native Sami songs – that were most influential in shaping his aesthetic. As he said in an interview with *Downbeat* magazine: 'What I see as a major force in this music [is] we have players from any part of the world now doing their own, shall we say, native version. They find their own direction, influenced by their own culture, but still using the strong basic elements of jazz.'[238]

Afro-Cuban Jazz

Afro-Cuban jazz is probably the most famous local dialect of jazz, despite emanating from within the borders of the United States. It originated at the hands of trumpeter Mario Bauza, who emigrated from Cuba to New York in 1925 to record with Antonio María Romeu's band after playing for three years in the Havana Symphony Orchestra. Once in New York he decided to pursue a career in jazz, becoming musical director of the Chick Webb and Cab Calloway bands, and it was with Calloway that he began thinking about combining the power of the American big bands with the exuberance of Cuban rhythms, contributing pieces such as 'Chili Con Conga', 'Rhapsody in Rumba' and 'Goin' Conga'.

In 1941, he left Calloway to form Machito's Afro-Cubans, a big band fronted by his brother-in-law Francisco Raúl Gutiérrez Grillo, who adopted the stage name Machito. Here Bauza was able to refine his ideas for creating a fusion of jazz and Afro-Cuban music. In 1943 Machito was called up for military service and Bauza took over the band during his absence. It gave him the opportunity of combining jazz and a Latin rhythm called the *clavé* on a piece called 'Tanga', making it what is generally accepted as the first performance of genuine Afro-Cuban jazz. The style was adapted by Dizzy Gillespie in his big band on numbers such as 'Manteca' and 'Cubana Be, Cubana Bop'. Gillespie's involvement effectively ushered Afro-Cuban jazz into the jazz mainstream, where other band leaders such as Woody Herman ('Bijou' from 1945), Charlie Barnet ('New Redskin Rhumba' 1946) and Stan Kenton ('Machito' from 1947, 'Cuban Episode' from 1950) helped establish it as a viable subgenre of jazz. In more contemporary times bands led by Ray Barretto, Eddie Palmieri, Mongo Santamaria, Chico O'Farrill and his son Arturo are among many who have continued the vibrant Afro-Cuban jazz tradition.

The African Connection

In South Africa of the 1930s, American big band records began reaching the main urban centres such as Johannesburg, Durban, Port Elizabeth and Pretoria and from there the tribal districts, where the music of the black bands like Ellington and Basie proved to be hugely popular. Township jazz emerged as an enduring and recognisable local variant of big band jazz, combining *marabi*, the oral tradition of African songs adapted by South African jazz instrumentalists with the sound of the American big bands. With the emergence of bebop, brass instruments had the effect of modernizing this tradition in the 1950s, which consolidated a style that still exists today in the hands of bands like the Jazz Pioneers. International jazz stars emerged from this tradition, such as pianist Dollar Brand, who changed his name to Abdullah Ibrahim and who was initially championed by Duke Ellington, trumpeter Hugh Masekela and vocalist Miriam Makeba. American big band recordings were also reaching West African countries such as Ghana where another local variant called Highlife emerged, inspired by big band question-and-answer riffs. Highlife quickly spread to Nigeria and Sierra Leone, where electric guitars were added to the mix to give the music greater rhythmic punch and popular appeal.

Brazil Adds Colour

In Brazil, Acácio Tadeu de Camargo Piedade, Professor of Music at the State University of Santa Catarina, has pointed out that when a Brazilian jazz musician solos, 'there are moments when he gives himself frankly to bebop, seeking the weight of the jazz tradition that gives him legitimacy and confers on him the symbolic status of global improvisor; but at the same time he tries to express something more Brazilian [or local], making use of other Brazilian genres, such as the *chorinho*';[239] the *chorinho* is a Brazilian popular music genre that often has a fast and happy rhythm and is characterized by virtuosity and improvisation. There are a huge variety of rhythms in Brazil, many derived from the samba, that have swept across the world since the 1930s. After the samba, probably the most popular is the bossa nova, which incidentally is derived from the samba and has come to personify Brazil to the rest of the world. Early on, local musicians such as Sergio Mendes combined the samba rhythm with jazz on songs written by the likes of Antonio Carlos Jobim and João Gilberto. Subsequently, musicians such as Laurindo Almeida, Charlie Byrd and Stan Getz were influential in popularizing the bossa nova in the USA, Getz especially successful with bestselling albums such as *Desifinado*, *Jazz Samba* and *Getz / Gilberto*.

Glocal Goes Global

Pianist Danilo Pérez is a gifted pianist from Panama who had the opportunity to perform with Dizzy Gillespie and his United Nation Orchestra from 1989 until the trumpeter's death in 1992. Pérez later noted that, 'One of the things Dizzy taught me was to learn about my own heritage even more than I knew already. He said it was more important for jazz for you to get to what your roots are, than to learn about other things'[240] – a clear signpost to the glocalization of jazz if ever there was one. Pérez duly obliged: his debut for the Impulse! label was the critically acclaimed *Panamonk* from 1996, which reflected the influence of his native Panama on a series of Thelonious Monk compositions – a fine example of the global and local coexisting alongside each other to produce something fresh and new.

In the United Kingdom, a feeling prevailed well into the 1950s that for jazz to be jazz, it had to be played 'the American way', a view that for some continues to the present day. This began to change for the majority in the 1960s when the

Vietnam war caused a crisis of conscience among many European musicians, causing them to question American values. In the United Kingdom, British jazz began a process of self-discovery, as Trevor Bannister observes in the introduction to pianist Michael Garrick's autobiography *Dusk Fire: Jazz In English Hands*: 'In the twentieth century British jazz was that [which was] played by British musicians putting the American ethos before everything else. By contrast, English jazz emerged with the culture and historical heritage of England foremost in mind. Michael Garrick was arguably the first to give expression to it.'[241] This can initially be heard in the Ian Carr/Don Rendell Quintet, where trumpeter Ian Carr and pianist Michael Garrick contributed compositions intended to reflect a home-grown component, and later in work under Garrick's name, such as a series of classic albums including *October Woman*, *Promises*, *Black Marigolds*, *The Heart Is a Lotus*, *Cold Mountain*, *Home Stretch Blues* and *Troppo* that consciously reflected Garrick's English heritage, so producing a glocalized approach to the music, as he later acknowledged.[242] Garrick was not alone, later writing: 'All the wonders that the great American prototypes so gloriously exhibited were no longer enough. What began to surface and receive delighted attention were those doing something fresh and home grown.'[243]

Bandleader Mike Westbrook was another musician working along similar lines – *Celebration*, *Release*, *Marching Song*, *Metropolis* and *Citadel/Room 315* – saying, 'One had to be very strong in one's convictions to question American orthodoxy and to work on developing an independent voice.'[244] These were sentiments that found consensus amid a broad cross section of musicians of the period, from free jazz musicians such as Trevor Watts of the Spontaneous Music Ensemble: 'In the '60s we reacted against the jazz music scene here, and the fact you were compelled to play like an American or not at all'[245] – to vocalists such as Norma Winstone: 'I worked in the 1970s with, shall I say, a lot of original voices in jazz in England, they were trying to do their own thing that felt right to sound English and not be so influenced by the Americans.'[246] It was a feeling that was also echoed by established British jazz stars such as bandleader Johnny Dankworth, who told *Melody Maker* magazine in 1963: 'I think ... musicians [should] say, "We will have a British style" and do something about it. I think that is tremendously important.'[247] Notable Dankworth albums from this period that practised what he preached include *What the Dickens!* (1963) a series of themes inspired by characters from the novels of Charles Dickens, *Zodiac Variations* (1964), *The Million Dollar Collection* (1967) and *Lifeline* (1974).

How Important is Glocalization?

Outside the United States, many musicians do not feel the degree of connection to the jazz tradition American musicians feel, arguing that the best people who play in the 'American tradition' are Americans themselves. They don't want to become copyists, but instead contribute something original to the music they love by bringing elements of their own culture into the jazz mix. This trend towards glocalization represents a major evolutionary shift in jazz since these various hybridized, or glocalized, forms of jazz contain properties that are not present in American jazz, and it is these differences that are attracting attention in a music that has shown no significant evolution since the 1970s. The following represents some examples of glocalization from around the world; it is by no means a definitive listing and is intended as a starting point for the reader to seek out examples of glocalized jazz in the global jazz scene for themselves.

The more you begin looking for examples of glocalized jazz the more you keep finding them – Jewish jazz musicians both inside and outside the United States introducing *klezmer* influences in their playing; jazz musicians from the former Yugoslavia incorporating Balkan folk themes with their complex rhythms,

EXAMPLES OF GLOCALIZED JAZZ FROM AROUND THE GLOBE

Argentina: Incorporating tango influences (tango is the national dance of Argentina).

Armenia: Pianist Tigran Hamasyan bringing elements of ancient Armenian folk music from the collection of the Armenian priest and musicologist Komitas Vardapet (1869–1935).

Austria: Jazz musicians incorporating *yodel* influences.

Azerbaijan: Jazz musicians incorporating *mugham* (local folkloric) influences such as Aziza Mustafa Zadeh and Shahin Novrasli.

Finland: Jazz musicians taking inspiration from the poetry of the *Kalevala*, the Finnish national epic that has been a major source of national self-esteem in Finnish culture and art since it was first published in 1835, influencing Finnish classical music (such as Sibelius's *Kullervo*), jazz and popular music.

France: During World War II France was cut off from American jazz and a localized form of jazz emerged in a 'French tradition' which has continued to evolve to this day.

Greece: Greek jazz musicians inspired by composers such as Míkis Theodorakis and Yannis Markopulo who incorporate *Eneknho* (Greek orchestral music using folk music) in their music.

Holland: Dutch jazz musicians have long incorporated large swathes of robust humour (an acquired taste!).

Hungary: Hungarian jazz musicians are using elements of Gypsy music (just as Bartok before them used similar influences in classical music) and Transylvanian folkloric themes.

India: Indian jazz musicians using elements derived from ragas and Carnatic singing styles.

Portugal: Portuguese jazz musicians incorporating *Fado* influences.

Phillipines: Philippine jazz musicians incorporating *Gamelan* influences.

Spain: Spanish jazz pianists in Barcelona are using elements of *Flamenco* in their music.

such as the pianist Bojan Zulfikarpasic – well, you get the point. Start doing your own research, and see how many imaginative reconceptualizations of jazz in local settings you can discover.

These changes are occurring in jazz now. It's an exciting time to be following jazz with new sounds and new ways of doing things just waiting to be discovered.

The Global Jazz Playlist

This playlist is intended to illustrate the effects of localization – or glocalization – of jazz that has followed the globalization of the music since 1917. It is not intended to be a complete list, nor should it be read as such. It merely seeks to illustrate how glocalization is producing unique outcomes in different geographic areas. Use this playlist to provide an aural understanding of localized – or glocalized – jazz by hearing the ways in which glocalized jazz differentiates itself from American jazz, yet retains certain aspects in common with it. Remember, this is just a starting point for the musically curious to begin their own journey into glocalized jazz and jazz itself.

1. Django Reinhardt: 'Minor Swing' from *The Django Reinhardt Anthology.*
2. Michael Garrick: 'Troppo' from *Troppo.*
3. Mike Westbrook: 'Awakening' from *Celebration.*
4. Jan Johansson: 'Visa från Utanmyra' from *Jazz går Svenska.*
5. Jan Garbarek: 'Lokk' from *Dansere.*
6. Gilad Atzmon: 'Al Quds' from *Exile.*
7. Jazz Jamaica: 'Bridge View' from *Skaravan.*
8. African Jazz Pioneers: 'Hellfire' from *African Jazz Pioneers.*
9. Tamba 4: 'O Morro' from *We and the Sea.*
10. Danilo Pérez: 'Panama Blues' from *Central Avenue.*
11. Michael Wollny: 'Phlegma Fighter' from *[em] live.*
12. Esbjörn Svensson Trio: 'From Gagarin's Point of View' from *From Gagarin's Point of View.*

Listening Notes to the Global Jazz Playlist

1. Django Reinhardt: 'Minor Swing' from *The Django Reinhardt Anthology*

What was striking about the Quintet of the Hot Club of France – and 'Minor Swing' is a typical example – was that they sounded quintessentially European at a time when everyone else in jazz sounded quintessentially American. The implication was clear – you didn't have to 'sound' American, or indeed *be* American, to play authentic jazz, as the astonishing virtuosity of Reinhardt, who died on 16 May 1953 at the age of forty-three, eloquently demonstrated. Reinhardt's virtuosity was all the more remarkable since a caravan fire as a young man (he was a Manouche gypsy) left the third and fourth fingers of his left hand – his fretboard hand – paralysed. You can watch a six-minute film of him called *Le Jazz Hot* – or *Jazz Hot* – online. It's the only known sound film of Le Quintette du Hot Club de France, from 1938. Reinhardt's disability is plain to see, but when the film cuts to an onstage performance of 'J'Attendrai' by the Quintette, Django's third improvised chorus is stunning. It's climaxed by a run, seemingly impossible for *any* guitarist, never mind a guitarist with just two fully functioning fretboard fingers.

2. Michael Garrick: 'Troppo' from *Troppo*

Troppo is for me one of Garrick's finest works, with a line-up that might be regarded as a best of British: Norma Winstone, voice; Henry Lowther on trumpet; Art Theman, Don Rendell on saxes and flute; Garrick on piano; Dave Green or Coleridge Goode on bass; Trevor Tompkins on drums. The title track was written by bassist Green as a tribute to Norma Winstone. The piece is loosely an AB structure with transitionary passages; the loping bass figure that underpins the A (longer) section is in 13/8, which changes to 13/4 under the (shorter) B section. Winstone's voice is used as an 'instrument' within the ensemble passages before taking an improvised, wordless vocal 'solo' on the A section. Trumpet, tenor and flute comment and add counterpoint before the piece decreases in volume and as it does it changes key. When you can barely hear the ensemble (is this a fade finish?) they return on the B section, the way prepared earlier by the key change, before a recapitulation of the A section.

3. Mike Westbrook: 'Awakening' from *Celebration*

How appropriate the title; this is indeed an awakening of British jazz. Recorded in the summer of 1967, it's Westbrook's debut as a bandleader on recording. It came at a time when a feeling was coursing through young British jazz musicians that you didn't have to sound American for jazz to be jazz. As Westbrook later observed: 'There was something in the air in the 1960s. Everybody loved the jazz that came out of America, but when we came to play it ourselves, it came out somehow differently ... British jazz musicians came at jazz from a different angle.'[248]

4. Jan Johansson: 'Visa från Utanmyra' from *Jazz per Svenska*

On 'Visa från Utanmyra' Johansson is the model of restraint, and with just Georg Riedel on bass, he allows the folkloric melody to speak for itself; one Swedish journalist described it as 'a rural symbol of security in a Sweden which in the '60s was marching towards anonymous, big-city wildernesses.'[249] Johansson captured a unique sound in jazz that's come to be known as the Nordic Tone.

5. Jan Garbarek: 'Lokk' from *Dansere*

Discussing *Dansere*, recorded in 1975, Garbarek told *Jazz Review* he considered it 'a breakthrough point for me, in trying to find the material I feel most at home with'.[250] That material was traditional Norwegian folkloric themes. 'Lokk', written by Thorvald Tronsgård, offers quite specific local, or 'glocal' characteristics and we are reminded by the liner notes that 'space is paramount'[251] in Garbarek's playing. This is very apparent from his opening clarion call, where he exploits the tone of his saxophone with a kind of poetic grandeur that is inflected by blues, yes, but a blues that's not shaped by black America, rather by a different place and a different kind of pain that is closer to a shipwrecked man shouting helplessly after a distant ship. Together with Bobo Stenson on piano, Palle Danielson on bass and Jon Christensen on drums, they convincingly demonstrated great jazz could be produced in the Old World too, and it didn't have to sound American.

6. Gilad Atzmon: 'Al Quds' from *Exile*

There can be no mistaking where the localizing, or glocalizing, elements of this performance come from, immediately evoking the Middle East. Listen how Reem Kelani's vocal uses melismatic pitch slides during the introduction, echoed by Atzmon on alto saxophone, to produce characteristics we associate with music from the Middle East. Then, having established the glocal elements, Atzmon's alto saxophone solo gradually assumes characteristics we associate with the global influence of John Coltrane. He is later followed by Frank Harrison on piano emulating the McCoy Tyner role (from the original 'classic' Coltrane quartet), so binding the global and the local into a convincing whole.

7. Jazz Jamaica: 'Bridge View' from *Skaravan*

If your first reaction to this piece is, 'Ah, reggae – Jamaica', then you're half right; take a look at the album's title. The difference between ska and reggae may be subtle and nuanced, but reggae tends to be slower and more laid back, while ska is brighter and punchier – as 'Bridge View' eloquently demonstrates. It's the product of first – and second-generation Jamaican immigrants to the UK reflecting *their* culture influences and the music *they* were brought up with, within jazz. 'Bridge View', originally by the Skatalites, has an energy and authenticity that's compelling. There is nothing intrinsically Jamaican about the solos, solidly in the jazz idiom, it's a 12-bar blues, but the rhythmic climate unmistakably derives from the local.

8. African Jazz Pioneers: 'Hellfire' from *African Jazz Pioneers*

South African township jazz is instantly recognizable as a global jazz dialect; its infectious rhythm makes you want to tap your foot, snap your fingers and get up and dance because this music is functional – it's dance music. Township jazz emerged as a recognizable glocal variation of American jazz that evolved out of the oral tradition of African folk songs passed down the ages and adapted by South African jazz instrumentalists. This early musical confluence of the global (big band jazz that had been copied from American jazz records) and the local was originally called *marabi*.

9. Tamba 4: 'O Morro (The Hill)' from *We and the Sea*

Perhaps the most famous and certainly *the* most recognizable of all the glocal variations of jazz comes from Brazil. Tamba 4 was a group immersed in the rhythms and harmonies of Brazil that date back four centuries to the time when the cultures of the African slaves and Portuguese missionaries began mingling with that of the Brazilian Indian. The musical outcome was an exotic mixture of the melancholy airs of Brazil with the insistent, structured beat from Africa and the loose, Moorish melodies of Portugal. The music of north Brazil is sometimes, and confusingly, called Afro-samba. It is darker in hue than bossa nova, more sombre, more gutsy. 'O Morro' tells of the hopes and fears of the shanty town community around Rio de Janeiro. It's an eight-minute tour de force of Brazilian-influenced jazz and the hypnotic rhythms of the samba. It's an example of how Brazilian musicians demonstrate their 'technical know-how and mastery of the jazz language, which symbolically is a passport to global communicability, but at the same time ... [pointing] ... to the need for dissolving bebop itself and expressing what distinguishes it from Brazilian jazz, that which is nearer to a root of Brazilian musicality and therefore more authentic'.[252]

10. Danilo Pérez: 'Panama Blues' from *Central Avenue*

Taking a field recording of folk singer Raul Vital from the Panamanian countryside, Pérez then built 'Panama Blues' around his singing in a New York recording studio. Here the virtual presence of Vital's voice allows Pérez to weave a fantasia of the global (hints of the American swing feel) and local (the Afro-Cuban *tumbao*) in this remarkable performance. In 2010 he reflected on the local elements in his music, saying, 'For me in my role as a musician, as a player of my music, I have explored a lot of the Spanish influences on [Panamanian] music ... I have used things from people singing on the street that are public domain, and I have worked with those, to create the essence of this community. I have taken a rhythm called *Tamborito*, very related to Panama, which means "a little drum" ... and I have used that rhythm a lot.'[253] In 2002 Pérez became a member of the Wayne Shorter Quartet, considered at the time by many to be the leading acoustic group in jazz, and it was fascinating to hear him bring a Latin (or glocal) influence to many of his solos with the group.

11. Michael Wollny: 'Phlegma Fighter' from *[em] live*

[em] live was recorded at JazzBaltica in July 2010, and numbers among the finest jazz albums of the previous quarter of a century. [em] – a trio comprising Michael Wollny on piano, Eva Kruse on bass and Eric Schaefer on drums – had refined a way of playing that has connected with contemporary audiences, as Wollny explained: 'The concept was to play it quite short and just make one atmosphere, one statement on one composition and make it as deep as possible, don't waste any "words" or "licks" or "phrases", make a really deep artistic statement.'[254] First recorded by the trio in 2005, this live version sees the written form quickly give way to inspired interaction and some breathtaking playing by Wollny. What is interesting is that while other European cultures often drew on their folkloric heritage as a localizing – or glocalizing – element, such a course was not available to German jazz musicians as the Nazis had used folk tunes for propaganda purposes during the 1930s and '40s, thus their use in German society today is frowned upon. As a result, many German jazz musicians (by no means all) draw on the influence of German classical music and modern European composers, such as Witold Lutosławski, as a localizing component.

12. Esbjörn Svensson Trio: 'From Gagarin's Point of View' from *From Gagarin's Point of View*

Probably the most important band to break into jazz during the early millennial years until his untimely death in a scuba-diving accident in 2008 was the Esbjörn Svensson Trio, or e.s.t.

as it later became known. Led by charismatic Swedish pianist Svensson, a piano virtuoso who had studied classical music at Stockholm's Royal College of Music and played in rock bands before establishing himself as a jazz pianist (winning the Swedish Jazz Musician of the Year award in 1995 and 1996), the trio made their breakthrough outside Sweden with this, their 1999 album *From Gagarin's Point of View*. From that point on they quickly became one of the most popular jazz groups in Europe, and were making significant inroads into the American market – they were the first-ever European band to feature on the cover of the American jazz magazine *Downbeat* – with a style that mixed a kind of Nordic Blues – or Nordic Tone – with subtle rock influences. Svensson was a very lyrical pianist, taking inspiration from Jan Johansson (the album *From Gagarin's Point of View* even opens with a similar bass figure to that which opens Johansson's 'Visa från Utanmyra'), Bill Evans and Keith Jarrett certainly, but he developed a highly individual style that has become a model for a younger generation of pianists around the world.

Acknowledgements

I'd like to thank those who kindly read early drafts of this book for their helpful advice, suggestions and corrections. Also to the countless musicians and commentators I have spoken to over the years who have helped shape my thoughts on jazz. Ultimately, however, an undertaking such as this depends on getting your head down and writing, a lonely task that needs an understanding and supportive wife, to whom this book is dedicated (as it is to my 'secretary' – our dog Gwladys). Once a book is written it then passes to an editor, and it has been my privilege to have worked with one of the best in the business in Shadi Doostdar, whose unfailing good humour, positive vibes, constructive suggestions and professionalism have given shape to the mountain of words she was originally confronted with. To her my extreme gratitude and thanks.

Stuart Nicholson, Woodlands St Mary, Berkshire.

January 2017

Visit Stuart Nicholson's website: stuartnicholson.uk

Notes

1   Donald Sassoon, *The Culture of Europeans: From 1800 to the Present* (London: Harper Press, 2006), p. 935.

2   Walt Whitman, 'I Hear America Singing', written in 1867.

3   The equivalent to the gap across five white notes in the upper middle section of a piano (octave five) see: Rossitza Dragnova, 'Serial Magnetoencephalographic Study of Foetal Newborn Auditory Discriminative Evoked Responses', *Early Human Development*, Vol. 83, pp. 199–207: www.earlyhumandevelopment.com/article/S0378-3782(06)00162-9

4   Carolyn Granier-Deferre, 'A Melodic Contour Repeatedly Experienced by the Human Near-Term Foetuses Elicits a Profound Cardiac Reaction One Month After Birth', PLOS ONE:www.plosone.org/article/info%3Adoi%2F10.1371%2Fjournal.pone.0017304

5   Gary Marcus, *Guitar Zero: The Science of Learning to be Musical* (London: Oneworld, 2013), p. 32.

6   Emmanuel Bigand and Barbara Poulin-Charronnat, 'Are We "Experienced Listeners"? A Review of the Musical Capacities That Do Not Depend on Formal Training', *Cognition*, 100, pp. 100–30.

7   Emmanuel Bigand, 'Abstraction of Two Forms of Understanding Structure in Tonal Melody', *Psychology of Music*, 18, p. 45.

8   Bigand and Poulin-Charronnat, *Cognition*, 100, pp. 100–30.

9   For example, by the end of 2014 it was estimated Apple had sold over 390 million iPods.

10 Adrian C. North, David Hargreaves and Jon J. Hargreaves, 'Uses of Music in Everyday Life', in *Music Perception*, Fall 2004, Vol. 22, No. 1, p. 72.

11 Ibid., p. 74.

12   Ibid., p. 75.

13   For example, 'When's the Last Time You Really Listened to an Album?' *Guardian*, 27 February 2008 and 'Is the Album Dead?', Edward Helmore, *Guardian,* 2 November 2013.

14   Helmore, 'Is the Album Dead'?

15   Daniel Levitin, *This Is Your Brain On Music* (London: Atlantic Books, 2008), p. 108.

16   W. J. Dowling, S. Kwak and M. W. Andrews, 'The Time Course of Recognition of Novel Melodies', *Perception & Psychophysics*, Vol. 57, Issue 2, 1995, pp. 197–210.

17   R. W. S. Mendl, *The Appeal of Jazz* (London: Philip Allan & Co. Ltd,1927), p. 186.

18   F. Scott Fitzgerald, 'Echoes of the Jazz Age', *Scribner's Magazine*, Vol. XC, Vol. 5, November 1931, pp 459–64.

19   Howard Goodall, *Big Bangs: The Story of Five Discoveries that changed Musical History* (London: Vintage, 2001), pp. 84–5.

20   According to *The Village Voice*, only thirty percent of Americans have passports: http://blogs.villagevoice.com/runninscared/2011/02/only_30_percent.php, and only thirteen percent travelled abroad in 2013–14 according to Fox News: /www.foxnews.com/travel/2014/08/28/americans-not-leaving-country-during-holidays-study-says/

21   Ivan Hewett, 'São Paolo Symphony Orchestra, Royal Albert Hall', *Daily Telegraph*, 26 August 2016, p. 23.

22   Ashley Ropati, 'Uri Caine: In Dialogue With Music History', www.stuff.co.nz/entertainment/78084857/uri-caine-in-dialogue-with-music-history, 21 March 2016.

23   'The Beginner's Guide Blues', lyrics by Stuart Nicholson.

24   Kenny Burrell *Midnight Blue* (Blue Note), 'Chitlins Con Carne' is the first track of an album well worth including in any collection of jazz.

25   Dan Morgenstern, quoted in Mel Tormé, *Traps the Drum Wonder: The Life of Buddy Rich* (London: Mainstream Publishing, 1991), p. 120.

26   Alec Wilder, *American Popular Song: The Great Innovators 1900–1950* (New York: Oxford University Press, 1972), p. 252.

27   Here's a few more examples of the 32-bar AABA form: 'Over the Rainbow', 'Blue Moon', 'Lady Be Good', 'September Song', 'Ain't

Misbehavin', 'Makin' Whoopee', 'Lullaby of Birdland', 'Take the A Train', 'The Four Brothers', 'Don't Get Around Much Anymore', 'Jordu', 'What's New', 'I Cover the Waterfront', 'Don't Blame Me' and 'Body and Soul'.

28   There are a few rare examples of AABA songs where the B section is the same melody as the A section, such as 'What's New?'. Here the B melody has been lifted into a different key, or pitch (up four notes) to become 'the middle eight'. Since it's a device that's not been too overdone it can be quite effective – go to iTunes and audition 'What's New?' by Linda Ronstadt and listen to the A melody shift upwards, unchanged, to become the B section.

29   For example: 'Jumpin' at the Woodside' and 'Miss Thing' both recorded by Count Basie, 'Cotton Tail' recorded by Duke Ellington, 'Apple Honey' and 'Northwest Passage' recorded by Woody Herman, 'Salt Peanuts' recorded by Charlie Parker and Dizzy Gillespie, 'Straighten Up and Fly Right' recorded by Nat King Cole, 'Oleo' recorded by Sonny Rollins, 'Rhythm-a-Ning' recorded by Thelonious Monk, 'Wail' recorded by Bud Powell and 'Hoe Down' recorded by Oliver Nelson – and this is only a partial list!

30   Keith Jarrett, interview with author, 27 August 2011.

31   Lewis Porter, *John Coltrane: His Life and Music* (Ann Arbor: University of Michigan Press, 2001), p. 196.

32   A haiku is a traditional form of Japanese poetry consisting of 3 lines. The first and last lines of a haiku have 5 syllables and the middle line has 7 syllables. The lines rarely rhyme.

33   See Alec Wilder, *American Popular Song: The Great Innovators 1900–1950* (New York: Oxford University Press, 1972), p. 190, 'A perfect song'.

34   *Independent Information Magazine*, 4–10 December 1999, p. 4.

35   *Guardian*, '1000 Albums to Hear Before You Die Volume 2', 19 November 2007, p. 5.

36   Robert Palmer, liner notes, *Kind of Blue,* Columbia/Legacy CK64935, p. 13.

37   For example, Krin Gabbard, *Hotter Than That: The Trumpet, Jazz and American Culture* (New York: Faber and Faber Inc., 2008), p. 192.

38   Setting a benchmark in recorded sound that influenced the German record producer Manfred Eicher in his approach to recorded sound on his ECM label.

39   A distinctive hollow metal mute held in the bell of the trumpet by a cork collar, so forcing the air through the mute and altering the sound of the trumpet to produce the highly distinctive tone heard here and on 'All Blues' and 'Flamenco Sketches'.

40   Bill Evans, liner notes to *Kind of Blue* Columbia CL 1355.

41   Kevin McSpadden, 'Now You Have a Shorter Attention Span Than a Goldfish', *Time*, 14 May 2015.

42   Ted Gioia, 'Five Lessons the Faltering Music Industry Could Learn From TV', *Daily Beast*, 3 August 2014.

43   At its most basic, the blues uses only three chords that correspond in our example to the colours, black, grey and white.

44   Paul F. Berliner, *Thinking in Jazz: The Infinite Art of Improvisation* (Chicago: University of Chicago Press, 1994), p. 201.

45   Sonny Rollins, interview with author, 10 September 2009.

46   For example, Elon University's Imagining the Internet Center and the Pew Research Center's Internet & American Life Project, 2012 Report, www.elon.edu/e-web/predictions/ expertsurveys/2012survey/future_generation_AO_2020.xhtml

47   *The New Yorker*, 31 July 1995, p. 16.

48   Vincent Pelote, liner notes, *The Complete Roost Johnny Smith Small Group Sessions*, Mosaic MD8-216, p. 4.

49   Dean Pratt, liner notes, *Big Swing Face* (Pacific Jazz 7243 8 37989 2 6).

50   'The Joy of a Genius', NPR, 19 September 2007, www.npr. org/2007/09/19/14501602/erroll-garner-the-joy-of-a-genius

51   Coda means the section which brings a piece to its conclusion.

52   Peter Van Der Merwe, *The Origins of Popular Style* (Oxford: Oxford University Press, 1989), p. 63.

53   Ibid., pp. 277–86.

54   'Paris Has Gone Rag Time Wild', *San Francisco Chronicle*, 10 June 1900.

55   Gunther Schuller, *Early Jazz* (New York: Oxford University Press, 1968), p. 32.

56   Larry Gushee, liner notes, *Steppin' On The Gas: Rags to Jazz 1913– 1927* (New World NW 269), p. 1.

57 www.pbs.org/jazz/biography/artist_id_bolden_buddy.htm

58 See Alan Lomax, *Jelly Roll Morton: The Complete Library of Congress Recordings* (Rounder 1161-1888-2 DG01 and DG02), an eight-CD set.

59 Gunther Schuller, *Early Jazz* (New York: Oxford University Press, 1968), pp. 142–3.

60 Ibid., p. 144.

61 Ibid., p. 140.

62 Ted Gioia, *The History of Jazz* (New York: Oxford University Press, 1997), pp. 20–1.

63 Marshall and Jean Stearns, *Jazz Dance: The Story of American Vernacular Dance* (New York: Da Capo, 1994), p. 24.

64 Larry Gushee, liner notes, *Steppin' on the Gas: Rags to Jazz 1913–1927* (New World Records NW269), p. 2.

65 YouTube is among the many sources on the Internet where it is possible to listen to this piece free, for example, www.youtube.com/watch?v=ZRQ5CU3l8tQ

66 Gushee, liner notes, *Steppin' on the Gas* p. 3.

67 This piece can be auditioned on iTunes and YouTube.

68 Catherine Parsonage, *The Evolution of Jazz in Britain, 1880–1935* (Aldershot and Burlington: Ashgate, 2005), p. 121.

69 Randall Sandke, *Where the Light and Dark Folks Meet* (Lanham: The Scarecrow Press, Inc., 2010), p. 84.

70 Ibid.

71 Ibid., p. 51.

72 See playlist for a brief summary of Beiderbecke's role in early jazz.

73 In Goodman's now legendary Carnegie Hall concert of 16 January 1938, he paid tribute to the ODJB with a hand-picked group of musicians in a take-off of 'Sensation Rag', perfectly imitating Larry Shields' clarinet playing.

74 Parsonage, *Evolution of Jazz*, p. 130.

75 Email to author, 20 September 2003.

76 *Talking Machine World*, October 1920.

77 Lawrence Gushee, liner notes, *Jelly Roll Morton: Birth of the Hot* (Bluebird 66641–2), p. 10.

78 Robert G. O'Meally, liner notes, *Louis Armstrong: The Complete Hot Five and Hot Seven Recordings* (Columbia/Legacy C4K 63527), p. 69.

79   Bunk Johnson's version of 'The Entertainer', a return to his ragtime roots, can be auditioned on iTunes and is from the album *Bunk Johnson: Bunk and the New Orleans Revival 1942–47*. It is also available on YouTube.

80   Orrin Keepnews and Bill Grauer Jr, *A Pictorial History of Jazz* (London: Spring Books, 1968), p. 209.

81   It is interesting to hear pianist Art Tatum's version, on iTunes or YouTube, where he turns the song into a stunning tour de force.

82   Charles Fox, *The Essential Jazz Records Vol. 1: Ragtime to Swing* by Max Harrison, Charles Fox and Eric Thacker (London and New York: Mansell, 2000), p. 140.

83   Ibid., p. 141.

84   Clyde Bernhardt, *I Remember: Eighty Years of Black Entertainment, Big Bands and the Blues* (Philadelphia: University of Pennsylvania Press, 1986), p. 62.

85   Gunther Schuller, *Early Jazz* (New York: Oxford University Press, 1968), p. 192.

86   Thornton Hagert, liner notes, *An Experiment on Modern Music: Paul Whiteman at Aeolian Hall* (Smithsonian Collection R028), p. 1.

87   *New York Times*, 12 February 1922, p. 1.

88   'Drum Taps', *Metronome*, July 1922, reproduced in *Jazz in Print (1856–1929): An Anthology of Selected Early Readings in Jazz History*, ed. Karl Koenig (Hillsdale, New York: Pendragon Press, 2002), p. 197.

89   Among countless references, see Stan Nussbaum, *American Cultural Baggage* (New York: Orbis Books, 2005), ch. 1.

90   Schuller, *Early Jazz*, p. 192.

91   Randall Sandke, 'Was Bix Beiderbecke Poisoned by the Federal Government?' *Journal of Jazz Studies*, Vol. 9, No. 2, p. 178.

92   Ibid., p. 179.

93   Ibid., p. 182.

94   Philipp Blom, *Fracture: Life and Culture in the West 1918–1938* (London: Atlantic Books, 2015), p. 62.

95   Among others, *Cleveland Press*, 20 May 1933.

96   Mercer Ellington with Stanley Dance, *Duke Ellington in Person: An Intimate Memoir* (London: Hutchinson, 1978), p. 34.

97　*Variety*, 29 January 1936, p. 45.

98　Mercer Ellington with Stanley Dance, *Duke Ellington in Person* (London: Hutchinson, 1978), pp. 68–9.

99　Based on the chords for the pop song 'Exactly Like You'.

100　ASCAP (American Society of Composers, Authors and Publishers) who collect royalties on behalf of their members.

101　Some claim Ellington's 1950s and 1960s band produced work of equal merit, but I disagree. The 1940–2 band is where Ellington's genius was in full flower, realizing the potential of the 78 rpm's 3-minute time limit to perfection. A lot is said in a short space of time with a great richness of tonal colour, which I do not believe is matched elsewhere.

102　Jeffrey Magee, *The Uncrowned King of Swing: Fletcher Henderson and Big Band Jazz* (New York: Oxford University Press, 2005), p. 97.

103　Helen Bullitt Lowry, 'Putting the Music in Jazz', *The New York Times Book Review & Magazine*, 29 December 1922, reproduced in *Jazz in Print (1856–1929): An Anthology of Selected Early Readings in Jazz History*, ed. Karl Koenig (Hillsdale, NY: Pendragon Press, 2002), p. 217.

104　Jeffrey Magee, *The Uncrowned King of Swing: Fletcher Henderson and Big Band Jazz* (New York: Oxford University Press, 2005), p. 38.

105　Dicky Wells, quoted in *The Uncrowned King of Swing: Fletcher Henderson and Big Band Jazz* (New York: Oxford University Press, 2005), p. 185.

106　For example, the opening of Gershwin's *Girl Crazy* that made a star of Ethel Merman and *Strike Up the Band*, plus Richard Whiting's *Free For All*.

107　Benny Goodman quoted in George T. Simon, *The Big Bands* (New York: Macmillan, 1968), p. 207.

108　Benny Goodman and Irving Kolodin, *The Kingdom of Swing* (New York: Fredrick Ungar Publishing Co., 1961), p. 198.

109　Ibid., p. 157.

110　Chris Griffin in Chip Deffaa, *Swing Legacy* (Metuchen, NJ: The Scarecrow Press, 1989), p. 45.

111　Liner notes, *Benny Goodman: The Complete Goodman Vol. 1 – 1935* (RCA Victor AXM2-5505).

112 Ross Firestone, *Swing, Swing, Swing* (London: Hodder & Stoughton, 1993), p. 287.

113 Gunther Schuller, *The Swing Era* (New York and Oxford: Oxford University Press, 1989), p. 43.

114 The reader is referred to two very different but informative books on the subject, *The Big Bands* by George T. Simon and *The Swing Era* by Gunther Schuller to discover more about a period of jazz that has become somewhat neglected in recent years.

115 Gunther Schuller, *The Swing Era* (New York and Oxford: Oxford University Press, 1989), p. 43.

116 Gunther Schuller, *Musings* (New York: Oxford University Press, 1986), pp. 44–5.

117 Schuller, *Swing Era*, p. 43.

118 Ibid., p. 225.

119 Loren Schoenberg, liner notes, *Count Basie and his Orchestra: America's Number One Band* (Columbia/Legacy 512892-2), p. 64.

120 Schuller, *Swing Era*, p. 704.

121 Ibid., p. 757.

122 These include three masterpieces under Davis's name: *Miles Ahead*, *Porgy and Bess* and *Sketches of Spain* (all Columbia/Legacy).

123 Rather than spend acres of ink in trying to explain a sound, it's quicker to *hear* what these chord extensions sound like. There is no shortage of piano and guitar teachers demonstrating the 9, 11 and 13 chord extensions or the flat 5 on the internet – just put 9, 11 and 13 chord extensions into your search engine.

124 In my book *Jazz and Culture in a Modern Age* (Boston: Northeast University Press, 2014) I detail a number of these early experimenters.

125 Nat Shapiro, Nat Hentoff, eds, Charlie Parker quoted in *Hear Me Talkin' To Ya: The Story of Jazz by the Men Who Made It*, (London: Peter Davies,1955), p. 315.

126 It is certainly worth checking out his early work with the Jay McShann Orchestra 1941–2, where Parker solos on 'Swingmatism', 'Hootie Blues', 'Dexter Blues' and 'Sepian Bounce'.

127 A more unbridled Parker can be heard on some of his live recordings now on CD, such as *The Complete Legendary Rockland Palace Concert 1952* (Jazz Classics Records) or *The Complete Royal Roost*

Broadcasts (Jazz Dynamics) which Parker fans swear by, but be warned, they don't come cheap.

128 Barry Kernfeld, ed., *The New Grove Dictionary of Jazz Volume One A to K* (New York: Macmillan, 1988), p. 429.

129 Remarkably, the adverts for the Real Gone Bop Glasses continued into the mid-1950s!

130 Ted Gioia's term, *The History of Jazz* (New York: Oxford University Press, 1997), p. 244.

131 Listen again to No. 21 of the Big Band Playlist.

132 Interestingly, Stravinsky had previously used the same principle of six instruments in three groupings an octave apart in *L'Histoire du Soldat*, although the combinations he chose were cornet and trombone, clarinet and bassoon and violin and bass.

133 *Time*, 2 February 1953.

134 Thom Jurek, allmusic.com see: www.allmusic.com/album/the-complete-verve-concert-band-sessions-mw0001353675

135 Bob Blumenthal, liner notes, *Art Blakey Quintet A Night at Birdland Vol. 1* (Blue Note 7243 5 32146 2 3) RVG edition.

136 David H. Rosenthal, *Hard Bop: Jazz and Black Music 1955–1965* (New York: Oxford University Press, 1992), p. 24.

137 Jack Cooke, 'Art Blakey: A Night in Birdland – Vol. 1', *Modern Jazz The Essential Records* (London: Aquarius Books, 1978), p. 69.

138 I'm sure most people reading this know what funky music is, since the meaning is the same as in pop music, but just in case you don't, the *Encyclopaedia Britannica* online says: 'Musically, funk refers to a style of aggressive urban dance music driven by hard syncopated bass lines and drumbeats and accented by any number of instruments involved in rhythmic counterplay, all working toward a "groove".'

139 Barry Ulanov, "How Funky Can You Get," *Downbeat*, 6 March 1958, p. 18.

140 Quincy Jones arranged this piece for his own big band, the whole trumpet section playing Nat Adderley's inspired solo on the album *Gula Matari* to powerful effect.

141 Today, original-issue Blue Note albums can fetch up to four-figure sums on Internet auction sites.

142 Note that the example of Sidney Bechet's playing included in the Blues playlist – 'Blue Horizon' – was also on the Blue Note label.

143 Such as 'a calamitous, self-presented New York Town Hall concert in 1962, a short-lived recording venture, Charles Mingus Records ... and other setbacks [that] broke his bank account and ultimately his spirit'. see www.allmusic.com/artist/charles-mingus-mn0000009680/biography

144 Gene Lees in *The Biographical Encyclopaedia of Jazz* (Oxford and New York: Oxford University Press, 2007).

145 Jerry Coker, *Elements of the Jazz Language for the Developing Improviser* (CCP/Belwin, Inc., 1991), pp. 12–13.

146 Coltrane's 'classic quartet' lasted from 1962 to 1965.

147 Albeit with the addition of Eric Dolphy on alto sax.

148 Check out Previn's playing on the bestselling *Shelly Manne & His Friends: My Fair Lady.*

149 'The Man on Cloud No. 7', *Time*, 8 November 1954.

150 Evelyn Lamb, 'Uncommon Time: What Makes Dave Brubeck's Unorthodox Jazz Stylings So Appealing?' *Scientific American*, 11 December 2012, p. 13.

151 Dave Brubeck, liner notes, *Time Out* (Columbia/Legacy CK 65122).

152 Charles Beale, 'Jazz Education' in *The Oxford Companion to Jazz*, ed. Bill Kirchner (Oxford and New York: Oxford University Press, 2000) pp. 760–1.

153 Ibid., p. 760.

154 Dave Brubeck, interview with author, 18 November 2002.

155 Leonard Feather, liner notes, *Supersax Plays Bird* (Capitol Jazz CDP 7 96264 2).

156 Lawrence O. Koch, *Yardbird Suite: A Compendium of the Music and Life of Charlie Parker* (Ohio: Bowling Green State University Popular Press, 1988), p. 66.

157 Jerry Coker, *Elements of the Jazz Language for the Developing Improviser* (CCP/Belwin, Inc., 1991), pp. 12–13.

158 Such as http://jazzstudiesonline.org/files/jso/resources/pdf/SonnyRollinsAndChallengeOfThematicImprov.pdf

159 Max Harrison, *The Essential Jazz Records* by Max Harrison, Eric Thacker and Stuart Nicholson (London and New York: Mansell, 2000), p. 381.

160 Lou Levy, quoted in the liner notes for *Stan Getz: West Coast Jazz* (Verve 557 549-2).

161 Ornette Coleman in John Litweiler, *The Freedom Principle* (Poole: Blandford Press, 1958), p. 33.

162 Edited from *Encyclopaedia Britannica* /www.britannica.com/art/free-jazz

163 For example, *Downbeat*, 15 May 1958, p. 40.

164 Paul Bley in Litweiler, *The Freedom Principle*, (Boston: Da Capo Press, 1990) p. 62.

165 Diatonic means all the notes come from one key, i.e. none of this funny business with flatted 5ths, 9ths, 11ths and 13ths, which are chromatic harmonies. A lot of folk songs and nursery rhymes are diatonic.

166 Charlie Haden, interview with author, 28 July 2008. The folk tunes Haden recalls are ones that he learned in his parents' country and western group called Uncle Carl Haden and the Haden Family which had their own radio show in the mid-West. Haden began singing on the radio when he was twenty-two months old and continued to sing with the family group into his mid-teens, when he took up jazz.

167 John Coltrane in *Coltrane on Coltrane: The John Coltrane Interviews,* ed. Chris DeVito (Chicago: Review Press, 2010), p. 286.

168 Jim Merod, 'What We Hear When We Listen To Music', *La Folia*, Vol. 3, No. 3, 2001.

169 Tony Whyton, *Beyond a Love Supreme* (Oxford and New York: Oxford University Press, 2013), p. 75.

170 Stanley Crouch, 'Coltrane Derailed', *Jazz Times*, September 2002, p. 28.

171 A. B. Spellman, 'Trane + 7 = A Wild Night at the Gate', *Downbeat*, 30 December 1965, pp. 15 and 44.

172 Stanley Crouch, 'Coltrane Derailed', *Jazz Times*, September 2002, p 28.

173 Rashied Ali, 'Trane's Last Stop', *The Sixties: The Decade Remembered Now, By People Who Lived It Then,* Lynda Rosen Obst, ed. (New York: Random House/Rolling Stone, 1977), p. 201.

174 Eddie 'Lockjaw' Davis in Arthur Taylor, *Notes and Tones* (London and New York: Quartet Books, 1983), pp. 85–6.

175 Richard Brody, *The New Yorker*, www.newyorker.com/goings-on-about-town/movies/name-albert-ayler

176 Charles Eugene Claghorn, *The Biographical Dictionary of Jazz* (New York: Prentice-Hall, 1982).

177 There is a shattering film clip of Ayler playing at John Coltrane's funeral in the film *My Name Is Albert Ayler*, directed by Kaspar Collins.

178 Gunther Schuller, *Musings* (New York: Oxford University Press, 1986), p. 17.

179 Anthony Shadduck, *Charlie Haden, Scott LaFaro, and Harmolodics: Bass Styles in Ornette Coleman's 'Free Jazz'* (California State University, Long Beach, 2006).

180 Steve Lacy, in Stuart Nicholson, *Jazz: The Modern Resurgence* (London: Simon & Schuster, 1990), p. 94.

181 *Downbeat Yearbook 1973*, p. 18.

182 Miles Davis, obituary, *Daily Telegraph*, 30 September 1991.

183 Miles Davis, with Quincy Troupe, *Miles: The Autobiography of Miles Davis* (New York: Macmillan, 1990), p. 262.

184 Ibid., p. 287.

185 Chick Corea in *Downbeat*, December 1991, p 17.

186 Davis in *Miles: The Autobiography*, p. 287.

187 Larry Coryell in *Downbeat*, May 1984, p. 16.

188 Ginger Baker quoted in the television documentary *Rock Family Trees: The British R&B Boom*, directed by David Jeffcock, BBC TV, 1995.

189 Eric Clapton in *Rolling Stone,* 15 October 1970, p. 22.

190 *Rolling Stone*, 11 May 1968, p. 11.

191 Ian Carr, interview with author, 14 December 1995.

192 John McLaughlin in *Wire*, July 1988, p. 37.

193 Most notably with the group VSOP, initially a reconvening of Miles Davis's Second Great Quintet comprising Wayne Shorter on tenor sax, Ron Carter on bass and Tony Williams on drums with Freddie Hubbard in Davis's stead, or in a trio with Carter and Williams.

194 Joe Zawinul from Bill Milkowski, *Jaco* (San Francisco: Miller Freeman Books, 1995), p. 74.

195 *Black Music & Jazz Review*, June 1978, p. 14.

196 The similarity between progressive rocker Rick Wakeman's *Myths and Legends of King Arthur and the Knights of the Round Table* from 1975 and Corea's *Romantic Warrior* becomes too much to ignore at this point, even down to the latter's cover art of a knight in shining armour mounted on a horse and song titles such as 'Medieval Overture' and 'Duel of the Jester and the Tyrant'. The French violin virtuoso Jean-Luc Ponty's *Mystical Adventures* also took up this theme.

197 Some of the Cellar Door sessions turned up on Davis's *Live Evil* album (1970).

198 *Melody Maker,* 1 April 1972, p. 28.

199 A fourth album, *The Lost Trident Sessions*, originally recorded 25–9 June 1973, was not released until 1999.

200 Chick Corea in *Downbeat*, September 1988, p. 19.

201 John S. Wilson, 'Miles Davis Leaves Them Limp, Waiting for More', *New York Times*, 7 September 1975.

202 David Hadju, 'Wynton's Blues', *The Atlantic Monthly*, March 2003.

203 Lewis Porter, *John Coltrane: His Life and Music* (Ann Arbor: University of Michigan Press, 1998), p. 264.

204 Ibid.

205 Bob Belden, liner notes, *The Complete In a Silent Way Sessions* (Columbia/Legacy C3K 65362), p. 74.

206 Laurens van der Post, *A Walk With a White Bushman* (London: Vintage Books, 1986), p. 68.

207 George Butler, 'Between Lions and Legends', *Newsweek*, 24 February 1992.

208 Eric Porter, *What Is This Thing Called Jazz?* (Berkeley: University of California Press, 2002), p. 291.

209 Interview with author, 17 March 2003.

210 'Between Lions and Legends', *Newsweek*, 24 February 1992.

211 Wynton Marsalis, interview with author 19 October 1991.

212 Paul Tingen, *Miles Beyond: The Electric Explorations of Miles Davis 1967–1991* (New York: Billboard Books, 2001), p. 177.

213 Quoted in Miles Davis obituary, *New York Times*, 29 September 1991.

214 Wayne Shorter in *Musician*, December 1991, p. 50.

215 Howard Mandel, 'Steve Coleman: Music for Life', *Downbeat*, February 1988, p. 22.

216 See http://m-base.com/essays/symmetrical-movement-concept/

217 See Michael J. West, 'Steve Coleman: Vital Information', *Jazz Times*, June 2010.

218 Mark Hudson, 'Groove in their Hearts', *Observer Music Monthly*, August 2006, p. 42.

219 Manfred Eicher, interview with author, 23 May 1999.

220 Ibid.

221 Ibid. 26 October 2007.

222 Ian Carr, *Keith Jarrett: The Man and his Music* (London: Paladin, 1992), p. 85.

223 Manfred Eicher, interview with author, 23 May 1999.

224 Peter Rüedi, liner notes, *Keith Jarrett, Gary Peacock, Jack DeJohnette: Setting Standards* (ECM 2030–32), p. 13.

225 By then, Jarrett was the youngster in the group at seventy, while DeJohnette was seventy-three and Peacock eighty.

226 For a full listing of the impressive awards both Eicher and the ECM label have accumulated see www.ecmrecords.com/story

227 Marius Gabriel, 'What Coltrane hears in Heaven', see www. amazon.com/review/RNHOW1MMLVJIQ/ref=cm_cr_dp_title ?ie=UTF8&ASIN=B000025IL0&nodeID=5174&store=music

228 Manfred Eicher, interview with author, 23 May 1999.

229 Ibid.

230 Jack DeJohnette, liner notes, *Jack DeJohnette Special Edition* (ECM 372 1965), p. 29.

231 See Marshall McLuhan, *The Gutenberg Galaxy: The Making of Typographic Man* (Toronto: University of Toronto Press, 1962).

232 It's a good idea to check this recording out first to help you understand what's going on here.

233 Tomasz Stanko, interview with author, 7 March 2001.

234 See Stuart Nicholson, *Is Jazz Dead (Or Has It Moved To A New Address)?* (New York: Routledge, 2005), pp. 163–94.

235 Thomas L. Friedman, *The World Is Flat* (London and New York: Penguin Books, 2006), p. 477.

236 Interview with author, 15 July 2008.

237 Tord Gustavsen, interview with author, August 2009.

238 Jan Garbarek, *Downbeat,* July 1986, pp. 26–7.

239 Acácio de Camargo Piedade, 'Brazilian Jazz and Friction of Musicalities', in *Planet Jazz* (Jackson: University Press of Mississippi, 2003), p. 54.

240 Danilo Pérez, *the Independent*, provenance unknown.

241 Trevor Bannister, *Dusk Fire: Jazz in English Hands* (Reading: Springdale Publishing, 2010) p. v.

242 Michael Garrick, telephone conversation with author, 19 March 2006.

243 Michael Garrick, liner notes, *Impressed with Gilles Peterson* (Universal 064 749 2).

244 Mike Westbrook, *Interviews with Modern and Contemporary Jazz Musicians, Composers and Improvisers by George McKay*, see http:// usir.salford.ac.uk/1654/1/Jazz_interviews_with_images.pdf

245 Trevor Watts, *Interviews with Modern and Contemporary Jazz Musicians, Composers and Improvisers by George McKay* see http://usir. salford.ac.uk/1654/1/Jazz_interviews_with_images.pdf

246 Norma Winstone, interview with author, 20 January 2011.

247 Johnny Dankworth, 'Our Jazz Is British!' *Melody Maker*, 7 December 1963, p. 3.

248 Mike Westbrook, liner notes, *Celebration* (Deram 844 852–2).

249 Erik Kjellberg, 'Swedish Folk Tone in Jazz', *Jazz Facts Sweden 1998* (Stockholm: Svensk Musik, 1998), p. 4.

250 Jan Garbarek quoted in liner notes, *Dansere* (ECM 2146–48), p. 21.

251 Michael Tucker, liner notes for Jan Garbarek, Dansere (ECM 2146–48), p. 21.

252 Acacio Tadeu de Camargo Piedade, 'Brazilian Jazz and Friction of Musicalities', in *Jazz Planet*, ed. E. Taylor Atkins (Jackson: University of Mississippi Press, 2003), p. 53.

253 Danilo Pérez, interview with author, 23 August 2010.

254 Michael Wollny, interview with author, 25 September 2010.

Index

Also by Stuart Nicholson:

Jazz and Culture in a Global Age
Is Jazz Dead? (Or Has it Moved to a New Address)
Reminiscing in Tempo: A Portrait of Duke Ellington
Jazz-Rock: A History
Ella Fitzgerald
Billie Holiday
Jazz: The Modern Resurgence (reprinted in the USA as *Jazz: The 1980s Resurgence*)

With Max Harrison and Eric Thacker
The Essential Jazz Records Vol. 2

With Will Friedwald, Ted Gioia, Peter Watrous, Ben Ratliff and others
The Future of Jazz